Newspaper Pennies CARDBOARD & Eggs

for Growing a Better Garden

More Than 400 New, Fun, and Ingenious Ideas to Keep Your Garden Growing Great All Season Long

RODALE

Roger Yepsen

and the Editors of *Organic Gardening* Magazine

Book design by Joanna Williams

Illustrations by Michael Gellatly

The designs and instructions for the potting bench (page 42), tool house (page 280), and garden gateway
(page 276) are adapted from *Building from the Yard and Garden* by John Kelsey and Ian J. Kirby (1997) with
permission from John Kelsey.

CONTENTS

Speedy Transformations

Gardening is something like professional sports. At the end of the season, you evaluate what went right, what went wrong, and what might make things better next year. The goal for next year's garden might be a more bountiful harvest of vegetables, or an impressive display of artfully arranged perennials. You may want to garden more efficiently, to free up time for other warm-weather activities. Whatever your particular bent, this book offers a generous range of ideas on getting better performance from your garden. You'll find new wrinkles, as well as variations on familiar themes such as coaxing seeds to sprout and dealing with pests and diseases.

The bottom line isn't only to produce more and toil less, but also to reap more enjoyment from your time out in the garden. Few of us really *have* to get out there and put in a few hours a day. Working in the yard is an elective activity (aside from obeying local weed ordinances, that is), and the more pleasure you take from it, the more care you're apt to invest. That's why especially helpful tips often are those that appeal to our sense of wonder. The most enthusiastic gardeners seem to be those who are curious, taking note of what works best.

In the chapters that follow, you'll find a mix of quick fixes, weekend projects, and intriguing plants that can give your garden a lift no matter what you grow or how many hours you care to invest. In the process, you may find that your very good garden is on its way to becoming a *great* garden—one that will welcome you each time you step out into the yard.

✦ Chapter 1, **Seed Starting and Saving,** tells how to enjoy the astounding variety of plants available only as seed, while saving money over buying plants. Starting from seed also allows you to plan for a midseason planting that will yield a late crop of vegetables or flush of flowers, at a time of year when nurseries are running out of stock and gardeners tend to run out of enthusiasm. And you'll save substantially over what you'd spend for plants.

✦ The most challenging stage in a young plant's life is adapting to the great outdoors. Chapter 2, **Planting and Transplanting,** offers approaches for easing this transition. Tips include using colored mulches that researchers have found to boost plant performance; gardening with elevated beds to bring the plants up to your level, rather than the other way around; and succeeding with inexpensive bare-root plants.

- Turn to Chapter 3, **Soil, Compost, and Fertilizing,** for ideas on making the most of the organic gardener's greatest ally, good soil. Compost, proper pH, nutrients, and custom fertilizer blends.

- Weeds happen, unless you are growing fungi in a cave, and Chapter 4, **Weeds and What to Do about Them,** shows how to meet this challenge with a creative arsenal that includes vinegar, hot water, flames, stone pavers, and sheets of transparent plastic.

- Chapter 5, **Getting a Leg Up on Pests and Diseases,** tells how to deal with everything from troublesome microbes to deer capable of leaping a 6-foot fence. The list of gardener's resources for this battle is long and growing, and includes row covers, natural pesticides, a remarkable number of beneficial insects and organisms, and even (your budget willing) high-tech robots.

- When planning next year's garden, you should consider your needs as well as those of your plants, advises Chapter 6, **The Vegetable Plot.** You'll read how to take best advantage of everything your particular site has to offer, while including a few amenities for yourself—a bit of shade, a bench, and paths that feel comfortable underfoot even after a couple of hours in the garden.

- Chapter 7, **Flowers in Beds and Pots,** coaches you on how to use flowering plants more effectively in the home landscape, as well as how to get them to perform indoors. Look here for ideas on doing well with bulbs and biennials, and harmoniously orchestrating blossom colors.

- Herbs combine fragrance, flavor, and flowers, as well as attracting certain beneficial insects and repelling certain pests. Chapter 8, **Growing and Enjoying Herbs,** gathers a potpourri of pointers on having these talented plants play a bigger role in the garden and landscape.

- Your very first garden probably didn't involve much more than a shovel, seed packets, and dirt. But as we dig deeper into this hobby, we're apt to find ourselves with a garage full of indispensable items. The idea behind Chapter 9, **Tools, Supports, and Storage,** is that well-crafted, properly sized tools can significantly increase your gardening pleasure—and that includes models designed with women or children in mind. Modest hand tools get most of the attention in this chapter, but there's also a small toolhouse that you can build where you need it most, right in the garden.

- Chapter 10, **Out in the Yard,** considers the whole works—garden beds, lawn, and whatever other features you may be fortunate enough to call your own. These last pages sketch possibilities for walks, lighting systems, a pool, and growing environments both high and dry (a rock garden) and wet and somewhat sloppy (a bog garden).

To sum up, you're not holding a gardening primer in your hands, but a collection of ideas that are passed along like certain plants, informally and over the garden fence. It's our hope that a few of these suggestions may take root in your yard, with results that bring you greater satisfaction in the years ahead.

CHAPTER 1

Seed Starting and Saving

Seeds are the tiny germs of life from which the garden grows. They need to be coaxed into sprouting, typically with warmth and moisture and sometimes with light as well. You then have to tend the seedlings, making sure that they make it through this vulnerable stage.

Why bother, when you can buy sturdy plants already well under way? Local nurseries may stock a selection of heirlooms, regional specialties, international favorites, and wildflowers. And mail-order nurseries offer an ever-expanding inventory of plants that will arrive at your door after a cross-country trip in excellent shape. One family-owned firm, Forest Farm in Williams, Oregon (www.forestfarm.com), lists more than 5,000 varieties of plants in its latest catalog.

Why bother? The main reasons can be summed up as economy, a mind-boggling selection, and taking part in a miracle of nature.

Starting with the last of these, many gardeners are both humbled and fascinated by the way in which little specks of matter turn into sprawling, musky scented tomatoes or a glowing bed of zinnias. Horticulturalists have described the process a thousand times—the sprout feeds on the starchy cotyledon, and so forth—but that doesn't explain what we see unfolding before us. The migration flight of monarchs to Mexico is no more amazing a feat than the way a single seed will grow into an acreage-commanding vine that will keep your household in butternut squash through the winter.

As for economy, that may not add up to much of an incentive if you are growing just a few plants for a modest yard and garden. But if your vegetable garden supplies a part of your diet, or if you want to plant flowers in drifts of a hundred rather than drifts of three, then seeds may be the way to go. One packet of seeds typically can generate several flats full of seedlings. All it takes is time and care, flats, and seed-starting mix.

Aside from commercial sources, thousands of gardeners share seeds of hard-to-find varieties through Seed Savers Exchange catalogs and various Internet groups. Nature itself has seen to it that seeds are an extremely transportable commodity, and they can be mailed safely and inexpensively.

While it's true that the seeds of some plants need babying, the tricks of seed starting are few and easily learned. You are apt to have better results with a modest investment in equipment, beginning with flats and pots and possibly including bright lighting and a source of bottom heat. Before long, seed starting can become an annual ritual that you look forward to season after season.

1

A NOTEBOOK FOR SEEDS

Unless you're a mouse or a bird, most seeds look pretty much alike. Here's a way to keep them in order.

Preventing Leaking Packets

Once you open a seed packet, it can be devilishly difficult to keep the leftover seed from spilling out. Save yourself a lot of frustration by keeping a roll of artist's tape or low-tack painter's tape wherever you keep seeds. This tape is available at artist's supply and paint stores and can be used with a sturdy dispenser. The tape will repeatedly seal the envelopes without tearing them to shreds.

If your seed packets tend to stray, and you habitually tear off the name of the plant, there is a tidy way to put whatever you're after right at your fingertips. Buy ring binder bags, place the packets in them, and use a three-ring binder to organize the packets as you see fit—by planting *date,* or by the *type of plant.* So, the tabs in such a notebook might be labeled by the weeks of the year, alerting you to the seeds that are to be started now; or, you might want to gather all the lettuces, the tomatoes, and the peppers in one section. The bags are available from office supply firms.

You can also store seed packets in three-ring binder photo sleeves. Choose sleeves that hold 3-by-5 or 5-by-7 photos, fold over the seed packet top, and insert the packets into the sleeve pockets.

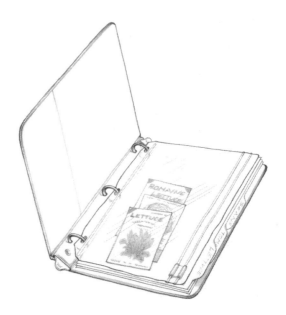

Seeds are tiny, and all the more difficult to store and organize because of it. Slip seed packets into resealable plastic ring-binder pages and come up with a system for putting them in order.

MAKE YOUR OWN GROWING MIXES

You probably go through a lot of bagged growing medium when you start your own seeds. Now's the time to economize by making your own in big batches.

What You'll Need

Seed-Starting Mix

1 part milled sphagnum moss

2 parts vermiculite

2 parts perlite

Potting Mix with Compost

1 part finished compost, screened through a mesh of ¼-inch hardware cloth

1 part vermiculite

Potting Mix without Compost

1 part commercial potting soil

1 part milled sphagnum moss

1 part vermiculite

EASY DOES IT

Moisten Mix Quicker

It can seem as though plant mixes take forever to absorb water, and there may be the temptation to plant seeds in a medium that's not thoroughly moistened. To save a bit of time, use warm water—it's soaked up somewhat more quickly than cold.

Just about anything costs you more if you buy it in small containers, and that goes for bagged seed-starting and potting mixes. Instead, come up with your own custom blends for both in large quantities, and store them neatly in plastic garbage cans rather than floppy plastic bags that tend to spill. The one thing you don't want to do is include ordinary garden soil in your recipes, with its weed seeds, disease organisms, fungi, and insects. Not only that, but most soils are just plain too dense to get plants off to an optimal start.

To combine the ingredients easily, use a plastic tub of the sort sold for mixing cement. Or for larger volumes, spread the measured amounts of each ingredient on a tarp spread over the driveway or patio. Choose a relatively windless day to work. Even so, the dust may fly, and you may want to occasionally mist the medium with a fine spray from a hose. Use a dull hoe or a metal rake (tines up) to mix thoroughly. Then place the mixture in a new plastic garbage can—use one for seed-starting mix, and a larger one for potting mix. Keep a plastic bucket on hand in which to moisten small amounts of mix by stirring in water. Allow enough time to ensure that the medium in the bucket is completely moistened. Dry mix may dehydrate young seedlings, killing them. If you do a lot of seed starting and potting over a short period each spring, you may want to have several buckets of soaking mix on hand so that you don't feel tempted to rush the moistening process.

There are any number of recipes for seed-starting and potting mixes, so feel free to adapt the suggestions for mixes on this page. Be sure to include compost only if it is thoroughly processed, rather than half-degenerated plant matter.

PUT THE DAMPER ON DAMPING-OFF

A tiny forest of just-sprouted seedlings may be felled by fungi unless you take precautions. Try these reliable remedies.

ADVICE OVER THE FENCE
Water Warily

Avoid casually splashing when watering seedlings, at the risk of spreading soil-borne diseases to many plants. Seedlings in plugs may avoid being infected by sick neighboring plants, but if you see signs of damping-off in one part of a flat, remove the entire flat from the area and discard it.

Damping-off is a fungal disease that can rapidly lay waste to entire flats of vulnerable young seedlings. You'll know it by the afflicted stems, which may take on a water-soaked appearance or turn thin and wiry at the soil line. The unsupported seedlings topple and die. As a preventive, moisten the seed-starting medium with a mild homemade fungicide. To 1 gallon of water, stir in 1 tablespoon of clove oil (available at supermarkets and drugstores, as well as by mail order) and a drop or two of dishwashing soap. Among various powerfully scented herbs and spices, clove has been found to be particularly effective against two principal soil-borne pathogens.

You also can buy a fungal control agent formulated to prevent damping-off, marketed as SoilGard. It contains dormant spores of a beneficial fungus. When mixed with water, the fungus comes to life and puts off an antibiotic substance. Another product, Mycostop, harnesses a beneficial bacterium that controls or suppresses damping-off and other soil-borne troublemakers as it grows among the seedlings' roots. It too can be mixed with water for use as a soil drench.

An additional step that takes little time is to scatter a dusting of milled sphagnum moss over the soil surface. This thin layer will help keep seedling stems drier, suppressing disease, and the moss also contributes a certain antimicrobial effect. Note that this product is marketed in small bags—don't confuse it with baled peat moss. To make it easier to apply a thin layer, you can give the moss a spin in a blender to reduce the particles to a dust.

SAVE WITH SOIL BLOCKS

Can you really save by spending? Sure! If you start a lot of plants each year from seed, a soil-block mold may be one of the best investments you make in your garden.

Instead of buying dozens of little pots or plug trays in which to seed next year's garden, you can skip the containers altogether by using a mold to make soil blocks. These blocks are nothing more than cubes of planting mix. They encourage a healthily branching root system that sets up plants for a happy transition to the garden. (Because the blocks are relatively shallow, however, they aren't the way to go with deep growers like carrots and beets.) The steps for converting damp mixture into planting blocks are easy enough, once you buy a blocker. These devices are available from nurseries and mail-order supply companies. You'll also need trays in which to place the blocks.

You can buy blockers in two sizes, with the smaller model making many little blocks that eventually will fit nicely within a square hole in the larger blocks, which look something like square doughnuts. This system avoids disturbing the seedlings as they're moved to a larger container.

1. Stir up a batch of planting medium that will keep its shape once popped out of the blocker. Johnny's Selected Seeds (www.johnnyseeds.com) sells a mix that will work well. Here's a recipe for making your own:
   - 2 parts peat moss, screened through a mesh of ¼-inch hardware cloth
   - 1 part vermiculite
   - 1 part finished compost, also screened through hardware cloth

   Do your mixing in a flat-bottomed container that's wide enough to allow you to press the blocker into the medium; a plastic tub sold for mixing concrete is ideal, and a clean wheelbarrow will also work. Make sure you allow enough time for the medium to fully absorb the water you add to moisten the mix.

2. Press the blocker into the medium so that the squares are filled. Then push the handle to eject the row of blocks into the tray.

3. Plant seed in the conventional way.

4. You can water the blocks from the top as you would seedlings in pots or flats. Use a misting nozzle or fine rosette on a watering can to avoid causing the block to come apart. The blocks will become sturdier as roots spread through them, but to avoid the risk of crumbling them, you can deliver water from the bottom up with capillary matting.

A PLUG-IN WELCOME MAT FOR SEEDLINGS

Instead of hoping your new plants are warm enough atop a water heater or furnace, steal a secret from professional growers—entrust them to a seedling mat.

ADVICE OVER THE FENCE
Use That Heat Twice

Heat rises. And the warmth from a flat with a heating mat or cable can be used to help to sprout the seeds in a flat stacked above (although at a lower temperature). Check seed packets for a variety of vegetable or flower that germinates best in cooler conditions and place it on the second tier.

At a cost approaching $100, a thermostatically controlled seedling mat may seem like a luxury if you're accustomed to using the secondhand heat from the top of a furnace or water heater. But assuming you start vegetables and flowers from seed each spring, you'll appreciate the convenience—and the dependable results, especially for seeds that are tricky to germinate. And because plants get off to a quicker start, they may be less vulnerable to damping-off. Small-scale greenhouses and specialty growers have discovered that seedling mats create ideal conditions, meaning less work, less reseeding, and less babying of weak plants.

A less expensive alternative is to snake a length of heating cable under the flats to provide gentle bottom heating. The cables cost roughly a dollar a foot; you can expect to pay more than that for shorter cables, and less for lengthy ones. Adding a thermostat substantially increases the price.

HEAT HELPS HEAPS

Supplying bottom heat can make a startling difference when starting seeds. Have a look at how long it took lettuce seeds to come to life at various soil temperatures, as reported in *Knott's Handbook for Vegetable Growers*, a resource for commercial market gardeners. If you're patient—fine. But if you're anxious for that first bowl of garden-grown salad, a heat cable or seedling mat makes good sense.

77°F—2 days	50°F—7 days
68°F—3 days	41°F—15 days
59°F—4 days	32°F—49 days

PRESPROUT FOR BETTER RESULTS

Know before you grow! Give your plants a head start even before you stick them in growing medium.

To increase the percentage of seeds that will make it as plants, presprout them rather than trusting that garden conditions will be favorable. The germinated seeds will get off to a faster start once they reach soil or planting medium. The system works particularly well for plants that need warmth to get under way, including cukes, melons, pumpkins, and squash. Here's what you do:

1. Dampen a sheet of paper towel that's been folded over once or twice to make a blotter.
2. Arrange the seeds over the surface without allowing them to touch.
3. Place a single damp sheet of towel on top of the seeds, press down to help hold them in place, then slowly roll up the toweling.
4. Place the rolled toweling in a plastic bag. Leave the bag open and put it in a warm place, out of direct sunlight. Take a peek at the seeds each day to determine when they've begun to sprout.
5. Plant the presprouted seeds in potting mix and place them under fluorescent lights or in sunlight.

SOWING IS CHEAPER BY THE DOZEN

Eggshells are the perfect biodegradable planting pots!

You're probably already tossing eggshells in the compost pile, but you can put them to good use in another way. Use eggshells to start your seeds. Try to crack your eggs in half, then rinse and save the shells in an egg carton. When it's planting time, add seed-starting medium and sow your seeds, one to a half-shell. When seedlings emerge, plant them outdoors, shells and all. The eggshells will break down, adding nutrients to your soil.

COLD FRAME, WARM PLANTS

Discover five simple steps for building a warm frame to stretch your gardening season.

A cold frame might better be termed a *warm* frame, its purpose being to make use of heat stored in the earth as well as solar energy. You can use it at both ends of the gardening year, when the weather isn't quite so hospitable.

A variety of mail-order frame kits are on the market, typically with polycarbonate glazing and framing of cedar, redwood, or metal. If you are reasonably handy, you can assemble the frames with just a couple of hand tools.

BUILDING A WARM FRAME

A warm frame made of cedar will hold up better than those made with other woods, and there's no need to rely on preservative chemicals. (Exterior-grade plywood works well, and it allows you to make the sides and back from a single piece rather than with two boards each.) If you are having a sheet of double-walled polycarbonate glazing cut to size, you can determine the overall dimensions of the frame. Or, to make use of an old storm window, adjust the length and width of the frame to suit it. Just make sure that the frame has a front-to-back slope to take better advantage of the sun.

1. Cut the pieces as shown, choosing the dimensions to suit the storm window, if you are using one, and your own needs. Typically, a frame will be about 3 feet deep by 6 feet wide. The front should be roughly 12 inches lower than the back, with the sides sloped accordingly, to pitch the glazing toward the sun. The front, sides, and back are from ¾-inch-thick stock; the cleats are from 2 × 4s ripped in two pieces roughly 1½ inches square.

2. Five cleats add rigidity to the frame. Assemble the back by driving 1¾-inch screws through the two back pieces into the back cleats. (For these and all screws used in the project, drill pilot holes.)

3. In the same way, attach the front piece to the front cleats.

Next Year's Garden
A Self-Venting Cold Frame

A cold frame can build up enough heat on a chilly but sunny day to cook the seedlings inside. Few plants will be happy if the air temperature within soars above 85°F. If you or someone in the household can't be around to vent the frame when necessary, consider adding an ingenious lifting mechanism that responds to elevated temperatures by elevating the lid. It's a cylinder containing a compound that expands when heated, something like a hydraulic piston. There are no batteries, no wires. The automatic lifters are carried by mail-order firms that sell cold-frame kits.

4. Assemble the frame by attaching the sides to the cleats, front and back. Note that the top inside edge of the back will be slightly above the sloping sides. Using a hand plane, bevel this edge to the angle of the sides.

5. Install the storm window using three exterior door hinges with the screws provided, attaching them to the outside of the back and underside of the window. Or, if you are using a sheet of polycarbonate, you can keep it in place with bungee cords, attached to screw eyes driven into the sides, front, and back, as shown in the detail. Keep the front two cords loose enough that a block of wood can be inserted under the front edge of the sheet to vent the frame.

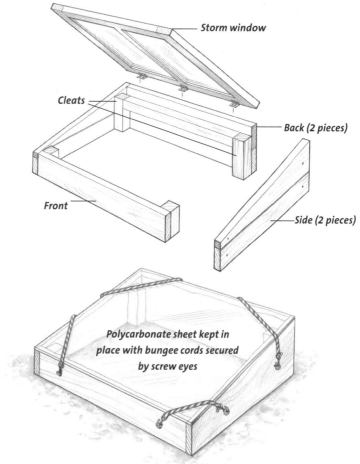

Storm window

Cleats

Back (2 pieces)

Front

Side (2 pieces)

Polycarbonate sheet kept in place with bungee cords secured by screw eyes

An old storm window can serve again as the lid of a cold frame. Or you can use a sheet of polycarbonate glazing.

WHEN A SEED'S BATTERY RUNS DOWN

As living things, seeds gradually will consume the food stored within them. If it is used up, the seeds die, becoming as lifeless as grains of sand.

EASY DOES IT

A Seed Dehumidifier

To keep seeds dry in a glass jar, first pour in a couple of inches of powdered milk. Place a few layers of paper towel on top of the powder, then add the seed packets.

If you start plants from seed, it's good to know how long the seed of each vegetable will remain viable. Otherwise, you risk planting a row from which nothing—except weeds—will appear. While some seeds can sit around for a few years without suffering a greatly reduced germination rate, cucumbers among them, others have to be purchased each year, such as parsnips. That's especially important if you have a modest-size garden and find yourself with leftover seed at the end of each growing season. It's also apt to be a factor if you save seed from your plants and can easily collect enough to last for the next several years.

Although it's possible to give general longevity figures for vegetable seeds (see the table below), you may find that your seeds are considerably more or less viable because of the way in which they're stored. Ideally, seeds should be kept cool and dry and out of direct sunlight. Jars with screw-on lids are a good choice. Place them in the refrigerator, if you have the space. For legumes, however, it's best to allow the seeds to breathe by storing them in a paper or cloth bag.

SEED	YEARS	SEED	YEARS
Asparagus	3	Muskmelons	5
Beans	3	Onions	1
Beets	4	Peas	3
Broccoli	5	Peppers	2
Cabbage	5	Pumpkins	4
Carrots	3	Radishes	5
Cauliflower	5	Spinach	5
Corn	2	Squash	4
Cucumbers	5	Tomatoes	4
Lettuce	5	Watermelons	4

IRON-CLAD SEEDS

No need to sign up for Plant Diseases 101 when you have helpful information at your fingertips—on seed packets and plant labels and in catalogs. The best time to think about bothersome plant diseases is when you're buying seed.

EASY DOES IT

Beware of Vectors among the Vegetables

Both troublesome viruses and bacteria can be spread to healthy plants by insects, so part of keeping plants healthy is keeping an eye on bugs, especially early in the season. Row covers can help you fend off some of these *vectors*, such as the cucumber beetles that carry bacterial wilt to cucumbers, melons, and squash.

Read before you reap. Catalogs, plant labels, and seed packets often alert you to any diseases to which a particular variety is resistant. The more common afflictions may be listed as abbreviations, such as TMV for tobacco mosaic virus and VFF for verticillium and fusarium wilt. Resistance to a disease means that the plant is less likely to show symptoms; it does not certify that the plant is immune. Plant varieties also may offer resistance to problems other than diseases, such as tip burn in lettuce and the effect of cold on tomatoes.

VEGETABLE	DISEASES RESISTED
Beans	Anthracnose, bacterial blight, bacterial brown spot, bean mosaic virus, halo blight, powdery mildew
Broccoli	Bacterial soft rot, downy mildew
Cabbage	Black rot, fusarium yellows
Cantaloupe	Downy mildew, fusarium wilt, powdery mildew
Corn	Common rust, northern corn leaf blight, smut, southern corn leaf blight, Stewart's wilt
Cucumber	Anthracnose, bacterial wilt, cucumber mosaic virus, downy mildew, powdery mildew, scab
Lettuce	Downy mildew, lettuce mosaic virus
Peas	Bean yellow mosaic virus, common wilt, fusarium wilt, powdery mildew
Pepper	Bacterial leaf spot, pepper mosaic virus, potato virus, tobacco etch virus, tobacco mosaic virus
Potato	Early blight, late blight, scab
Spinach	Downy mildew
Squash	Cucumber mosaic, powdery mildew, watermelon mosaic, zucchini mosaic
Tomato	Alternaria blight, alternaria stem canker, fusarium wilt, gray leaf spot, late blight, tobacco mosaic virus, verticillium wilt

A PLUG-IN HOTBED

A new idea for a tried-and-true garden! A hotbed will keep plants happy even through cloudy, cold spells.

ADVICE OVER THE FENCE
Overheating: Too Much of a Good Thing

Guard against overheating young plants in a frame. On sunny days, the interior temperature may soar into the 90s or above, and the lid should be lifted—automatically or manually—for ventilation. Watering is another concern even though a closed lid will conserve moisture. Bottom-heating tends to dry out plants relatively quickly. Water the bed early in the day, so that the leaves of the plants have a chance to dry before evening comes on.

What's the difference between a hotbed and a cold frame? Generally speaking, a hotbed is used for starting plants, which then can be moved to a cold frame to harden off and grow a bit before transplanting to the garden. Unless you have a good deal of horticultural activity going on, a single frame can perform both functions.

Hotbeds once relied on a layer of composting manure to generate heat. Today, the warmth is more likely to come from the sun (through the transparent or translucent top), from the earth, and from an electrical cable or pad. To make the most of these sources, choose a spot that faces south and gets some protection from the chill of prevailing winds. And when scouting the yard for the ideal location, don't forget the need for a nearby plug. Often, it's wise to nestle the hotbed next to or near a shed or a garage or in close proximity to the house.

Thermostatically controlled heating cables are sold by mail order and in garden supply centers. Run a few loops of cable between layers of vermiculite and sand, as shown. The extension cord running to the cable should be plugged into a ground-fault-interrupter (GFI) outlet or circuit. A 60-foot-long cable will warm a bed measuring 6 by 6 feet.

PREPARING THE SITE

Place the hotbed over a 6-inch-deep recess in the ground. Add the following in layers:

❖ 6 inches of gravel for drainage

❖ Burlap or landscaping cloth to keep vermiculite from settling in gravel

❖ 2 inches of vermiculite for insulation

❖ Loops of heating cable

- 1 inch of builder's sand as a buffer between cable and hardware cloth
- Hardware cloth (¼-inch metal mesh) to protect cable
- 2 inches or more of builder's sand on which to put plant containers

HEATING AND VENTING

Only a modest-powered cable is needed for a small hotbed; you may want to buy a higher-rated model to heat two adjacent beds. To help conserve heat, berm soil around the lower edges of the frame. Set the thermostat at between 70° and 75°F for germinating most seeds. Then follow the temperature recommendation for the plants you're growing. Cool-season vegetables (salad greens, cabbage, and cauliflower) do best with a daytime setting of 60° to 65°F. Warm-season crops (tomatoes, peppers, and melons) like a temperature of 65° to 75°F. It's best if the temperature is allowed to drop 5° to 10° at night. Finally, when the spring weather warms up, you may want to place the frame under shelter so that it will have a longer life.

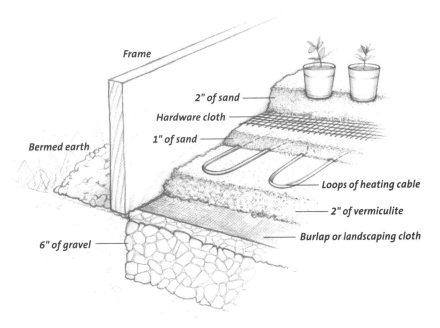

Frame
2" of sand
Hardware cloth
1" of sand
Bermed earth
Loops of heating cable
2" of vermiculite
Burlap or landscaping cloth
6" of gravel

A plug-in hotbed generates a dependable source of heat for starting plants.

(continued)

GOING TRADITIONAL WITH MANURE

Have a horse farm next door, or a horse of your own? If so, you can use the fresh manure twice—as fertilizer, of course, but also as a natural source of heat as the manure composts. For centuries, growers have placed a bed of composting green manure beneath young plants to ward off frosty temperatures. To harness this free horse heat for a hotbed, you'll need to dig down 16 inches or so and lay down a 12-inch layer of well-packed green manure (not older, mature manure), followed by 4 inches of good garden soil. Then place potted plants on this surface. As the manure "works," the temperature in the frame may reach 75°F or more. But the heat won't last forever. As the biological processes in the manure layer slow down, the frame will cool off. To keep the heat on, you'll have to remove the plants and the soil layer, then replace the old manure with fresh.

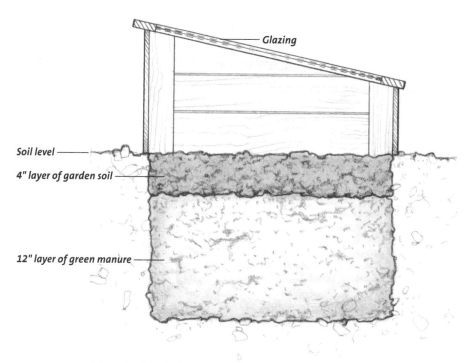

A traditional hotbed uses the biological action in composting manure to keep plants warm.

LOW-TECH COLD FRAME, HIGH-TECH GLAZING

Leave the old storm windows in the garage! Try using straw and plastic for this quick-to-make insulated cold frame.

Here's a cold frame you can put together in a matter of minutes, combining a centuries-old material—bales of straw—with a double-walled panel of polycarbonate. Both are good insulators, helping to conserve the warmth of the sun. Unlike glass, once the standard glazing, these plastic panels are resistant to breaking, and the ribs between the layers act to diffuse sunlight evenly. Polycarbonate panels may be available at home centers; if not, check with greenhouse supply firms.

1. As a trial run, arrange the straw bales end to end to make a frame sized to support the panel. The long sides of the frame should face north and south.
2. Put the bales aside and prepare the soil, unless you're placing the frame in an existing garden bed. To admit more sun into the frame, pitch it toward the south by removing some soil where the bales will go along the front. Also make a sloping trench for both ends, as shown. Note that the bed within the frame remains level.
3. Put the bales in place and rest the panel on top. Keep a couple of 2 × 4 scraps on hand so that you can prop up the panel when it's necessary to vent excess heat.
4. Come spring, use the bales for mulch and store the panel out of the sunlight.

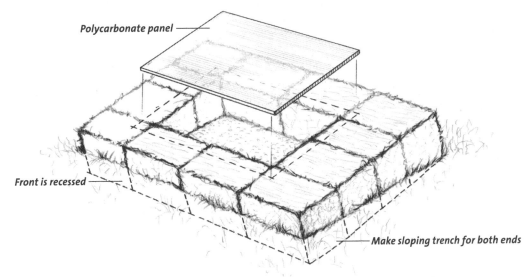

For a low-cost, biodegradable cold frame, construct the sides with bales of straw.

IS THIS YOUR YEAR FOR A GREENHOUSE?

Think outside the house! The controlled climate in a greenhouse presents all sorts of possibilities for gardeners.

Kids on bikes dream of motorcycles, sailors in dinky sailboats dream of yachts. And gardeners, many of us, dream of having a greenhouse. Not a hoop house with its plastic flapping annoyingly in the wind, but a traditional shelter of glass, one that we can spend pleasant, comfortable hours in growing vegetables off-season or growing plants from warmer climes—orchids, citrus, you name it.

Greenhouses can stand alone or can be attached to an existing structure. Talk to gardeners and other greenhouse owners before selecting a model to get advice on what works best for your growing plans and site. Greenhouse gardening is similar in many ways to gardening outside. The plants need water, nutrients, and tending but in a greenhouse you are able to control the environment to benefit you and your plants.

So just how expensive would it be to have a greenhouse on your property? The price range is considerable. Aside from obvious differences because of size, the cost is influenced by both the structure and the glazing material.

Elegant, it's not. But a plastic-covered hoop house brings greenhouse growing within the budget of many gardeners.

The shape of a gothic greenhouse yields more usable space along the sides.

❖ The least expensive way to go is to construct a **Quonset** greenhouse, which is simply a larger version of the familiar hoop house. Curved conduits or pipes are bent into hoops high enough to allow you to walk around inside. The inverted U shape makes the area along the sides less useful because of the low overhead clearance. Quonsets typically are covered with some sort of plastic sheeting, a material that is affordable but has a relatively short life.

❖ A **gothic** greenhouse has curving sidewalls meeting at a point, similar to a gothic window. These are made with a rigid frame, often using curved wooden beams. The interior space is more fully usable than in a Quonset because the long sides are vertical or nearly so.

The gable-roofed shape allows better headroom to either side, and it may fit in better with the home landscape.

- **Gable** structures have straight sides and a peaked roof, like a typical house. They are attractive, offer good headroom, and tend to have good ventilation because of all the space under the roof. But they can be costly to construct, with their relatively complex framing, and the vertical side walls bear enough weight that they may need a footer of some kind.

Then there's the skin that covers the greenhouse. Each choice has its advantages and drawbacks. Whereas glass was once the rule, plastics have gained in popularity and continue to be improved.

- **Glass** is the traditional material for greenhouse glazing. It is durable (unless you're troubled by hailstorms or stone-throwing kids) and remains highly permeable to light over time, admitting about 90 percent of the sun's rays. *Tempered* glass is less prone to breakage but costs more. Because glass is heavy, it's necessary to have a sturdy (and more expensive) structure for support.

- **Fiberglass** is light in weight, strong, durable, and as permeable to light as glass, although cheaper versions may become less so with age.

- Double-walled **polycarbonate** holds up well and acts as an insulating barrier to conserve heat, while admitting somewhat less light than other materials. The panels can be bent somewhat for curved walls.

- **Plastic films** don't last as long as other alternatives, but they are considerably cheaper in the short run and their light weight can be supported by inexpensive hoop structures. Polyethylene typically lasts a couple of years. Polyvinyl chloride (PVC) and vinyl films may cost two to five times as much but hold up for 5 years or so.

Although the clear surfaces of a greenhouse admit plenty of light, supplemental heating is usually required in cold months—electric, gas, or oil. You also can hold on to more of the sun's free energy by placing black water-filled drums in the greenhouse. A fan will help keep the space within at a constant temperature. And if

(continued)

Next Year's Garden

Don't Keep Your Greenhouse in the Dark

Our crazy granite planet tilts and wobbles while making its orbit, which means the sun shines down on us from different angles through the year. It's all too easy to place a cold frame or greenhouse in a spot that basks in the sun in June, only to discover long shadows stretching across the same area come late fall. Check to see how sunlight is distributed in the crucial months, from dawn to dusk, and record your findings on a simple sketch of the property.

the greenhouse is to be used in summer months, there must be some means of venting or shading. You can use shade cloth and netting to cut down on the sunlight. And the yard itself may come to the rescue from spring to fall, if you have deciduous trees that leaf out to the west of the greenhouse.

A greenhouse makes good use of free solar energy, but it will need help on cold winter nights. Your home heating system may have surplus capacity, allowing you to tap into an existing unit rather than buying a new one. But supplemental heat usually is necessary. A relatively simple solution, at a modest initial cost, is to install a 220-volt electric heater. A small propane or natural gas heater may be less expensive to run over time. But you should note that an unvented gas heater will produce combustion products that can be harmful to many plants.

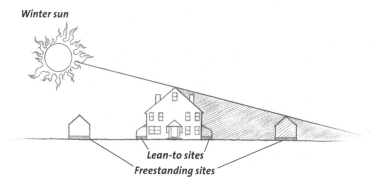

When siting a greenhouse, don't overlook the obvious—precisely where sunlight falls at the crucial times of year.

ROTATE THOSE BEDS!

Just like some gardeners, many vegetables need their distance from family members. This is the latest advice from expert gardeners.

If you are one of those gardeners who tend to habitually plant the same crops in the same places each year, remind yourself that the plant wastes in the soil may harbor family-specific diseases and pests that will lurk over winter to attack a similar crop the following year. And it's key to think in terms of vegetable *families* so that you don't afflict this season's eggplants, for example, with the problems that troubled last year's tomatoes. Here's a roll call of family members.

Cabbage family: Broccoli, Brussels sprouts, cabbage, cauliflower, Chinese cabbage, kohlrabi, mustard greens, radish, rutabaga, turnip

Cucumber family: Cucumber, gourd, muskmelon, pumpkin, squash, watermelon

Onion family: Chive, garlic, leek, onion, shallot

Tomato family: Eggplant, husk-tomato, pepper, potato, tomato

Umbelliferous family: Carrot, celery, parsnip

A whole sick ward of diseases can be discouraged by swapping beds. You can spare beans from anthracnose; the cabbage family from fusarium wilt; cucumbers from anthracnose and scurf; lettuce from drop (producing water-soaked spots); sweet potatoes from black rot; and tomatoes from early blight and septoria leaf spot. It's not enough to simply change addresses. You also should promptly clear out and destroy any diseased plant material. Don't add it to the compost pile because the temperatures within may not be high enough to deactivate the troublesome organisms.

READY, SET, SOW

Early bird? Johnny-come-lately? It's easy to put off starting seed until it's too late— and almost as easy to jump the gun and begin too early. Let's set the record straight.

When starting seedlings in spring, timing's the thing. Get them started too soon, and the plants are apt to be spindly or rootbound. If you procrastinate, you may be dealing with a seriously shortened growing season. Here's a chart to help you determine when to sow seed for a number of common crops.

TEST TIME FOR SEEDS

To determine if there's much life left in a batch of seeds, you can run your own germination test. Count out a round number of seeds—20, 30, or more, with a greater number helping to ensure a more accurate result. Dampen several layers of paper towel, distribute the seeds over it, then roll up the towel carefully so that the seeds stay in place. Don't allow them to clump together. Label a plastic bag with the type of seed and tuck the rolled paper into it. Seal the bag and keep it at room temperature. Have a look at the seeds every day, looking for signs of germination. Allow the seeds one week after the first ones have sprouted to give the rest a chance, then calculate the germination percentage. Divide the number of germinated seeds by the total number of seeds in the test, and multiply by 100. You can make use of the sprouted seeds, by the way, if it's time for them to be planted. Carefully place them in cell packs or out in the garden.

SAFE SETTING-OUT DATE FOR PLANTS

Use this chart to help you determine how early and how late you can plant seeds. Working from your region's frost-free date, use the chart to figure out how many weeks before and after the frost-free date you can plant and still harvest vegetables during the growing season.

CROP	WEEKS BEFORE FROST-FREE DAY						FROST-FREE DATE:	WEEKS AFTER FROST-FREE DAY							
	6	5	4	3	2	1		1	2	3	4	5	6	7	8
Basil								x	x	x	x	x	x		
Beans (snap)									x	x	x	x	x	x	x
Beets			x	x	x	x									
Broccoli			x	x	x	x		x	x	x					
Brussels sprouts			x	x	x	x		x	x	x					
Cabbage		x	x	x	x	x		x	x	x					
Carrots			x	x	x	x									
Cauliflower			x	x	x	x		x	x						
Celery			x	x	x			x	x	x	x				
Corn									x	x					
Cucumber										x					
Eggplant									x	x					
Kale		x	x	x	x	x		x	x						
Kohlrabi		x	x	x	x	x		x	x						
Leek		x	x	x	x	x		x	x						
Lettuce					x	x		x	x	x					
Okra									x	x					
Onion, bulb	x	x	x	x	x	x		x	x						
Parsley	x	x	x	x	x	x		x	x	x	x	x	x		
Parsnip			x	x	x	x		x	x	x	x				
Peas			x	x	x	x		x	x	x					
Pepper									x	x					
Potato			x	x	x										
Pumpkin											x				
Radish	x	x	x												
Spinach	x	x	x	x											
Swiss chard			x	x											
Tomato									x	x					
Turnip			x	x	x	x		x	x	x	x				

LUNAR WISDOM, OR LUNAR WHIMSY?

For centuries, people have been planting according to the heavens rather than what's written on a seed packet. Maybe they're on to something.

Not much clinical research has been done on the traditional practice of planting by phases of the moon, or by the astrological signs determined by the position of the stars. But that doesn't keep gardeners from being guided by the heavens. The only way to settle the issue is to experiment in your own backyard.

PLANTING BY THE MOON

It may be that the gravitational pull of the moon draws fluids up through plants, much as the moon creates ocean tides. A study by the federal Agricultural Research Service suggested that weeds could be discouraged by tilling at night under a new moon (the phase in which it isn't visible), but that may be explained simply by the relative darkness at this time of month.

It's said that aboveground crops will do better if planted during a waxing moon (the illuminated portion of it is increasing); for root crops, the best planting time is during the waning (decreasing) phase. Leafy plants should be planted between the new moon (when it's dark) and the first quarter (when the right half of the moon is illuminated). When the moon is between the first quarter and the full phase, it's time to plant crops with seeds borne inside the fruit. Between the full moon and last quarter, concentrate on planting bulbs and root crops. And forget planting between the last quarter and the new moon.

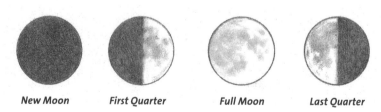

New Moon   **First Quarter**   **Full Moon**   **Last Quarter**

In cultures around the world, the phases of the moon have served as a celestial guide to planting here on Earth.

PLANTING BY THE STARS

So much for the moon. Here are the 12 signs of the zodiac, with the activities that are promoted or discouraged by each.

- **Aries:** Favors tilling the soil, and planting garlic and onions.
- **Taurus:** A good sign for planting root crops.
- **Gemini:** Cultivating and weeding are appropriate activities.
- **Cancer:** A fruitful sign, and the best for general planting and transplanting.
- **Leo:** Suspend planting and transplanting, and attend to weeds instead.
- **Virgo:** A good sign for cultivating and weeding.
- **Libra:** Favors planting flowers and crops harvested above-ground.
- **Scorpio:** A very good time for planting most crops.
- **Sagittarius:** A barren sign.
- **Capricorn:** Planting root crops is appropriate.
- **Aquarius:** Cultivate and weed the garden under this sign, rather than plant.
- **Pisces:** A good time for planting bulbs and fruits in particular.

NAMING THE FULL MOONS

Traditionally, people have lived much of their lives out of doors, and in many cultures each of the year's full moons has become associated with weather and growing conditions. In parts of the United States, gardeners continue to be guided by the moon; for example, they might wait until May's Planting Moon to set out tender plants. Here are some of the names that have come down through the years.

January	Old Moon	July	Hay Moon
February	Snow Moon	August	Green Corn Moon
March	Sap Moon	September	Harvest Moon
April	Grass Moon	October	Hunter's Moon
May	Planting Moon	November	Frosty Moon
June	Strawberry Moon	December	Long Night Moon

SEED TAPE SIMPLIFIED

Here a dab, there a dab! If you've found that making homemade seed tapes was a messy, sticky proposition, try using an icing decorating bag to plop down the paste.

What You'll Need

Yardstick or other straightedge

Newspaper (black-and-white sections only) or newsprint

Wheat flour

Disposable icing decorator bag (or heavy-duty sandwich bag)

Seeds

Plastic food storage bags

This pleasant off-season gardening project is one that's suited to doing along with kids. Using an icing decorating bag and a few household materials, you can manufacture your own seed tapes with the varieties (and spacing) of your choosing. Look for decorating bags at craft stores.

1. Using the straightedge as a guide, tear off strips of newspaper about 1½ inches wide.
2. Make a paste of flour and water.
3. Fill the decorating bag or sandwich bag with paste, and cut off the very tip to make a hole. With the yardstick establishing the spacing given on the seed packets, make generous dabs of paste by squeezing the bag. (A decorating bag coupler and a star-shaped decorating tip will make the job even easier.)
4. Place one seed on each dab, tapping so that it will stay put.
5. When the paste has completely dried, gently fold or roll the strip and place it in a plastic bag along with the seed packet for identification.
6. Once it's time to plant, place the seed tape at the depth recommended on the seed packet.

WHERE THE (CAPILLARY) ACTION IS

Need a time-saver you can depend on? Leave the watering of flats to a do-it-yourself capillary mat.

You can buy all sorts of self-watering trays with which to get seeds off to a good start, or make your own with things you probably have around the house. The heart of the system is a capillary mat that draws water from a reservoir and distributes a moderate supply to flats or individual pots. Begin with a sturdy plastic tray in which to pool water. Add a support to elevate seedlings; a simple solution is to use a scrap piece of Styrofoam insulation and press a nail into the underside of each corner for legs, as shown. For the mat, either a rectangle of quilt batting or an old wool blanket will do; it runs over one edge of the platform and into the water. The flat or pots sit on the mat. To conserve moisture, place lightweight plastic over the tray. To simplify matters, you can buy seed-starting kits with self-watering capillary mats.

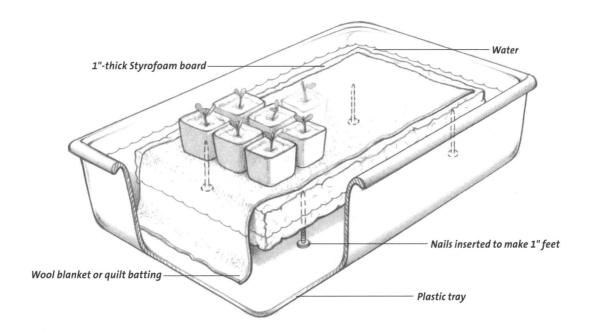

1"-thick Styrofoam board

Water

Nails inserted to make 1" feet

Wool blanket or quilt batting

Plastic tray

A simple home-constructed capillary watering system can provide plants with a steady supply of moisture.

OPEN-POLLINATED OR HYBRID SEED?

Both traditional open-pollinated and hybrid varieties have their advantages.

Next Year's Garden
Pollination Transportation

If you are saving seed and want next year's crop to look like this year's, then the parent plants should be pollinated with pollen from the same variety. That may be a challenge for vegetables that have airborne pollen, such as corn, spinach, and Swiss chard, because those tiny particles can float up to a mile in the wind, meaning that cross-pollination is very possible. Bugs don't distribute pollen quite so freely as a good breeze, so a general recommendation for insect-pollinated plants, such as broccoli, cucumber, eggplant, and squash, is to ensure at least ¼ mile between varieties. Self-pollinated crops, such as beans, peas, and tomatoes, aren't as likely to have a problem because the pollen goes straight to the stigma within the flower. Nevertheless, some pollen may reach a neighboring variety unless you take the precaution of planting it on the other side of the garden.

If you have your choice between open-pollinated or hybrid varieties, what do you do? The answer depends largely on what you're looking for.

OPEN-POLLINATED

Open-pollinated varieties were once the only way to go. They've been selected over the centuries for desirable characteristics—flavor, color, ease of harvest, productivity. They tend to reflect the tastes of people of a region and to do well in that region's climate. Many thousands of varieties came to be, some of them given names and others are anonymous favorites passed down within a family over the generations. Brandywine tomato and Moon and Stars watermelon are two well-known open-pollinated varieties you can buy today.

HYBRID

Plant the seed of an open-pollinated variety, and you'll get something that closely resembles the parent. But plant the seed of a *hybrid* vegetable, and there's no telling what it will grow into. It won't "breed true." That's because hybrids are bred by intentionally crossing two different parent plants to see what comes up. A promising offspring might be bred with others of its kind, and so on, resulting in a complex family tree. A first-generation hybrid is designated as *F1*, and a second-generation hybrid as *F2*, as you've probably noticed in seed catalogs.

So why, as a resourceful gardener, would you want to buy plants that make all-but-useless seed? First, you may not be able to find anything else among certain vegetables, either in a catalog or at a local nursery. But hybrids do have advantages worth investigating. They may exhibit what is known as hybrid vigor, meaning that they perform vigorously. They often are resistant to troublesome diseases. And they are apt to perform uniformly, an advantage to commercial growers who might have trouble with a long, gradual harvest.

TOMATOES: BUSH OR VINE?

Matchmaking isn't just for singles! Tomato varieties differ a lot in their growing style, so pick a style that matches your own.

Next Year's Garden
Make Your Own Hybrid

Although creating hybrid varieties is usually left to plant geneticists, there's no reason you can't attempt it at home, given good eyesight and considerable patience. And you may want to look at a basic horticulture textbook or Web site for help in identifying plant parts. Here's how you might begin with tomatoes.

First, identify desirable characteristics in two varieties; one may have good size while the other has an especially interesting color. Remove the anthers from the flower of one plant (this will be the female parent) before it forms pollen and pollinates itself. Use an artist's paintbrush to collect pollen from the other parent (the male) and transfer it to the stigma of the female flower. Harvest the resulting seeds, plant them, and see what comes up. Chances are very slim that you'll get great plants, because undesirable characteristics from past generations will crop up. But you can keep at it, picking the best performers in each generation of tomatoes and self-pollinating them. You may arrive at a hybrid that is stable genetically.

Broadly speaking, tomato varieties grow as either bushes or vines. *Determinate* varieties mature to a bushy, moderate size and then are genetically programmed to put on the brakes. *Indeterminates,* on the other hand, love to grow and grow—until they are reined in by frost or disease. Which type should you choose?

- **Determinates** reach just 2 to 4 feet. That's an advantage if you don't have a lot of space. You may also welcome the freedom of not having to stake these mild-mannered plants, although low cages can help keep them off the ground. Determinates ripen their tomatoes over a shorter period, usually from 2 to 3 weeks, and that's a boon if you don't want to be bothered with harvesting over a longer season. Once this period is over, the foliage yellows and production slows dramatically.

- **Indeterminate** tomatoes can grow 10 feet or more—unless you do something to restrain them, as you probably will. Most gardeners pinch back the suckers that grow from the fork between branches, so that the plant grows just one, two, or three main stems. This pruning not only keeps plants more manageable but also can increase the size of the tomatoes you harvest by an ounce or two. Indeterminates produce later in the season than determinates, and keep on producing so that you don't have a glut of tomatoes turning to pulp all over the kitchen and attracting every fruit fly in the neighborhood. Most backyard favorites, by the way, are indeterminate, including both the popular "beefsteak" sort and quirky heirlooms that have been handed down over the years.

FREE TOMATO SEEDS FOR LIFE!

Be a part of the future. Save seeds from tomatoes (and other open-pollinated vegetables) for use next year and to give to fellow gardeners.

Next Year's Garden
Healthy Tomatoes from Healthy Seed

The bacterial diseases that tend to plague tomato plants may get their start early, by hitching a ride on seed. If you've been having trouble getting your plants through the season in good shape, try disinfecting the seed. Mix 1 part household bleach to 4 parts water, and stir in a few drops of dishwashing liquid. Add the seed and stir for 1 minute. Then rinse the seed thoroughly by placing it in a sieve and running water through it for 5 minutes. Spread the seed over a few thicknesses of paper towel and allow it to dry.

If you are growing open-pollinated tomatoes (that is, not hybrids), you can save seed from each year's crop to sow for the following year. That's the way varieties have been kept alive down through the centuries, and the system still works—with a little care but not much trouble.

Keep that phrase "open-pollinated" in mind. Pollen blows or is carried from plant to plant—and sometimes from one tomato variety to another. The results can be interesting and even valuable, if this cross produces an exceptional tomato. But if you want the seeds to preserve the qualities of a given variety, then allow some distance between plants in the garden. Just how much distance is needed to isolate one variety from others is a matter of debate, but 5 feet in all directions ordinarily should do it.

1. When collecting seed, choose good-looking and fully ripe tomatoes from healthy plants.
2. Scoop out the seeds from the tomatoes.
3. Ferment the seeds. This can be a disagreeable task, but it helps to both kill plant diseases and also inactivate a naturally occurring compound that keeps seeds from germinating prematurely in the fruit. Place the juicy contents of the tomatoes in a disposable container and set it aside for a few days.
4. When the tomato innards have begun to bubble, dump them in a bucket and hit them with a stream of water from a faucet or hose to help free the seeds.
5. Collect the seeds and place them on a couple layers of paper towel to dry.
6. Store dry seeds in plastic sandwich bags or the container of your choice, using an indelible marker to label the variety and year collected.

SEED-SAVING SPECIFICS

Seeds are programmed to bide their time until conditions are favorable. So, when saving seed, it's good to know what it will take to keep the seeds resting quietly until you start them.

ADVICE OVER THE FENCE

Saving the Seeds of Biennials

Biennials add a wrinkle to seed saving: they require two seasons to mature and produce seed. Among vegetables, the biennials include beets, Brussels sprouts, cabbage, carrots, cauliflower, celery, kale, leeks, onions, parsley, parsnips, rutabaga, salsify, Swiss chard, and turnips. Biennial flowers include Canterbury bells (*Campanula medium*), delphinium (*Delphinium ajacis*), forget-me-not (*Myosotis sylvatica*), foxglove (*Digitalis purpurea*), hollyhock (*Alcea rosea*), sweet William (*Dianthus barbatus*), and verbena (*Verbena bonariensis*). When sowing and growing biennials, it helps to keep in mind the old saying, "Patience prospers."

When collecting seeds from the following vegetables, think in terms of survival of the fittest and look for plants that have been the best performers that season. And once you identify these plants, collect seeds that seem plump and healthy (although peas, to name one exception, will appear somewhat shrunken). Allow damp seeds to dry thoroughly before storage by placing them on several thicknesses of paper towel, out of direct sunlight.

Beans. Allow the pods to remain dry on the plant until they rattle when jostled. This typically takes 6 weeks after picking beans for fresh use in the kitchen. Harvest the pods and remove the seeds.

Eggplant. Leave the eggplants on the vine until they have reached full size and are beginning to turn brown and shriveled. Halve the eggplants, scoop out the insides, and rinse away the pulp.

Cucumbers. It's best to grow just one variety of cucumber in a garden patch if you plan on saving seed, because of cross pollination. Leave the cukes on the vine until they turn yellow. Cut them in half and spoon out the seeds. To rinse off the slimy coating, place the seeds in a sieve under running water and rub them against the mesh. Dry the seeds on paper towels.

Lettuce. After flowering, seedheads should stand for 2 to 3 weeks before you gather seed. To dry the seed, cut off the tops of the plants and place them upside down in a paper bag left open for air circulation. Shake off the dried seed.

Peppers. Choose a pepper that has reached its mature color. Scoop out the seeds, and remove any pulp attached to them before drying on paper towels.

Summer squash. The seeds should be ready when the rinds of the squash harden on the plant. Cut the squash open and scrape out the seeds. Rinse the seeds to remove the pulp and then allow them to dry on paper towels.

BROADCASTING SYSTEMS

Forget all those spacing rules you've heard. Try sowing thickly so that plants form their own weed-squelching, moisture-conserving mulch.

Next Year's Garden

Swapping Meat-Eating Seeds

Strange as it sounds, there is a group of enthusiastic gardeners who trade seeds programmed to eat meat—tiny pieces of winged, multilegged meat, that is, such as flies. The International Carnivorous Plant Society maintains a seed bank through which members can swap seed at very reasonable prices. Seeds of some varieties are offered free of charge to teachers for use in the classroom, as well as to conservation organizations. To learn how to become a member, visit the Web site, www. carnivorousplants.org.

Seed packets usually tell you to allow generous amounts of space between plants, and not without reason. You can get better performance from a plant that isn't crowded cheek by jowl with its neighbors. But until plants reach a mature size, there is unused real estate between rows—prime territory for weeds, and also nicely prepared soil that isn't growing anything at the moment.

THE BENEFITS OF BROADCASTING

For some crops, both of the shortcomings mentioned above can be met by *broadcasting* seeds—that is, scattering them evenly over the entire bed rather than confining them to rows. Lettuce, arugula, mesclun mixes, and Asian greens all lend themselves to sowing this way. Left on their own, the young plants will quickly form a living mulch that discourages weeds. You can go into the garden with a pair of scissors and make a succession of three or four cuttings from the top few inches of these greens. Or, you can pull some seedlings (and put them in salads) to allow a reduced number of plants to reach their normal size.

PRECISION SOWING

Some gardeners prefer to take more care, planting seeds one by one in rows or bands and being mindful of the spacing. You use less seed with this method; there isn't the need to spend time thinning; and you avoid disturbing the soil around the roots of the seedlings that will remain. To make it easier to sow seed in a controlled way, you can use a clever gadget known

A simple precision seeder can make it easier to distribute seeds evenly.

as the Precision English Seeder. It's just a handheld plastic pump that creates a vacuum to pick up individual seeds, then deposits them singly. There are tips of various diameters to match the size of the seeds.

AUTOMATIC SOWING

If you sow long rows each growing season, you may want to save time and spare your back with an Earthway Seeder, selling for about $100. Looking something like a kid's scooter, it rolls along on two wheels and drops seed into a furrow at a preset depth. Not only that, but the furrow is covered and the next row is laid out, all in a single trip. The device comes with seed plates sized for planting everything from corn to radishes. You'll only have to do deep knee-bends when it comes time for the harvest.

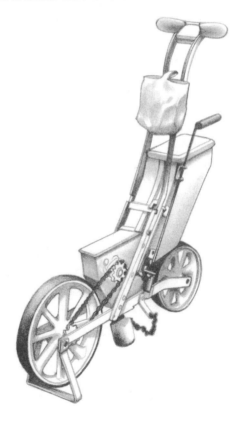

If you sow a lot of seed, a wheeled seeder will save you time and trouble, while guaranteeing neat, straight rows.

SOWING ISN'T JUST FOR SPRINGTIME

In midsummer, consider a second round of crops that are improved by freezing temperatures, as well as those that will slumber through the winter and appear as if by magic the next spring for harvesting.

ADVICE OVER ⌂THE⌂ FENCE
Coming to the Aid of a Late Planting

You occasionally may not get around to starting plants until a few weeks after the date given on the seed packet. If so, you can help nurse a late crop through the first fall frosts in order to get a harvest. Beans, cucumbers, squash, peppers, and tomatoes all may reward you for the warmth of an old blanket or overturned cardboard box on a cold fall night. Just remember to remove the covering early the following morning so that the plants can take full advantage of the sun's warmth and light.

The first warm days of spring excite seeds to sprout. The balmy weather also excites gardeners to get in gear. But we are apt to be distracted by other activities once summer is here in earnest, and gardening can enter something of a slump by August. For evidence, take a look at the local gardening center or at your neighbor's backyard. All too often, gardening is a seasonal activity that starts off with a bang and ends with a horticultural whimper. And yet there are many weeks of good growing weather ahead, continuing even after the first frost blackens the basil—although you might not know that from reading seed packets or catalogs, which often give growing directions only for a first planting in spring or early summer. In midsummer, there's still time to dash off to the gardening center to see what's left on the seed racks, or to buy cool-season seeds from a favorite mail-order catalog.

A SEED GROWS IN SUMMER

It's blazing hot, and your planting window is long over. Think again. You've already done the hard work of preparing the soil and dealing with weeds, so why not take advantage of those vacant beds?

- **Arugula.** This spicy green turns downright hot in response to summer heat, and a late-sown crop will remain less assertive in flavor.

- **Asian greens.** Pak choi, komatsuna, and other East Asian greens can be sown through to late summer. Many will keep growing well after hard frosts and under snow cover. Cool, even downright cold weather suits them, whereas plantings may bolt if they run into an early heat wave.

- **Basil.** True, basil is wasted by the first frost, but you can sneak in a late crop up until as little as a month before that day is expected to arrive.

- **Beans.** For a late planting, choose a filet bean that you can harvest in just 50 days.

- **Beets.** Count back 8 weeks from when you can expect hard frosts, and that's your cutoff date for a fall crop of beets. Even if the plants don't have time to mature their belowground crop, you can add small leaves to salads and steam the larger ones.

- **Cabbage.** July and August sowings will yield a late-fall crop. Or, you can have a second harvest from cabbage planted in spring if you remove the mature head and allow smaller heads to sprout from the stump. Encourage sprouting by cutting off the head as high up on the stem as possible, without removing the loose outer leaves. Pick the sprouts when they reach 2 to 4 inches in diameter and feel firm.

- **Carrots.** You can get in a late-July sowing of carrots, with the assurance that the crop will be secure belowground for the first frosts. Dig up all the carrots before the ground freezes up.

- **Cilantro.** Count back just 55 days from the first frost to plant this herb for a harvest of the foliage. A light frost won't necessarily do them in.

- **Daikon radish.** Some varieties of this large, moderately flavored East Asian radish can be planted in late summer. Use them along with Chinese cabbage for homemade kim chi, a Korean staple similar to sauerkraut and a traditional way to preserve late-season vegetables.

- **Kale.** One of the sturdiest cold-weather crops, kale tastes better after being frostbitten. Small leaves of the delicate, tender 'Red Russian' kale can be harvested in just 25 days for salads and steaming.

- **Kohlrabi.** Look for newer varieties that can be harvested in just 40 days—and harvest before the odd-looking orbs become woody and unappealing. You may want to put up temporary shade to protect midsummer seedlings from the worst of the day's sun. The first frosts of autumn aren't usually a problem for kohlrabi.

- **Peas.** Most of us think of peas as one of the ultra-early crops, planted when the ground is still soggy and cold. But they also

(continued)

*The Joys of Late-Season
Gardening*

Working in the garden becomes
especially enjoyable as summer
winds down, for a number of
reasons. The heat and humidity
have relented. There may be
fewer biting insects. The hard
work of turning beds is already
behind you (although you may
want to rake them and add
another round of compost and
fertilizer). One easily overlooked
requirement is that seeds
planted in July and August are
vulnerable to the hot midsummer sun, and you have to take
care to ensure that at least the
top $\frac{1}{2}$ inch of soil is kept moist.
It may help to run a length of
permeable row cover over the
just-seeded beds to conserve
moisture. And if you see young
seedlings wilting in the heat,
block the afternoon sun with
any sort of object you have lying
about—boards, bricks, or cardboard boxes weighted with
stones.

will do well when planted 2 months before freezing temperatures
return in fall. They may be able to handle a light frost or two.

✤ **Rutabaga.** This sturdy root crop can be planted up until the
middle of July, so that it does much of its growing as fall temperatures come on—rutabagas typically need 90 to 100 days to
mature. If you want to leave them in place well into fall, toss
straw mulch over them to help retain the ground's warmth.
Their flavor will become milder and sweeter as starches gradually are converted to sugars.

✤ **Shallots.** Plant the bulblets in fall and you can look forward to
green onions coming up at winter's end, followed by an early
crop of mature shallots.

✤ **Spinach.** Don't count on a good showing from seeds sown in
soil that's heated by the midsummer sun, but when temperatures
moderate, you can start a fall crop. Or plant seed from September right up until hard frosts for picking next spring.

✤ **Swiss chard.** With varieties named 'Magenta Sunset' and 'Pink
Passion,' as well as the now-famous 'Bright Lights' Technicolor
mix, Swiss chard will bring brilliance to a late-season garden if
sown in midsummer. Allow 50 to 55 days until harvest, although
you can pick little leaves earlier to add visual punch to salads.

✤ **Turnips.** Turnips mature more quickly than rutabagas and can
be planted from July through early August for a fall crop after
early potatoes, cabbage, beets, and peas. The greens may be ready
in just a month, with roots needing nearly 2 months to form.

MIDSUMMER LETTUCE?

If you sow beds with lettuce during a hot stretch of summer weather,
nothing much will happen. That's because the seeds are programmed
to be inactive when temperatures climb into the 80s. Instead, go
indoors. Find the coolest room of the house and start seeds in flats.
Once the seedlings have two sets of true leaves, move them out to
the garden and shield them with a floating row cover.

You also can erect a temporary shade barrier—a fence that
blocks the sun at the hottest time of day. Observe where the lettuce-
wilting sun comes from in the afternoon; drive metal garden posts

along the side of the bed at roughly 6-foot intervals; string wire along the tops of the posts; and use clothespins to hang up a piece of shade cloth or row cover. The plants will be spared the brunt of the afternoon heat while still benefiting from good air circulation. And you are spared the work of rolling back a cover each time you want to harvest or have to weed.

SCARIFYING AND STRATIFYING

Scarify and *stratify* are a couple of scary sounding words that it's good to be familiar with if you like to start plants from seed. These are processes for breaking the dormancy of seeds, which are programmed to germinate only in favorable conditions. Both methods work by mimicking natural conditions.

Many seeds have a waterproof coating that prevents moisture from triggering germination, and to get past this device you can scarify the seeds by roughing up the protective layer. Depending on the species, this may involve scraping, sanding, or even treating with a solvent (as if the seed were subjected to the acids in an animal's stomach).

Stratification exposes the seed to low temperatures (typically from 33° to 41°F) for a month or more, as if they were subjected to overwintering. The specific technique varies with the plant species, but a common approach is to place the seeds between layers of dampened (not soaking) paper towel within a resealable plastic bag and then refrigerating. At the end of the stratification period, plant the seeds as you would otherwise.

A SANCTUARY FOR SEED

Seed Savers Exchange is a valuable network for preserving rare and old-time varieties. Sign up, and you can help maintain endangered vegetables, flowers, and fruits.

As smaller seed companies are gobbled up by takeovers and mergers, and as mass-marketed hybrid varieties take over more slots on seed racks, there's a danger that unique heirloom varieties may disappear. And they *will* disappear in time unless someone grows the plants and generates new seed. Here's where you come in! To help ensure that precious heirlooms and lovable oddities are kept alive, you can join Seed Savers Exchange, or SSE. (To join, write to 3094 North Winn Road, Decorah, IA 52101 or log on to www.seedsavers.org.) For the price of membership, you receive a catalog the size of a small phone book crammed with listings for more than 11,000 varieties, both well beloved and obscure. And you are invited to submit your own listing for seed you collect and are willing to supply to other members for a nominal charge. SSE also publishes *Garden Seed Inventory,* giving the sources for more than 8,000 nonhybrid varieties, and *Fruit, Berry, and Nut Inventory,* with more than 6,000 listings.

SSE isn't your only option. Many seed catalogs now make an effort to stock open-pollinated heirlooms. For example, Johnny's Selected Seeds (955 Benton Avenue, Winslow, ME 04901-2601; www.johnnyseeds.com) offers a rotating selection of old-timers, the idea being that once you buy a certain variety, you can continue producing your own seed and won't need to rely on the company's catalog. For other sources, just do an Internet search for "heirloom variety."

CHAPTER 2

Planting and Transplanting

Entrusting seeds and seedlings to the outdoor garden environment is a time of transition, for both the plants and you, the gardener. A plant has a certain amount of security when isolated in a plastic pot of its own. Its needs for water, light, and nutrients are easily met. But out in the yard, it has to take on the elements with much less help. Wind, direct sunlight, foot traffic, pests, diseases, drought, drenching rain—all may conspire to do in your young plants in what amounts to the survival of the fittest.

The best medicine is attention, focusing in on the needs of the garden at this crucial period. Each variety of plant will have its particular requirements for soil, moisture, temperature range, fertilizer or compost, shade, pest and disease control—the list is long, but this is a fascinating time to be out in the yard. Watching the plants come into their own is a reward in itself, even before they yield something to eat or to arrange in a vase.

You can help seedlings weather the transition to outdoor living by "hardening off," in which the young plants are gradually exposed to the vagaries of the natural world. They are taken outside for longer periods each day over a week or two, so that they become accustomed to sunlight, temperature swings, and the wind. It's best to begin when the weather is particularly mild, treating these babies to just a couple of hours of filtered sunlight in a sheltered spot. If strong winds or especially heavy rains are forecast, skip that day's session. You can spare yourself some of the trouble of moving plants around if you have a cold frame with a lid that opens automatically to vent solar heat.

Plants differ in how quickly they can adjust to the warming garden. While parsley seedlings shouldn't be fazed by a cold snap, a chilly turn in the weather may cause Chinese cabbage and pak choi to bolt.

MINIMUM TRANSPLANT TEMPS

Hardy	40°F	Broccoli, Brussels sprouts, kohlrabi, leeks, onions, parsley
Half-Hardy	45°F	Celery, endive, Chinese cabbage, lettuce, pak choi
Tender	50°F	Pumpkin, squash, sweet corn
	60°F	Cabbage, cauliflower, celery, cucumber, eggplant, muskmelon
	65°F	Basil, peppers, tomatoes

GARDENING WITH GROCERIES

Your shopping bag may contain seeds, roots, and stems that can be planted in pots or the garden.

EASY DOES IT

Willow Root for Me

You can encourage cuttings to grow roots and become self-sustaining plants by dipping the cut end in a rooting hormone powder, sold by garden supply centers. Or take advantage of the root-promoting properties of the willow tree, as has been done for centuries. Cut several short pieces of willow branch and cover them with warm water. Allow them to sit for a few days. Soak the cuttings you want to root in this tea for a day or so, then plant them.

Next time you visit the produce department of your local supermarket or ethnic grocery, look at the vegetables and fruits as potential sources of plants for the garden or windowsill. Increasingly, markets carry fresh herbs as well, ready for propagating. There are a few ways to bring these plants to life—by rooting cuttings, by sticking rooted ends in soil, or by collecting seeds and pits.

STARTING WITH PLANTS AND CUTTINGS

To help plants become established, you can raise the humidity by slipping a clear plastic bag over them, leaving it open at the bottom for some air circulation. Place the plants in a warm place, out of direct sunlight. Look for new growth as a sign that there is activity belowground.

- **Basil, parsley, mint, and cilantro.** Try to find entire plants with roots, and stick them in a container with potting mix. Or simply take a 4-inch cutting, place it in water, and wait for the roots to form.

- **Oregano, thyme, rosemary, and sage.** Take short tip cuttings, remove the lower leaves, and stick at least the bottom 1 inch in moistened potting mix, with one or more nodes (where a leaf was attached) below the surface.

- **Potatoes.** For considerably less money than buying seed potatoes by mail order, you can pick up a few interesting spuds at the market and tuck them into the ground. Trouble is, these potatoes may be treated to retard their sprouting. Even so, you can plant them for a modest harvest, then use this crop to plant a new chemical-free crop the following year. You also might pick up your potatoes from a farmers' market or roadside stand, where you can be reasonably assured the tubers haven't been treated.

The easiest way to create a lot of plants quickly is to plant their seed, as nature intended. But with seeds (and the pollination process) comes variability. Some herbs won't grow true from seed, their offspring having an insipid taste and scent. Oregano and the various mints are examples. To bypass the problem, start new plants from cuttings, by division, or by layering a parent plant. You'll get a clonal copy of the original.

❖ **Lemongrass.** This tall, graceful grasslike herb is central to Thai cooking, and you're apt to find it in East Asian groceries. Plants with roots may get off to a quicker start, but even if they've been trimmed, you can root them in water before moving them to pots or a garden bed with full sun.

Lemongrass adds a haunting fragrance to East Asian recipes. It can be grown easily in a sunny spot.

STARTING WITH SEEDS AND PITS

As long as foods from the market haven't been cooked or canned, there's a chance they still have the ability to make more of their kind from seeds or pits.

❖ Even if spice seeds have been sitting around in a jar for many months, they may sprout and grow. Try anise, celery, cumin, coriander, dill, fennel, sesame—whatever you have on hand. Some herb plants also have flavorful foliage as a bonus, including coriander and dill.

❖ Dried beans don't look very lively, but they may just be waiting for a bit of soil and moisture. Generations of schoolkids have sprouted beans in paper cups as a nature lesson, so you, as a gardener with some experience, stand a good chance of raising a crop. For interesting dried beans in a fascinating array of colors and patterns, walk down the international aisle of your supermarket or visit a Latino grocery. Depending on the variety, you may be able to harvest early for fresh beans or later, allowing the beans to dry in the pod before collecting them.

❖ If you buy a squash that looks attractive and has great flavor, save the seeds. Rinse them well and allow them to dry thoroughly on a couple thicknesses of paper towel. Then put them in a sealable plastic bag labeled with the variety and the year, and keep them until it's time to plant.

(continued)

- You can grow interesting tomato and pepper varieties with a few dollars' worth of these crops from a roadside stand or farmers' market. Why not buy them at a supermarket? The fruits you find there likely are hybrids rather than open pollinated, and they won't grow true from seed. Local growers also are apt to offer interesting varieties not readily available through the usual channels. Just make sure that you'll be collecting seed from open-pollinated tomatoes and peppers.

- And then there are the plants that simply are interesting to look at, even if you live in the wrong part of the world to raise a crop. Try cardamom and citrus seeds, avocado pits, and gingerroot.

FREE GARDENING GUIDES!

For informative how-to publications on gardening, just walk out to the mailbox.

Many mail-order seed companies issue catalogs with reliable, condensed information in an easily accessed form. To plant kohlrabi, you merely turn to the listings for kohlrabi. If the company produces much of its own seed, then their printed information is apt to be based on firsthand experience: These people *must* have a good growing season, or they won't have seed to sell.

Another excellent (if less reliable) free source is the Internet. Do a search for your pet peeve or your pet plant, and chances are you'll get a dizzying amount of free advice. For ad-free, dependable information, try limiting your search to educational institutions and agricultural research stations by searching only for site addresses ending in .edu.

MADE IN THE SHADE

Yes, it's true what you've heard—in order to get a good start, seedlings need light. But what you may not know is that typical full-bore sunlight is too much for most plants.

EASY DOES IT

A Shady Workspace

A shady nook can also be a hospitable place for you, the gardener—a pleasant spot in which to do any number of garden-related tasks. You might want to add a lawn chair or two, as well as a small bench as a work surface. Keep a plastic toolbox on hand in which to store plant labels, indelible markers, and perhaps a seed catalog that includes good planting directions.

Set up a propagation area in an area of the yard that affords some shade—under the broad branches of a tree, or along the north side of your home or an outbuilding. If you don't have a favorable site, consider placing lattice panels atop a simple structure. One quick answer is to attach lattice panels atop the stand-alone monkey bars that are available in knocked-down form at home centers. To filter strong sunlight from the south or west, you might also want to attach a vertical panel. Secure the panels with nylon cord or wire.

You can use this shady spot for starting seeds, handling transplants, repotting, and encouraging cuttings to root. Even though seedlings may look robust, they lack the well-developed root systems necessary to replace the water lost to heat and direct sunlight. Gradually expose the plants to more light to help them adapt to the big, bright world of the garden.

You can make a comfortable outdoor workstation with a lattice panel set on top of monkey bars or a simple structure of your own devising.

STOOP-FREE POTTING BENCH

This sturdy, counter-height potting bench can keep you upright by allowing you to do all sorts of tasks at a comfortable level.

What You'll Need

- 96 feet 5/4 × 6 pine
- #6 × 2-inch galvanized screws
- #8 × 3-inch galvanized screws
- 2½-inch galvanized finishing nails

You can make this potting bench in about a weekend, if you have basic woodworking skills. If not, show the drawings and general construction steps to a carpenter or woodworker and have them do the job. This design includes a few optional features: a tool shelf below the work surface, and a seed packet shelf and herb-drying bar above. The bench is made from 5/4 pine, which typically measures just over 1 inch thick. You can paint, stain, or varnish the piece, or leave it unfinished.

A standard height for a work surface is 36 inches, but that may not be right for you. If your kitchen counters are comfortable to work at, measure their height and use this dimension for the bench. Overall, the bench measures 72 inches high, 48 inches wide, and 28 inches deep.

The bench is put together with both screws and water-resistant polyvinyl acetate glue (such as Titebond II). Parts are assembled with glue on their mating surfaces, then clamped before driving the screws.

1. The legs are "sandwiches" of several pieces, which allows you to make sturdy joints without the need for tricky cuts. Assemble them as shown in the detail view, together with the apron and cross rails.

2. Construct the rear legs, attaching them to the cross rails and then slipping in the rear apron.

3. Nail the boards for the lower shelf, with a little space between them to allow the wood to expand and contract. Attach the narrow tool shelf to the underside of the cross rails with screws.

4. Make the tabletop, with the boards running front to back rather than the usual lengthwise configuration. This allows you to make use of short scrap pieces and also will make it easier to brush off the surface. Attach the small support blocks to the rear legs, then

A Midsummer Soil Cooler

Compost is most often thought of as a soil ingredient, to be stirred in well. But it also can work as an insulating top dressing in garden beds, lowering soil temperatures and conserving moisture. Apply a 2- to 3-inch layer around plants. When the weather moderates at summer's end, work the compost into the soil.

nail the narrow fillers. Next come the end boards, and finally the boards in the middle. Nail the boards into the aprons.

5. Assemble the upper shelves, fitting the upper shelf spacers into the slot between the rear legs. Attach the upper shelf supports to the rear legs with screws. Trim the back of the upper shelf to fit between the rear legs, then nail it in place. Nail the upper shelf front onto the supports. Also nail the seed packet shelf onto the bottom of the shelf supports, and the herb-drying bar between the rear legs.

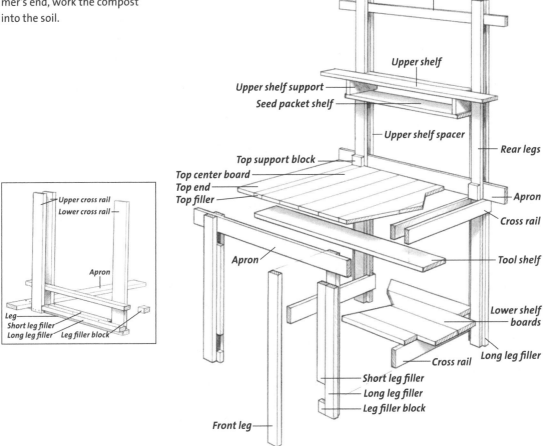

A potting bench puts pots and labels—as well as many common tasks—right at your fingertips. It also helps keep you organized because there's one central spot for gardening odds and ends.

FILTERING SUNLIGHT WITH A SANDWICH BOARD

"Why didn't I think of that?" That's what you'll say when you assemble this attractive lath structure to help moderate the full force of the sun and protect vulnerable plants.

What You'll Need

- 38 pieces 1 × 2 × 36, for laths and support pieces
- 4 pieces 1 × 2 × 48, for legs
- #8 1½-inch flat-head screws
- 3 butt hinges with fasteners
- 2 screw eyes and nylon cord, optional

ADVICE OVER THE FENCE

Growing Vegetables on a Lean-To

When the lath sandwich board isn't being used to shade seedlings, you can move it to where you want to grow plants that need support, such as cucumbers.

There are times of the year when plants can benefit from a sunscreen—some way of reducing the power of the sun. Transplanted seedlings may wither under direct sunlight, as can midsummer beds of lettuce and other heat-sensitive greens. Fabric row covers and shade cloth are easy short-term alternatives, but a sturdy sandwich board of 1 × 2-inch lath will hold up well over the years, and it isn't likely to blow away, as can happen with fabrics. Consider painting the sandwich board to match the garden fence, so that it will be an attractive addition to the yard rather than a makeshift eyesore.

1. Just one side is shown in the plan views. Cut pine or cedar 1 × 2s into the lengths shown, for two sides. If you are using pine, you can finish the cut pieces with exterior paint for better durability, before assembling them.

2. Assemble the sides of the sandwich board by drilling pilot holes and driving screws for the laths. Note that laths are attached to the narrower (¾-inch) side of the legs, and the support piece for each side is attached from the underside.

3. Install butt hinges to join the two sides at their support pieces, using the screws that come with the hardware.

4. To help keep the sandwich board upright, you can install screw eyes toward the lower end of the legs on either side and tie a nylon cord between them.

5. When plants are able to make use of more sun, or if late summer shadows are providing shade, remember to remove the sandwich board and store it for use next growing season.

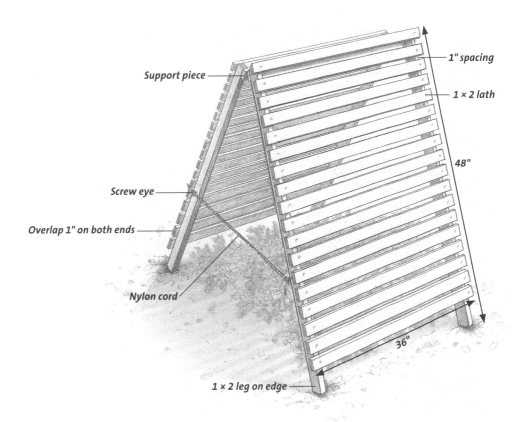

Support piece

1" spacing

1 × 2 lath

48"

Screw eye

Overlap 1" on both ends

Nylon cord

36"

1 × 2 leg on edge

A homemade sandwich board can provide seedlings and sensitive plants with a break from direct sunlight.

LUMBERING FOR MORE LIGHT

If you love plants and your yard is your favorite spot on earth, it can be painful to part with a single sapling. But trees have a way of hogging great swaths of sunlight, subjecting nearby plants to a deep gloom. Take note of how tree shadows move over the yard throughout the day and at various times of the growing season. It may help to make a simple plot diagram and then indicate the arcs of shadow, color coding them according to times of year. Then it's time to think boldly about whether or not to sacrifice one or more trees for the greater good of your gardens. The process of losing trees may be less wrenching for you if these old friends are replaced by species of smaller stature, such as semi-dwarf fruit trees.

MINI VARIETIES FOR PINT-SIZE PLOTS AND POTS

Long gone are the days when gardeners think bigger is better. For vegetables on a very small scale, it helps to choose very small varieties.

EASY DOES IT

A Pot within a Pot for Automatic Watering

Do you frequently forget to water container plants, outdoors or in, to be reminded only by the sad sight of drooping, discouraged leaves? Aside from your faulty memory, the problem may also have to do with unglazed clay pots. Water rapidly evaporates from them. You can use this characteristic to your advantage. Try recessing a terra-cotta pot in the center of a large pot full of planting medium. Put fine gravel in the smaller pot, and set plants around it in a ring. By filling the terra-cotta pot with water, you can keep the surrounding planting medium moist while making fewer trips with the watering can.

Some varieties are just *inherently* small. They never attain what we think of as the normal size for that particular vegetable because they are genetically different. Some have been bred only recently, while others are old standards. If you have a limited area for gardening, and particularly if you want to try gardening in containers, check for these dwarf selections in seed catalogs. Even if they aren't clearly identified as being smaller, the name ("tiny," "mini") may give you a clue. They're also a great choice for young gardeners, because of both their kid-size form and their novelty.

As with growing any sort of plant in a container, the smaller the volume of soil, the more prone the plant will be to drying out, especially in a clay pot. You'll need to get into the routine of watering regularly. For container gardening, use potting medium rather than garden soil to better retain moisture. And pay special attention to feeding plants in containers. They are particularly vulnerable to both overdosing and being malnourished. Fertilize regularly but moderately for the best performance. Finally, allow enough room for the roots to grow—use a pot at least 6 to 8 inches in diameter. Your aim isn't to starve the plants into bonsai.

Chances are that if you grow a lot of vegetables in pots, you set yourself up for *moving* a lot of pots—into or out of a shaded area, closer to a garden hose, or into the house if an out-of-season frost is predicted. To spare your back, place those pots on dollies equipped with casters. These mobile wood or metal stands are made for the purpose, and some can support a couple hundred pounds or more. Place the pot on the stand, then add the planting medium—in that order. When shopping for a dolly, pay particular attention to what's underneath. Dollies with larger casters will make it easier for you to negotiate a bumpy brick patio, flagstone walk, or doorsill.

Plastic Pots That Mimic Terra-Cotta

You now can buy polystyrene pots that have an uncanny resemblance to aged terra-cotta. Even the most tradition-bound gardeners may do a double take at the sight of these artful polystyrene planters, some complete with water staining to suggest that they've been in service for years. And these plastic containers lack a few drawbacks for which terra-cotta is known—they aren't heavy, they don't wick the planting medium's moisture to the atmosphere, and they are less likely to crack if the medium freezes in winter.

If you buy a polystyrene container without drainage holes, it's up to you to make them. That's easier than with a terra-cotta pot, which is apt to chip and shatter in the process. Drill one or more holes, depending on the size of the container.

GENETICALLY SMALL VARIETIES

Basil	Spicy Globe, Mini Greek
Beets	Little Egypt
Cabbage	Baby Head, Little Leaguer, Pee Wee
Cantaloupe	Minnesota Midget
Carrot	Lady Finger, Little Finger, Planet, Thumbelina, Touchon
Corn	Golden Midget
Cucumber	Patio Pik, Little Minnie, Tiny Dill
Eggplant	Bambino, Modern Midget, Pirouette
Lettuce	Little Gem, Tom Thumb
Okra	Dwarf Long Pod
Pea	Dwarf Grey Sugar, Knight, Little Marvel, Mighty Midget
Pepper	Redskin
Pumpkin	Baby Boo, Baby Pan, Jack-Be-Little
Summer Squash	Gold Rush
Tomato	Florida Basket, Pixie, Spoon, Red Robin, Tiny Tom
Watermelon	Golden Midget
Winter Squash	Bush Butternut

POTTED ROSES

Miniature roses (*Rosa chinensis* 'Minima') typically top out at just 3 to 8 inches, making them an excellent choice for growing in containers, either outdoors or on a windowsill that receives at least 5 hours of direct sunlight a day. You'll need to pay particular attention to watering. Probe the planting medium with a finger, and when the top inch feels dry, give the plants a good soaking. Fertilize moderately to avoid stimulating vegetative growth at the expense of flowering. Blossoms also may be shy if the temperature drops below 50°F.

Indoor potted minis will thrive if you move them outside once temperatures moderate in May. Allow them to acclimate themselves by exposing them to longer periods each day, and provide a sheltered, somewhat shady spot for the first week or two. You can keep them in their pots, or allow those roots to roam by placing the plants in beds. At the end of the season, bring the roses back indoors when there's a danger of a fall frost.

CLOSET SEED STARTING

Time to think outside the box and inside the closet. Clear out the winter coats and start seeds for spring planting.

EASY DOES IT

Turn Modular Shelves into a Plant Stand

Furniture stores sell easy-to-assemble wooden shelving that is intended for books or storage, and you can use the shelves as a rack to support fluorescent lights and flats. You may be able to find shelves that fit nicely into a spare closet, allowing you to build the system right in place.

To start seedlings successfully, you need to keep them reasonably warm, expose them to plentiful light, and water them—three conditions that can be met in a closet of your home. Yes, a closet. And the best part of it is that when you are finished dealing with messy potting mix and plant labels and seed packets, you can shut the doors on the whole operation. If the closet doesn't have an outlet, you'll need to snake an extension cord to it from an adjacent room or to extend an electrical circuit. Suspend tiers of fluorescent grow lights either from joists in the ceiling or from a 2 × 4 frame constructed within the closet. Store bags of potting mix and fertilizer containers in a plastic litter box on the floor. Better yet, buy a large plastic tub used for mixing concrete; it will cover much of the floor and catch spills. Seeds are best kept on a high shelf, where they won't get wet.

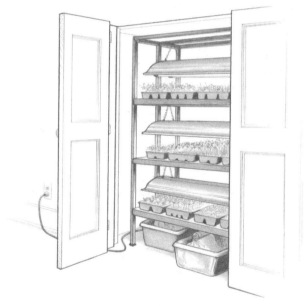

If you have a spare closet, consider using it for starting seeds. Once you're done with that part of the gardening season, you can simply close the doors and everything will be out of sight and out of mind until next year.

SOIL-SURFING POTATOES

Need a new idea for growing potatoes? Here it is. Use mulch to grow spuds without a spade.

EASY DOES IT

Cleaner Spuds

Even if you plant potatoes conventionally, in the ground, you can make the harvest a little easier by incorporating generous amounts of rotted leaves, pine needles, and peat moss in the holes at planting time. Potatoes will come out of the ground with less of the garden clinging to them, meaning less cleanup.

ADVICE OVER THE FENCE

Presprouted Potatoes

To get a jump on the season, *presprout* your potatoes. A couple of weeks before planting the potatoes, place them in a shallow box in a glassed-in porch or cool room so that they get some light but are out of direct sun. They will produce green sprouts (and take on a greenish tinge themselves) as they gear up to hit the ground running.

Potatoes are one of those crops that require you to dig twice—once to plant them, and again to harvest them. Unless, that is, you plant them right on top of the ground and top them with mulch.

1. Prepare the soil as you would to plant seeds, working compost or well-rotted manure into the top foot of soil.

2. Poke seed potatoes or chunks of potato with one or two eyes into the soil, eyes up.

3. Cover the potatoes with mounds of 6 to 12 inches of straw or leaf mulch. Water as needed to keep these piles moist.

4. As vines appear, add more mulch. Make sure that the forming spuds aren't exposed to daylight. The mounds will round up to a depth of up to 2 feet, so be sure to have a good deal of mulch on hand.

5. Once the flowers appear, you can begin reaching into the mulch to snitch a few new potatoes.

6. At the end of the growing season, as the tops begin to die, scoop away the mulch to harvest the full-size potatoes.

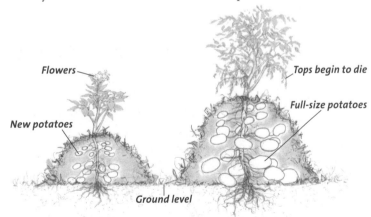

When the plants bloom, that's your signal to reach in for a few new potatoes. When the tops turn yellow, it's time to harvest the mature crop.

TOWARD BETTER TOMATOES

For many vegetable gardeners, tomatoes are the main event—and the main challenge—of the growing season.

Tomatoes rank as the most popular of backyard vegetables, with good reason. You can't buy tomatoes as good tasting as those you grow. You can't find, at any price, hundreds of rare varieties for which seed is readily available. And tomatoes are remarkable plants. There's nothing subtle about them—size, vigor, the scent of the foliage, the brilliantly colored fruit. Even their best-known insect pest, the tomato hornworm, is outrageously large and threatening looking.

Part of the interest in tomatoes must have to do with the challenge of growing a tropical plant in a less-than-welcoming climate. There are dozens of tricks for getting tomatoes to produce earlier, produce more—even to produce at all in the cooler zones. It's particularly important to see that the plants get off to a good start.

The trouble with the warming rays of the sun is that they are intermittent and unavailable to plants at night. A water jacket retains solar heat into the dark hours, protecting plants from frost and promoting growth.

A WATER JACKET TO WARD OFF CHILLS

You can protect young tomato plants from late frosts and growth-slowing cold temperatures at night by surrounding them with plastic water-filled "teepees." The water absorbs the sun's heat by day, then radiates it at night. You may be able to set out plants a month early and begin harvesting a month early as well. The jackets also will keep peppers and eggplants cozy and happy.

BURY SPINDLY SEEDLINGS UP TO THEIR CHINS

If tomato seedlings are started a little too early, get insufficient light, or are purchased in crowded flats, they may be thin and weak. You can take advantage of the plant's ability to grow roots from its stem when in contact with the soil. Dig a trench and lay the lower half to two-thirds of the plant in it, nearly horizontal, and strip the foliage from this section of the stem. The top will look odd, projecting from the ground at an angle, but it soon will right itself. And with the extra roots, the once-puny seedling should grow rapidly.

Tomatoes have been credited with a number of health-promoting benefits of late, including a possible reduced incidence of certain cancers. A beneficial antioxidant, lycopene, is also responsible for the tomato's characteristic rich red color. But according to professor Steven Schwartz, head of a study at Ohio State University, there's a hitch. The body isn't able to readily absorb that substance from red tomatoes. But a particular *orange* variety, 'Tangerine', contains another form of lycopene that seems to be more available. This is according to a test in which subjects ate spaghetti topped with red or orange sauce.

As of this writing, this particular 'Tangerine' variety isn't commercially available, although there are other tomatoes by that name or similar names on the market. But the researchers say that familiar orange-colored or golden varieties might also offer something of the same benefit as the variety used in their trials.

BAGGED TOMATOES

If you've put cages around young tomato plants, you can use these structures to support a plastic barrier against chilly temperatures. Cut the bottom off of large, clear plastic garbage bags and slip them over the cages. This enclosure will help collect heat from both the sun and the soil and keep the heat-loving plants a good deal warmer on nippy nights.

FROM TOMATO SUCKER TO TOMATO PLANT

Many gardeners routinely prune the suckers that grow from the V between two tomato stems, the goal being larger tomatoes. The usefulness of this strategy is a matter of debate, but you can have it both ways by clipping off at least several suckers early in the season and rooting them to make more plants for a late harvest. Just put the cuttings in water until roots appear, then pot them up and treat them tenderly.

CRACK ATTACK

Tomatoes that develop cracks are quick to spoil and attract bugs, not to mention rather unappealing on the plate. They typically develop the problem following a dramatic fluctuation in soil moisture. If plants are subjected to scant rainfall (and you haven't been diligent with your watering), and a cloudburst comes along, they are apt to take up more moisture than the fruits can hold. If you have been troubled by cracking in past summers, give the plants a steady supply of water throughout the growing season and keep the moisture in the soil by mulching.

A PLOP-DOWN, PULL-UP BASKET FOR BULBS

When your flower bulbs need double protection from subterranean troublemakers and the weather, try planting bulbs in a removable basket.

Next Year's Garden

Give Spring-Flowering Bulbs a Lift

Even though you may not *have* to exhume your tulip bulbs each winter because of a gentle climate, give some thought to doing so. They'll appreciate being stored in a nice, dry, temperate place until next spring, performing better for you in years to come.

Imagine solving two problems at once. A barrier basket, either homemade or purchased, keeps voles from tunneling to your flower bulbs. And if you are in the practice of lifting bulbs to store them over winter in a cool, dry place, a basket greatly simplify matters; there's no need to go fishing around in the dirt, because you just lift the basket. Make your own basket out of two pieces of either chicken wire or the sturdier hardware cloth—a circle for the bottom, and a strip to wrap around for the sides, bending the cut ends for a seam that will hold the basket together. Plastic bulb-planting baskets are inexpensive and hold up well to exposure to the soil.

You can avoid a good deal of frustration by planting flower bulbs in vole-proof planting baskets.

PREEMIE VEGGIES

Maybe you should ignore the "Days to Maturity" information! You can harvest super early for tenderness as well as the novelty of cute, dollhouse-size vegetables.

ADVICE OVER THE FENCE
Watch These Babies Closely

Monitor the growth of mini-vegetables on a daily basis. They are apt to have a growth spurt and no longer look quite so cute.

Certain vegetables go in and out of fashion, and now *miniature* vegetables are causing a buzz. Micro greens and baby vegetables turn up as cute adornments at upscale restaurants and are increasingly common in supermarket produce centers. Most of these baby vegetables are in fact babies—conventional varieties that are picked early. Certain varieties will develop their full color and flavor earlier in their growing season and are good candidates for picking young; take note of catalog recommendations for harvesting in the baby state.

When sowing seed or setting out transplants for an extra-early harvest, you can reduce the spacing with an eye to the size the plants will be when you do your picking. A familiar example of this is broadcasting seed for a patch of mesclun greens—lettuces and other leafy vegetables that are harvested young.

HERE A BEAN, THERE A BEAN . . .

The best defense for bean pests may be a good offense—in this case, divide and conquer.

Plant all your beans in the same spot, and you're setting the stage for a pest paradise. As an alternative, try planting a succession of mini-rows, no longer than you can reach with the spread of your arms. To keep pests guessing, place the rows here and there around the garden. The scattered planting will help discourage the spread of diseases, too. And be sure to experiment with bush bean varieties first; because they mature so quickly, you'll probably be harvesting beans before the first pests show up to dine.

A MULCH THAT MAKES PLANTS SEE RED

Plants respond positively to certain colors of the spectrum, and colored mulches can give you a better yield.

Next Year's Garden

Experiment with Colored Mulches

The jury is still out on the benefits of colored mulches, as researchers ponder why test results are inconsistent from year to year. But you can be the judge, by growing a portion of a crop with a colored mulch and the rest as you would normally. Compare the yield when you harvest, either by eyeballing the difference or (more scientifically) by weighing samples from both plots.

It sounds mystical rather than methodical, but research suggests that you can get tomatoes to perform better by placing red plastic mulch in garden beds. Peppers may yield more if grown over yellow or silver mulch. Cucurbits seem to benefit from red or blue, while potatoes favor a pale blue or white mulch. And preliminary studies found that turnips taste more "turnipy" with a blue mulch!

While black mulches are widely used to warm the soil early in the season, colored mulches are believed to trigger changes in the plants by reflecting a certain part of the spectrum at the foliage. The studies with tomatoes found that a red mulch can increase yields by 10 to 15 percent. That impressed the Agricultural Research Service of the USDA so much that they introduced a patented version.

Colored mulches also have been found to discourage plant pests. Research shows that a shiny, reflective mulch will reduce the number of aphids that land on squash and pumpkin plants, with a corresponding decrease in the incidence of the viral diseases spread by these insects. A reflective mulch will keep soils cooler, and while you might guess that would slow plant growth, the increased light level on foliage more than compensates. In one trial, pumpkins with reflective mulch had considerably longer vines than those grown over black mulch.

COOL AIR FLOWS LIKE SYRUP

Protect your plants from cold, growth-inhibiting night temperatures by finding the yard's hot spots.

It's cold on top of tall mountains, right? That's a commonly accepted fact, so much so that we tend to forget that air becomes heavier as it cools, traveling downhill into what are known as frost pockets. If your property has a low spot where cool air tends to drain, a garden laid out there may have a shorter growing season than one placed on higher ground or a slope. To determine what you'd gain from the elevation, place two or more thermometers of the same manufacture out in the yard and take readings at various times of day, in spring and summer and fall.

To see just how the cold air flows and what deflects it or causes it to pool, tour your property on a windless day with ground fog. The fog serves to make air currents visible. Or, if your area isn't visited by fogs, you can walk around with a helium balloon on a string and note which way it is being blown. If that makes you feel ridiculous, have a child carry the balloon while you follow behind with a pencil, a clipboard, and a no-nonsense expression.

Although you probably think of fences in terms of keeping out critters, they also can direct cold nighttime air as it flows downhill. A simple barrier will help divert the chilling draft if placed on the north or uphill side of the garden; it also can conserve the day's heat as temperatures fall. While a fence or rock wall would be an attractive way of accomplishing this climate control, you also could stack a row of straw bales for the same effect.

Another (if unconventional) way to redirect cold air is with a powerful fan. Use a window or shop fan and direct its flow into the foliage of vulnerable plants. This method has been used to protect papayas from overnight freezes in Arizona. If you have several frost-sensitive trees, you may want to invest in a few fans, as well as heavy-duty extension cords. Make sure that you plug into a GFI (ground fault interrupter) circuit to avoid the hazard of shock.

PLANTING IN A GOOD NEIGHBORHOOD

It's not fully understood why certain vegetables seem to flourish in the company of certain others, but nevertheless, companion planting has its followers.

ADVICE OVER THE FENCE

Transplanting Forecast: Clouds, Sprinkles, No Wind

The kind of weather that makes you feel like going outside to stick transplants in the ground may not be suited for the little plants themselves. They would prefer to step out into the big world on a day with cloud cover and perhaps a light shower. The air should be relatively still—no seedling-shredding gusts. Whatever the weather brings, your plants will stand up to the elements much better if they've been *hardened off* by gradually introducing them to longer periods of outdoor temperatures and filtered sunlight.

The practice of companion planting goes back to Native Americans who interplanted what became known as the Three Sisters—corn, beans, and squash. Keep in mind that plants aren't passive, but highly responsive to factors in their immediate environments that we ourselves might overlook. For example, a crop can provide shade, cool the soil, and attract beneficial predators and parasites, benefiting plants growing on all sides. As a general rule, gardens tend to flourish when plants of *any* kind intermingle. Monocropping, as growing huge patches of a single crop is known, may work for farmers, but it acts as a welcome mat for pests and diseases in the garden.

Here is a list of plants and the neighbors that seem to bring out their best.

PLANT	COMPANION
Asparagus	Basil, parsley, tomato
Bean	Beet, cabbage family, carrot, chard, corn, cucumber, eggplant, pea, potato, radish
Beet	Bush bean, cabbage family, lettuce, onion
Cabbage family	Bean, beet, celery, chard, cucumber, lettuce, onion, potato, spinach
Carrot	Bean, lettuce, onion, pea, pepper, radish, tomato
Corn	Bean, cucumber, melon, pea, potato, squash
Cucumber	Bean, cabbage family, corn, pea, tomato
Eggplant	Bean, pepper, potato
Lettuce	Beet, cabbage family, carrot, onion, radish
Pea	Bean, carrot, corn, cucumber, radish, turnip
Pepper	Carrot, eggplant, onion, tomato
Potato	Bean, cabbage family, corn, eggplant, pea
Squash	Corn, melon, pumpkin
Tomato	Asparagus, carrot, celery, cucumber, onion, parsley, pepper

SUCCESSION PLANTING

Gardening isn't a one-act performance, unless your garden happens to be up around the Arctic Circle. To keep those beds attractive and productive from spring through fall, it's important to think of a sequence of two or more plantings.

Next Year's Garden

Stretch Your Garden Space

If you always run out of garden area before you run out of seed, consider broadcasting the seed of smaller plants rather than going with conventional rows. This can work well for beets, carrots, lettuce and Asian greens, parsley, and spinach. After spreading the seed thinly, rake the bed so that you just cover the seed, then tamp down with the flat tines of the rake and water. Harvest young plants to thin the beds to the spacing indicated on the seed packet.

For larger plants, you can save space by staggering plants rather than slavishly setting out rows. Go with the spacing stated on the seed packet, so that each plant is that distance away from all of its neighbors.

Perhaps the toughest gardening chore is preparing beds and then keeping them fertile and relatively weed free. That said, it makes sense to work those beds for most of your area's growing season. Think in terms of three acts—spring, summer, and fall.

Start with cool-season crops that will germinate in chilly spring conditions and won't be done in by a light frost. They include asparagus, broccoli, Brussels sprouts, cabbage, collards, garlic, horseradish, kale, kohlrabi, leek, lettuce, onion, peas, radish, shallot, spinach, and turnip. These crops typically don't fare as well in warm stretches of weather. (There also are the "in-between" plants that may be injured by frost but don't flourish once temperatures stay above 70°F. Among them are beet, carrot, cauliflower, celery, chard, Chinese cabbage, endive, mustard, parsnip, and potato.)

Warm-season crops are those that do best once temperatures rise to 50°F or more. Their seeds tend to rot in cold, damp soil. The plants that do appear may be killed by a frost, and survivors will grow slowly. These include cantaloupe, cucumber, eggplant, lima bean, New Zealand spinach, pepper, pumpkin, snap bean, squash, sweet corn, sweet potato, tomato, and watermelon.

Round out the gardening year with another planting of cool-season vegetables, including those that can be expected to overwinter and even keep on producing right through the coldest months.

In order to have a seamless succession, start seeds indoors for transplanting rather than sow seeds in the garden. This can effectively add a few weeks to your growing season. You also might plan on making more than one planting of a vegetable, sowing them at intervals to ensure that this crop keeps producing in its time slot. Alternately, you can plant a few varieties of that crop that all have different days-to-maturity figures on the packets.

BUYING BARE ROOT

No soil? That's right! Bare-root plants cost less for mail-order firms to ship, meaning lower prices for you and a world of varieties to explore—affordably.

ADVICE OVER THE FENCE

Tear Your T-Shirts

Nothing feels softer to the skin than an old broken-in T-shirt, and plants prefer them too. Strips torn from old cotton are soft and have some give, unlike twine. Begin by tying a knot around the stake, making it good and snug. Keep the ends long enough to tie a second, looser knot around the main stem of the plant. Or pass the loop under a side stem, something like a sling, to support weighty melon or tomato stems.

To gently support tomatoes and other plants vulnerable to breaking and chafing, use strips of well-washed cotton.

It may seem cruel and unusual to ship plants long distances without a speck of soil around their roots. But there are clear advantages to transporting them that way, for both the grower and you. You just need to make sure that the plants are treated with extra care as soon as you receive them.

BARE-ROOT BONUSES

Here are some advantages that bare-root stock has over potted-up plants.

- ❖ You stand to pay less, often saving from 40 to 70 percent, because these plants aren't as expensive to produce and ship.
- ❖ You can find hundreds of rare and unusual varieties not available in pots.
- ❖ Bare-root plants may adapt more quickly to your particular soil.
- ❖ The plants often arrive with more-extensive root systems.

CODDLE YOUR BARE-ROOT BABIES

Bare-root perennials, shrubs, and trees look awfully vulnerable when you pick them up at the nursery or take them out of a mail-order carton. In fact, they *are* vulnerable and need your immediate attention, unlike plants parked in generous-size pots.

To make sure they survive in good shape, you have to take action as soon as they arrive at your doorstep. If you can't promptly pop them in the garden, there are a couple of temporary stopgap measures.

- The simplest strategy, good for a couple of days, is to allow the plants to remain in the packing material. Open the carton and pour a bit of water around any roots that feel dry to the touch. Then keep the carton in a cool, dry place until you can get into the garden.

- Pot them up. Use any old plastic pots you have about the place, and set the plants in a mixture of good soil, compost, and peat moss. Don't forget to tuck identification tags in each pot. If there is just one label for a number of plants of the same type, this is the time to make more—before you forget what's what in the rush of spring planting. Keep the pots in dappled shade where you can water them conveniently.

- Heel them in. Make a shallow trench in a partly shaded area, again choosing a handy spot that will be no trouble to visit with a hose or watering can. Lay the plants on their sides with the roots in the trench, and cover them with a mixture of good soil, compost, and peat moss. Make sure each plant or trench is identified with a label.

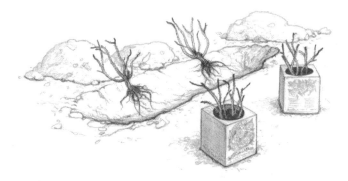

Plants with bare roots are easy to transplant but require prompt attention once you receive them. For a makeshift holding area, place their root systems in a shallow trench, fill with soil, and water as necessary.

MAP YOUR BEDS

It's easy to get lost in your own yard if your plant labels fade or disappear altogether. Try this trick for keeping track of your acquisitions.

Plant labels have a way of wandering away, bleaching out, or simply disappearing. You're left with mystery plants or, just as bad, labels for which you can't find the plant. Until someone comes up with a perfect tip for labeling plants, you can get some insurance by mapping perennial and vegetable beds.

1. Dedicate an inexpensive spiral notebook with unlined pages to mapping your garden. This will help ensure that these diagrams don't disappear along with the labels. Tie a mechanical pencil to the spiral binding.

2. Draw an outline of the bed. To help orient it, you might include the points of the compass or a landmark such as a fence post or tree.

3. Indicate plantings with Xs or whatever symbol you choose. Also note the year you planted a perennial, or the date you planted garden crops.

4. Use the other end of the pencil to delete plants that haven't made it in order to keep the map up-to-date—unless you find it instructive to be reminded of your gardening misfires as well as your successes! Or keep a list in the back of the notebook of plants that didn't make it, along with your best guess as to why (such as too little water, never established itself, or fell victim to deer nibbling).

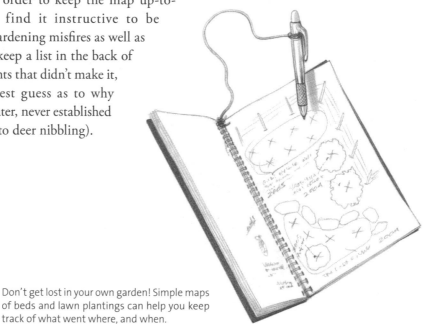

Don't get lost in your own garden! Simple maps of beds and lawn plantings can help you keep track of what went where, and when.

ELEVATED BEDS FOR WHEELCHAIR GARDENING

If you have trouble getting down to reach the garden, bring the garden up to you.

Gardeners in wheelchairs or walkers can till the soil if beds are raised to between 24 and 30 inches. Ideally, these beds should be just 2 feet wide if they will be accessed from one side, or from 3 to 4 feet wide if the gardener can work from both sides.

The beds can be an attractive addition to the garden if constructed with sturdy materials. One approach is to stack and spike landscaping ties. Be sure to avoid using ties that have been pressure treated or preserved with pentachlorophenol. For a highly durable base, pour a concrete footer, then build low walls of concrete block, faced on the outside with a layer of brick. For better drainage, you can place a layer of gravel in the bed before adding soil.

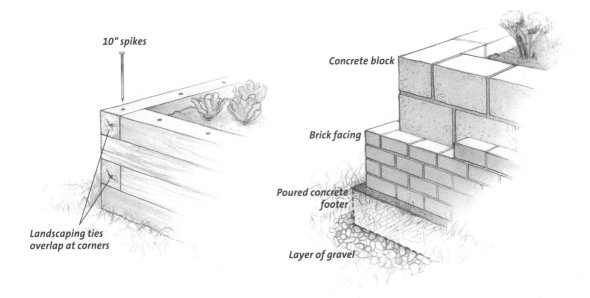

10" spikes

Landscaping ties overlap at corners

Concrete block

Brick facing

Poured concrete footer

Layer of gravel

A sturdy, long-lasting way to elevate beds is to construct a frame from landscaping ties.

For a good-looking piece of garden architecture, construct an elevated bed of concrete block and brick. A poured, recessed footer will support the weight of the walls.

PLANT LABELS, CHEAP

Frugal gardeners, gather 'round. Turn a spare piece of lumber into a hundred plant labels.

Wooden plant labels aren't inexpensive, and they're usually flimsy by the end of the growing season. If you have a table saw, or are handy with a handheld circular saw, you can quickly reduce a scrap length of lumber, such as a 2 × 4 or 2 × 6, into a bunch of sturdy labels. Wider boards (such as a 2 × 6 or 2 × 8) are easier to handle because you can saw off a good number of label-thickness slabs and still have some stock to hold on to. It also can help to begin by cutting boards to a manageable length that is a multiple of the desired label length. If you want 12-inch labels, for example, make cuts at 2- or 3-foot intervals.

These won't be ultrasmooth, rounded pieces of art, but they'll do the job. And if they're thicker than the commercial kind, they may hold up better. Wear safety eyewear when sawing. Either rip the board by running it through a table saw, or clamp the board securely and run a circular saw along it with a ripping guide attached. Use a chop saw, table saw, circular saw, or hand saw to cut the strips to length.

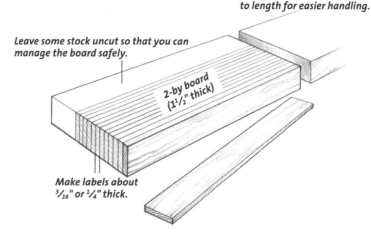

Begin by cutting a long board to length for easier handling.

Leave some stock uncut so that you can manage the board safely.

2-by board (1½" thick)

Make labels about ³⁄₁₆" or ¼" thick.

A circular saw or table saw can quickly rip a scrap board into a bunch of plant labels.

GARDENING WITH A CALCULATOR

Growing your own vegetables can produce an attractive bottom line if you concentrate on planting the garden with "cash crops."

Next Year's Garden
Grow These for the Love of It

How about vegetables that save you the *least* by growing your own? Here are four according to the Virginia Cooperative Extension: corn, melon, winter squash, and pumpkins. Not only are they apt to deliver less financial benefit, but also there is less value in harvesting fresh-from-the-garden winter squash and pumpkins. Still, if you have the garden space, you can find several good reasons for troubling with this quartet. You have your choice of variety, and there is a significant range of tastes and colors to be had for each. All four can be fascinating to watch as they grow, which you might not say of bunching onions. They can be grown organically. As for corn, this is one vegetable that begins to degrade within minutes of being picked. You can't buy corn fresher than your own.

We gardeners tend to be all too familiar with the outlay of money that our avocation requires, for seeds and potting soil and fencing and so on. Let's not lose sight of the money *spared* by making fewer trips to the produce section of the local market.

Some garden vegetables are worth more than others on a per-square-foot basis, figuring their value in terms of what they'd cost at the supermarket and how much of the growing season they take to produce a crop. According to a Virginia Cooperative Extension study, you save substantially if you grow your own tomatoes, for example, while winter squash is priced relatively low at the market and also hogs a lot of garden area. Have a look at the following list when ordering seed for next year to get an idea of crops that are more economical to grow yourself.

Tomatoes

Green bunching onions

Leaf lettuce

Turnip (green and roots)

Summer squash

Edible-podded peas

Beans

Beets

Cucumbers

Peppers

Broccoli

Head lettuce

Swiss chard

PERPETUAL EDIBLES

Don't overlook vegetables and fruits that you plant once and then harvest over the years.

Until not all that long ago, you'd expect a good-size American backyard to have at least a few perennial crops: asparagus, rhubarb, and horseradish, as well as all manner of berries and a fruit tree or two. For example, a 1927 book on root crops said about horseradish that "a few clumps are found in nearly every home garden."

Landscaping and gardening fashions change, and traditional perennial vegetables are often overlooked today. But they deserve consideration. Once planted, asparagus, rhubarb, and horseradish can be counted on to perform year after year without demanding much of your time. Choose the site with care, because you're planting for the long term. As with many garden crops, this trio prefers well-drained soil with plenty of organic matter. Rhubarb leaves and the lacy tops of asparagus look attractive throughout much of the growing season, so you might give some thought to placing these plants in a relatively visible site. Horseradish is no beauty, however, and it's apt to wander intrusively, so many gardeners park it in a spare corner of the yard rather than in the garden.

RHUBARB, THE FRUITY VEGETABLE

In an era of larger backyards, rhubarb was as common as barbecue grills are today. It's still worthwhile growing, especially to provide a tart counterpoint to strawberries in pies and jams. Plant it once, and you won't have to worry about it for a decade, at which time you may want to restore its vigor by dividing the clump. Older stands of rhubarb become less productive and may send up more flowering stalks, which should be cut off as they appear to avoid sapping the plant's energy.

Choose a site that gets full sun. The plants are started from crowns because rhubarb doesn't grow true from seed. Either buy crowns from a nursery or beg a few from a gardening friend. In early spring, plant the crowns with their budding tops just 1 inch below the surface. Top dress with compost each following spring for

Toward Tender Asparagus

Tender asparagus is delectable. Tough asparagus can be a challenge to swallow. The troublemaker is lignin, a fiber that is more concentrated toward the lower end of the spear. There are steps you can take in the garden and in the kitchen to ensure that spears are at their best.

First of all, don't pick skinny ones on the theory that they'll be extra tender; in fact, they are packed with more lignin per ounce than fatter spears. Cool temperatures increase the production of lignin, so harvest asparagus after a spell of warm weather if possible. The best way to store asparagus is not at all. That's because the fiber content continues to increase even after harvest. You can significantly slow its development by chilling the spears immediately after harvest. Place the bottom ends in a jar of cold water, place a plastic bag over the spears, and refrigerate.

best performance. And hold off harvesting for at least 2 years, allowing the plants to get established. Begin a normal harvest in the fourth year, cutting stalks that are at least 1 inch in diameter and allowing the rest to grow.

PLANTING ASPARAGUS WITHOUT A BACKHOE

Well, it's not really necessary to bring in heavy equipment to make an asparagus patch. But you might not know that from reading traditional planting advice for this crop, with directions typically calling for a hip-deep trench. In the venerable *Gardening for Pleasure*, published in 1886, horticultural authority Peter Henderson recommended planting rows totaling 300 to 360 feet to feed an average family. "Pleasure" indeed! Instead, if your soil is reasonably good, you can get away with making a much more modest trench. And in exchange for your labor, you can look forward to 20 to 25 years of harvests.

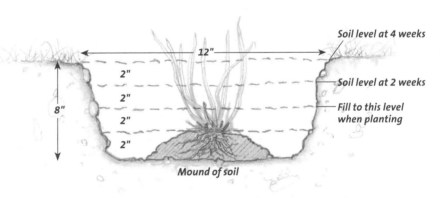

By gradually filling in a new asparagus bed, you can help to support the young plants as they emerge.

(continued)

Gardeners now have their choice of all-male varieties that dramatically outproduce old standards such as 'Mary Washington'; look for 'Jersey Giant', 'Jersey Knight', and 'Jersey Pride', among others. Choose a site with full sun, keeping in mind that the tall ferns will cast shade later in the season; if you are planting alongside the vegetable garden, place the asparagus bed to the west (to filter hot afternoon sun) or to the north.

Set out plants in spring, after the chance of frost is past. Typical spacing is 1½ to 2 feet between plants, and 3 to 4 feet between rows. Make the trenches 8 inches deep and 12 inches wide. Perch the crowns atop 2-inch-high mounds of soil, spreading out their roots in every direction. Cover the crowns with 2 inches of soil. Then add another 2 inches in a couple of weeks, and fill the trench to ground level 2 weeks after that. Every year, treat each row to a 1- or 2-inch layer of compost or aged manure and work it into the top foot or so of soil. Come the end of the season, cut down the dried foliage with a mower or scythe and distribute a layer of leaf mulch for protection through the winter.

ASPARAGUS UPDATE

Some things are eternal in the garden—weather, the seasons, the soil—while others are subject to change, such as the horticultural information for asparagus.

- The recommendation for planting depth has become shallower over the years.

- All-male varieties can give you three times the yield of older selections with females that fritter away their energy producing seed.

- You may be able to disregard the old rule of thumb that it's important to wait 2 years before beginning to snip spears for the table. Recent research has shown that a modest harvest in the first year after planting might in fact stimulate the plants to produce more buds (and more spears) in subsequent seasons.

- If you live in Florida or the Gulf states, you may have been disappointed to read that you can't grow asparagus because the weather doesn't get cold or dry enough to bring on the crop's necessary dormant period. In fact, gardeners in central and northern Florida can get a decent yield, and in central Alabama and Mississippi as well.

PUTTING A HARNESS ON HORSERADISH

EASY DOES IT

Corralling Horseradish

If horseradish gallops off into adjacent beds, you may face digging up all of the root you can, then sieving the surrounding soil with a compost sifter (see page 82) to catch tiny pieces that might become volunteers. Even then you're not ensured of control—the roots of well-established horseradish plants have been found a remarkable 15 feet below the surface. To prevent trouble, plant roots in terra-cotta flue liners or 12-inch-diameter PVC pipes, 2 feet long, sinking them into the ground with their tops just above the surface.

Those little jars of store-bought grated horseradish tend to get lost in the refrigerator, and unfortunately, the characteristic zippy flavor doesn't last for long. You can have your own fresh supply simply by tucking a root or two in an edge of the garden. *Somewhat* simply, that is. Horseradish loves to roam. Once you establish horseradish, you can't very easily get rid of it.

Planting is usually in March or April. You might want to experiment with a couple of different varieties, available as small roots from mail-order sources (horseradish doesn't grow easily from seed). Or start plants with supermarket roots; they aren't treated to keep them from sprouting as potatoes tend to be. Divide the crown into four pieces, each with some root and some of the leafy top, and allow the cuts to heal for a few days. Set roots or pieces at a 45-degree angle, with the top about 2 inches below the surface. Horseradish is best harvested after a couple of good frosts have improved the flavor. You can keep the roots in the ground through the winter, digging them as needed until just before the tops begin growing again in spring.

To prepare horseradish, wash and peel the roots, then grind them in a food processor with white vinegar and salt to taste. Vinegar helps moderate the root's pungency by slowing the release of key enzymes. For a lovely magenta-tinted horseradish, toss in a bit of beet. For a creamy condiment to accompany beef, mix in mayonnaise with the prepared horseradish.

SQUEEZE IN ONE MORE PLANTING BEFORE FROST?

All too often, gardeners throw in the trowel when there's still enough time to plant another cool-weather crop. This year, give it a whirl and plant late.

The challenge with planting late-season crops is that you can't rely on the "number of days until harvest" figures on seed packets. That's because plants mature more slowly when the temperature drops. Here's how to compensate for fall's chilling effect on plant growth.

1. Calculate the number of frost-free days left in the season.
2. Subtract 14 days to compensate for lower temperatures.
3. Check the days-to-maturity figure on the packet to see if you can make it.
4. If you're short by a couple of weeks—well, there's next year to begin planning for. If you're short by only a few days or a week, use a row cover to help buy a little extra time.

INFORMATIVE STAKES

If you use ruler-size wooden garden stakes, you can record all sorts of information on them. Plant stakes are like name tags at a conference, telling you who's who. But they can carry other useful information as well—if the stake is big enough or your writing is small enough, that is. And stakes likely will be handier than carrying around (and leaving out in the rain) a spiral notebook or clipboard. You might include the planting date, for a couple of reasons. It can help you determine if next year's planting should be a week earlier or later, depending on the crop's performance this season. The date also will be an aid if you are making staggered plantings of a vegetable for a sustained yield. The stake can be used to record how many parallel rows you've seeded, with a symbol of your own devising. That might spare you the frustration of cultivating a strip of soil where seedlings are about to nose forth. You also might want to note the source of the seed, so that if this year's patch of mesclun mix is particularly beautiful and tasty, you'll remember to reorder from a certain catalog.

CHAPTER 3

Soil, Compost, and Fertilizing

You could treat your garden soil as a neutral medium into which you mix synthesized nutrients. And, yes, plants would grow. But that would mean short-circuiting the uncountable natural processes that go on in a living, healthy soil. You need fewer amendments if the soil is an active participant in gardening, in which organic matter and minerals are broken down into a form that plants can use. Plants even need less watering. And microorganisms in the soil help to combat diseases that afflict plants.

So, perhaps the most important garden improvement you can make is to bring up the quality of your soil a notch or two. This isn't the most dramatic or immediately rewarding of garden activities. Great soil just doesn't *look* that impressive, compared to a backyard gazebo or a splashy new flowering crab apple tree. But you'll soon see results in the form of vigorous growth, with plants needing less from you in the way of nutrients, water, and pest and disease control.

A first step is knowing what sort of soil you're working with. The performance of both plants and weeds that crop up will give you a clue.

✤ If a handful of the stuff feels gritty, it may contain a lot of *sand*, the largest sort of particle that makes up soil. Sandy soils drain quickly—perhaps too quickly for much of what you're trying to grow. The most common fix is to add plenty of organic matter to help the soil retain not only water but also the nutrients that otherwise would wash away.

✤ If that handful of soil feels smooth between your fingertips, chances are it is *silty*, composed of particles much smaller than sand. Those small particles tend to make the soil dense, slowing drainage. Again, organic matter will increase permeability. Silty soils are apt to develop a hard, stubborn surface layer if walked on; raised beds can help keep them from becoming compacted because you're less likely to traipse across them.

✤ Not surprisingly, *clayey* soil will feel like clay when moistened. The particles are smaller still. If you've tried to work in a wet, clay-rich garden bed, you know why this is termed a heavy soil. It holds on to water, so that you have to put off turning the garden until later in spring when the soil is drier. As with the soil types above, organic materials can come to the rescue, loosening the soil and making it friable, or crumbly, while improving drainage.

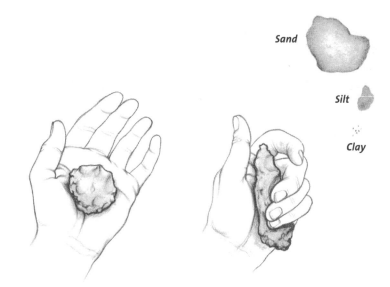

Good soil is a mix of mineral particles of various sizes, along with a healthy helping of organic matter. You can try squeezing some garden soil in your hand or pressing it into a riboon shape to see if you have clayey soil.

A *loamy* soil, by the way, is made up of relatively equal amounts of the above three. It's considered the ideal soil type for gardening because it retains moisture while draining well, allowing sufficient air to reach the roots.

The next step is to get a bit technical and test the soil. You can buy home test kits that will give you a fairly accurate idea of the levels of major nutrients, as well as the pH. For a more extensive analysis, contact your county agricultural agent or state department of agriculture and ask where to mail samples for testing. The soil's

THE STRUCTURE OF SOIL

The ability of soil to hold on to nutrients has to do with the particles in its makeup. A soil that's rich in organic matter will be especially good at retaining them. Not only that, but organic matter itself delivers nutrients as it decomposes. Another important benefit of good soil structure is that air and water will be freer to travel down to the roots. If you've been amending your beds with compost and other sources of humus over the years, you probably can feel the difference by picking up a handful of this soil. It will be friable—loose, crumbly, and not compacted.

Wisdom from the Weeds

Listen to what weeds have to say. A flourishing stand of a particular weed can tell you something about the soil.

- Lots of healthy dandelions, knotweed, goosegrass, speedwell, plantain, or spurge may mean the soil is compacted.

- Soils that don't drain well often are host to yellow nutsedge.

- Chamomile and goosefoot are resplendent in alkaline soils, while sheep sorrel (with the rocket ship-shaped leaves) and hawkweed favor acidic conditions.

- If you're growing a good crop of thistles, the soil likely is high in clay.

- Black medic, spurge, and purslane succeed when nitrogen levels are low.

- Crowfoot appears in soils with a pH of from 4 to 5.

report card will tell you what you have and what's wanting, including phosphorus, potassium, magnesium, calcium, nitrogen, sulfur, and boron, as well as the level of organic matter and a reading for pH. If you have a test done for you, the results should come with suggested sources for nutrients. You have your choice between synthesized and organic amendments.

The organic gardener's favorite amendment is compost, of course. Compost contributes nutrients necessary for optimal growth—not only the Big Three of nitrogen, phosphorus, and potassium, but also such micronutrients as manganese, copper, iron, and zinc. Although by definition micronutrients are needed only in small doses, they nevertheless are crucial to allowing a plant to make use of other nutrients. Commercial fertilizers typically skip the micros unless otherwise stated on the packaging.

Compost is precious stuff. It seems there's never quite enough to go around, especially if you follow gardening books (like this one) that instruct you to distribute mammoth amounts all over the yard. But once you understand the role of compost in many aspects of gardening, generating it becomes a rewarding task.

DECIPHERING WHAT PLANTS TELL YOU

Don't jump to conclusions. Plants that look diseased or have stunted growth may be suffering from poor soil, and not some horrible affliction. Until the results of a soil test come in, here are some telltale signs.

- Leaves that are yellowed, small, or withered may be the result of a generally inadequate soil.

- Stunted roots often are attributable to low levels of potassium and phosphorus.

- Poor performance from potatoes and legumes signals insufficient potassium.

- If young potato vines are a sickly yellow green, suspect too little nitrogen.

- Low nitrogen and phosphorus may be to blame for low-growing, oddly shaped celery.

A COMPOST PILE THAT REALLY COOKS

Yes, compost happens no matter what. But did you know that just a few degrees can make a big difference?

If you can get a pile of compost ingredients to heat up with bacterial action, it will take less time to produce the finished product. That heat also can zap weed seeds and some plant diseases, if the temperature rises above 140°F.

Where does the heat come from? It's created by countless microorganisms as they break down organic matter. Depending on the temperature of the pile, different types of microbes may be at work. Even though you can't see them, it's good to know how they accomplish this all-important process.

Bacteria known as *psychrophiles* get the compost off to a good start, doing their digesting at cooler temperatures and staying on the job even when the weather turns frosty. If all goes well, they heat up the pile to the point at which *mesophilic* bacteria thrive, at around 60°F. These are the principal agents of decomposition, and they can complete the composting process. But if they really get going, and the inside of the pile goes above 100°F, *thermophilic* bacteria take over. These heat-loving microbes generate enough heat—from 140° to 160°F—to wipe out disease-causing organisms and inactivate weed seeds. Three to five days of 155°F is enough for the thermophiles to do their best work.

Here's what you need to do.

1. Set up a bin, purchased or homemade, measuring 4 or 5 feet in each direction.
2. For aeration at the bottom of the pile, where it's difficult to turn materials, place a wooden shipping pallet or a lattice of a few scrap boards.
3. Add an even mix of nitrogen-rich and carbon-rich materials (see the lists on the opposite page). Achieving a good mix will be easier if you keep a stock of both near the pile.

4. Alternate layers of composting materials and soil.

5. Slip sticks, scrap lumber, or corn shocks horizontally into the pile.

6. Water the pile in dry weather to moisten it, but be careful not to turn it into a sodden mass. Turn the pile regularly to aerate it.

HIGH-NITROGEN INGREDIENTS	HIGH-CARBON INGREDIENTS
Fresh grass clippings	Dried leaves
Weeds	Tree prunings
Kitchen scraps	Straw
Manure	Aged sawdust

TAKE YOUR COMPOST'S TEMPERATURE

This won't make your compost pile any hotter, but you can monitor the activity in it with a special-purpose thermometer, available from garden supply firms. A low reading suggests that the biological activity within has stalled, and that may prompt you to give the pile a good toss or to supplement the mix with other ingredients.

A BETTER BIN

Build it to last. This sturdy three-sided bin takes a few hours to construct, but it will serve well for years.

Sure, you can make a simple compost bin out of a hoop of chicken wire (and you probably have!). But if you, like many gardeners, have found that composting is a cornerstone to a great yard, then you may want to build a more lasting structure. Concrete block is a humble but durable material. It's easy to make low walls of the block if they aren't going to bear a load; you just stack them up and drive metal garden stakes through the holes to keep them in place. There's no need for mortar, as is used in a foundation wall. If you want to always have some compost ready for taking and some in the process of decomposing, you can expand this bin to two or three bays. You'll only need concrete blocks (42 to build the bin as shown) and metal garden stakes to stabilize the bin.

1. Use a straight-bladed shovel to make the surface as level as possible.
2. Lay the first row of 12 blocks, taking care that the sidewalls meet the back at right angles. Leave a vertical gap of about ½ inch between blocks to allow air to circulate.
3. Lay the remaining three rows of 11, 10, and 9 blocks.
4. To stabilize the bin, use a sledgehammer to drive metal garden stakes through holes in the blocks and into the ground. If there is a chance that children will try climbing on the bin, use enough stakes to make it sturdy and pound them nearly flush with the top of the walls to prevent injury.

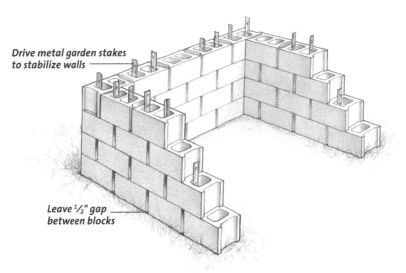

Drive metal garden stakes to stabilize walls

Leave ½" gap between blocks

For a compost bin that will stand up over the years, build it of concrete block.

A BACKYARD COOKOUT FOR STERILIZING SOIL

There's no need to mess up the oven when baking soil to sterilize it—not if you have an outdoor grill.

Make a fire in the grill as usual, building up hot coals with either wood or charcoal briquettes. Place equal amounts of garden soil and builder's sand in a roasting pan or other metal container. Either cover the container or use the grill's lid, if it has one. Bake for 1 hour, stirring occasionally, then remove from the heat. When the mixture has cooled, add an equal amount of milled peat moss and mix thoroughly. Store the mixture in a plastic tub or garbage can wherever you do your seed starting and potting.

READ THIS ISSUE OF COMPOST DAILY

What's read and white and brown all over? Why, it's your newspaper doubling as a countertop compost station.

Attractive they may be, but ceramic or stainless steel countertop compost bins still need to be rinsed and emptied. Need a tidier, faster alternative? Spread a sheet or two of newspaper on your countertop when you're cleaning vegetables, peeling fruit, or emptying coffee grounds, and let the compost-bound waste fall right onto the newspaper. Crumple up the paper and head right outside. The newspaper composts as nicely as the green and brown wastes.

STEEP COMPOST TEA IN A PILLOWCASE

A threadbare or dollar-store pillowcase makes the ideal tea bag for compost tea.

Aerosol cans are a handy way of dispensing liquids, including foliar fertilizers, and you can buy reusable containers that you pressurize yourself with a hand pump.

You may already know of the considerable benefits of compost tea. Plants readily uptake nutrients in liquid form, and seedlings and transplants will respond particularly well to a dose. And a simple tea bag made of a pillowcase can help you create potent compost tea.

You'll need to start with an old or new pillowcase and completely processed compost—your best stuff. The compost should have a uniform consistency and be pleasant smelling, not slimy and objectionable to the nose. Place the compost in the pillowcase. Tie off the top or seal it with clothespins. Dip the pillowcase into a 5-gallon bucket of water as you would a tea bag. Then allow the compost to leach its goodness into the water for a few days, in a cool and shaded part of the yard. Although some directions call for adding molasses or another sweetener to encourage the growth of beneficial bacteria, recent research suggests that this may instead give a boost to plant pathogens.

Pour the finished tea as a soil drench around the roots of established plants. Or use it as a foliar spray to deliver a hit of nutrients that young plants can begin absorbing almost immediately. To nourish seedlings, it's best to dilute 1 part tea with 3 parts water before spraying. You may be able to get three or more batches of tea out of the compost before working these spent "grounds" into the garden soil.

FOLIAR FISH EMULSION FOR A PHOSPHORUS BOOST

Seedlings are especially dependent on phosphorus if they are to develop a good root system. But once they are transplanted, cold spring weather is apt to slow the uptake of nutrients, in part because beneficial microorganisms in the soil have yet to get up and running. Use a dilute fish emulsion, following the directions on the packaging. And don't rely solely on foliar feeding—plants also need good soil, because the leaves alone can't absorb enough nutrients.

POTTING SOIL ISN'T JUST SOIL

When you open a bag of potting soil, you typically see a lot of peat moss—an aerating, water-absorbing ingredient that is slow to decompose. There also may be ground-up or partially composted bark, which also serves to aerate the mix but doesn't hold on to moisture as well. You're also apt to find white, featherweight pieces of perlite, a volcanic rock that is expanded with heat to add air spaces, absorb moisture, and improve water drainage. Another mineral, vermiculite, is expanded by heat into an accordion-like shape; it has a similar role in mixes and also contributes some potassium, calcium, and magnesium. Also look for beads of Styrofoam, an inexpensive substitute for perlite that tends to float to the surface during watering or blow away in the wind. The mix may contain little translucent water retention crystals, which are able to absorb a great volume of water. Limestone may have been blended in to counteract the acidity of the moss, with its pH of from 3.5 to 4.0. Many commercial mixes are prepared with wetting agents to increase water absorbency. Most of these are prohibited from use in organic mixes. Finally, if you prefer to measure out a fertilizer of your own choosing, stay away from mixes that come packaged with plant food.

MAKE YOUR OWN CUSTOM FERTILIZER BLENDS

There is no one perfect organic fertilizer for all plants in all seasons, so consider making a variety of homemade mixes.

Many gardeners mix their own fertilizers, saving money by buying materials in larger quantities and also by incorporating a vital free ingredient, compost from the backyard. The numbers for the recipes below refer to the N-P-K balance of nitrogen, phosphorus, and potassium. That doesn't make for very memorable names for these backyard blends, but you can make up your own—Betty's Blossom Booster, or whatever. Do your mixing in a wheelbarrow, using a hoe. Store the fertilizer in plastic tubs, recycled drywall compound containers, or small garbage cans.

A LOW-NITROGEN FERTILIZER TO ENCOURAGE FLOWERS, NOT FOLIAGE

To coax flowering plants into putting on a good display of blossoms, try one of these blends. They also can be used in fall to encourage good root growth for shrubs and trees, without triggering them to send out foliage that would be vulnerable to the cold weather ahead. The numbers express a ratio of nitrogen, phosphorus, and potassium.

0-5-4	2-8-3
1 part rock phosphate	1 part bloodmeal
3 parts greensand	2 parts rock phosphate
2 parts wood ashes	3 parts greensand
	2 parts kelp

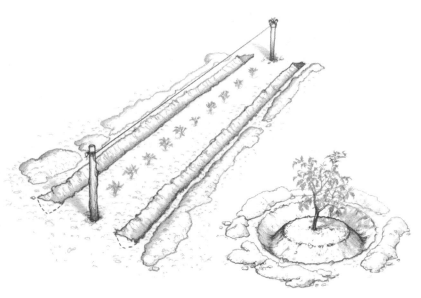
Banding Practice

You can plant seedlings and distribute fertilizer in a band, all in one step. Dig a 3-inch-wide, 3-inch-deep trench on both sides of the rows, or in a circle around larger individual plants such as tomatoes. Place the fertilizer in the trench and cover with the soil you removed. As the plants grow, their roots will gradually make contact with the nutrient-enriched soil.

To release fertilizer gradually, place it in a trench near the plants rather than directly over their roots.

COMPOST-BASED FERTILIZERS

Tap that steaming source of goodness for an important fertilizer ingredient. Generally speaking, 10 pounds of compost equals the nitrogen, potassium, and phosphorus in 1 pound of 10-10-10 fertilizer. (For ease in measuring, figure that a cubic foot of compost weighs 45 pounds.) These three blends are ideally suited for leafy greens, including lettuce, spinach, and Swiss chard.

LOW OCTANE	MEDIUM OCTANE	HIGH OCTANE
40 pounds compost	100 pounds compost	200 pounds compost
1 pound bloodmeal	3 pounds bloodmeal	5 pounds bloodmeal
3 pounds fish meal	5 pounds fish meal	10 pounds fish meal
3 pounds kelp	5 pounds kelp	10 pounds kelp

WAKE UP SLUMBERING COMPOST

What do you do if the compost won't cooperate? Change just one thing, and presto!

You know how it's *supposed* to work. You mindfully pile up kitchen and yard wastes, and they magically turn into a fragrant, nutrient-rich substance beloved by plants. But sometimes the alchemy doesn't quite click. The stuff just sits there month after month, sodden and defiant. Here are a few fixes for broken compost.

AERATE IT

A compost pile needs to breathe. Simply tossing scraps into a heap may not be enough. Be sure to use a compost container with open sides that allow air into the pile. You also can run branches, old corn stalks, or pieces of scrap lumber vertically through the pile and give them an occasional shake to introduce oxygen. Or equip the pile with a "smokestack," a vertical length of perforated PVC drainpipe. And then there's elbow grease: Get out a garden fork and give the pile an occasional toss.

WATER IT

A compost pile needs moisture. If the weather hasn't brought much rain, you may need to hose down those uncomposted ingredients to encourage them to decompose. But don't overdo it. A handful of the stuff should feel moist, not soggy.

DRY IT

So what do you do if heavy rains have turned the pile into a sponge? There's no easy answer. Turn over the pile to help dry it; mix in dry ingredients such as dead leaves; and cover the pile with a lid of hay, plastic sheeting, or scrap plywood to shed additional rain.

HEAT IT UP

A compost pile may stall in cold weather. Try surrounding it with walls made by stacking straw bales. Straw is a good insulator. Then, once the bales begin to break down, you can use them for mulch.

MAKE IT BIGGER—OR SMALLER

That's right, a compost pile is apt to work better if it's a certain size—roughly 4 or 5 feet square and 4 or 5 feet high. If it's too big, the contents are apt to be mashed down so that oxygen can't reach them; if it's too small, there may not be enough mass to generate the heat necessary for breaking down weed seeds and disease organisms.

SUPERCHARGE IT

You can buy commercial compost boosters that contain both dehydrated microorganisms and also protein, but you should be able to introduce these microbes simply by adding good garden soil in layers and mixing it in. Rotted manure or finished compost also can give a pile the boost it needs.

PULVERIZE IT

Just as you wouldn't swallow your dinner without chewing, a compost pile will appreciate having larger kitchen scraps reduced to a pulp in the blender. Citrus rinds and winter squash shells are particularly resistant to decomposition. You might take a look at your compost pile to see just what sorts of objects are still identifiable, then resolve to mince these materials in the future.

FREE SEEDLINGS FROM THE COMPOST PILE

A hot, steaming compost pile is supposed to mean certain death for the weed seeds and plant disease organisms within. But the warmth and nutrient value also may act as an ideal incubator for vegetable seeds that were carried out with the kitchen scraps. Keep an eye out for tomato and squash seedlings, in particular. Lift them out with a good-size divot of the surrounding compost, and pot them up until they're large enough for transplanting. You then can look forward to seeing just what sort of item these freebies will turn into. If you tend to eat open-pollinated vegetables, the seeds will replicate the parent; if the seeds came from hybrids, there's no telling what will happen.

MAKING A COMPOST SIFTER

Frustrated by lumpy compost or dry clumps from your compost bin? Try refining your technique with a sifter. Sifted soil is ideal for filling pots and containers.

Kitchen Scrap Smoothies

If you don't have the time or the space to construct and maintain a compost pile—certainly the case with most apartment dwellers—there's another way to make good use of kitchen scraps. Gather carrot peelings, coffee grounds, withered lettuce, eggshells, and what-have-you in a small countertop container. Process a batch of scraps at a time in a blender to make a slurry with plenty of worthwhile nutrients. Scoop away some of the surface soil from around potted or garden plants, pour in the slurry, and cover up with the soil.

To sift compost (as well as peat moss) on a small scale, all you need to do is place a rectangle of ¼-inch-mesh hardware cloth in one of the plastic open-bottomed plant trays handed out by nurseries. Cut the mesh with metal shears and keep it in place with a few twist ties.

To process bigger quantities of compost, make the sifter shown here, sizing it so that the frame will rest atop your wheelbarrow or garden cart. The sides are 1 × 6s, held together by drilling pilot holes and driving screws. Cut a piece of hardware cloth so that its sharp edges will be safely within the perimeter of the sides. Attach it by hammering U-shaped wire staples. To make shaking the sifter a bit easier, you can install 1-inch-diameter cabinet knobs on the sides.

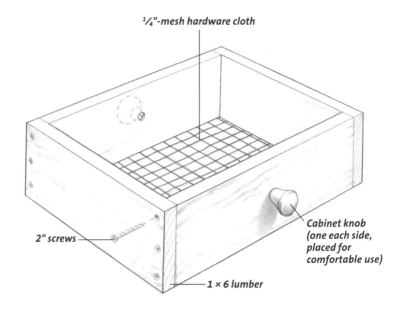

For fine, garden-ready compost, give the stuff a shake with this sifter.

COLD COMPOSTING

Don't go around with a compost complex if the backyard pile doesn't steam like a locomotive. Cold composting works, too.

Cold Compost Kills

Here's a surprising bit of news. Cool-temperature compost piles can control soil-borne diseases better than hot compost, according to researchers. That's because the lower temperatures are apt to preserve the beneficial bacteria that offer a natural control to these diseases.

A compost pile doesn't have to steam like a locomotive and be toasty inside. *Cold composting* may be the way to go if you don't have the time or sufficient interest to manage a pile that will heat up and digest its ingredients rapidly. All you need to do is heap grass clippings, garden and yard waste, and dry leaves in a bin—or even in a freestanding mound. It's best to exclude weeds with seeds and sickly plants because the pile may not reach the temperatures necessary to render them safe. Also, the finished product might not have the fine texture of conventional compost, and you may want to sift cold compost before using it.

What if you have more yard waste than even a couple of compost piles can accommodate? A good-size yard is apt to generate tangles of leafy branches, heaps of weeds, and wheelbarrows of not-so-wonderful soil. They'll all turn to compost, eventually, and without your participation. Deposit the materials in a long, continuous mound at the edge of the property where they won't be conspicuous. Then forget about them. Within a year or two, you should be able to begin sliding a shovel into the base of the pile to pull out compost. Harvest as much of it as you can without getting large, undigested chunks, and then allow the piles to sit another year before revisiting them.

COMPOSTING SHORTCUTS

Read on for a few ways to get compost sooner—and with less work.

Anchoring Outdoor Pots

When placed outside, potted plants can be toppled if their foliage acts like a sail in a strong wind. Consider giving these pots a weighted keel by including a good measure of sand in the potting mix. Sand is the heaviest ingredient in a typical mix, and it also promotes drainage and maintains air spaces. You might use a sandy blend for the bottom few inches, then top off with a standard potting mix.

No doubt you'd rather be gardening (or golfing) than composting, and there are easier alternatives to the standard process.

MOW YOUR COMPOST INGREDIENTS

A compost pile will have better digestion if you feed it shredded material. To chop up prunings and garden waste, place them on a seldom-visited part of the yard and run over them with a lawn mower. If the mower doesn't mulch clippings but directs them out a shoot, place a piece of plywood or a tarp a couple of feet from the shoot to make it easier to collect the pulverized compostables. Then add the shreds to the pile.

LET NATURE DO THE SHREDDING

Chipper-shredders allow you to quickly (if noisily) convert yard wastes to mulch or compostable material. But, pick up a handful of rich, loamy soil from the forest floor, and you have evidence that machines aren't necessary for reducing brush, clippings, and leaves to a useful form. If you have a patch of woods, try piling up yard wastes there and allowing the forces of nature to do the work.

TRENCH COMPOSTING

If you want to have the benefits of compost but lack the space to maintain a compost pile, consider composting in a trench right in the garden. The soil there is equipped with the microorganisms and earthworms needed to do the job. Dig a trench along the edge of a bed, making it deep enough for you to scatter compostable materials, and then top them with about 6 inches of soil. That's all there is to it. Next spring, when you work the soil, remember to incorporate the composted materials from the trench. Note that trench composting (and the following tip) may be best suited to *fenced* gardens, to keep wandering animals from rooting around in the beds for your edible scraps.

AN EASY PATH TO RICHER SOIL

You can do your composting underfoot by scooping the top several inches of soil from garden paths in spring, then distributing the garden's scraps and litter along them through the growing season. Keep a few bales of straw on hand to cover the compost so that you can navigate the paths without the danger of stepping on something unpleasant. The following spring, rake the finished compost into the beds.

SKIP THE COMPOST PILE WITH THESE INGREDIENTS

Not every type of kitchen waste has to be processed in the compost pile. Here are several that you can carry right out to the garden. Scratch them into the soil to help them become incorporated more readily (and to keep the beds from looking trashy).

Coffee grounds

Used loose tea leaves

Carrot and potato peels

Leftover oatmeal

Burnt toast

Water used to steam vegetables

Eggshells

Flour and grains that have gone past their expiration date

Soups and low-fat sauces

Unfinished bowls of breakfast cereal

Stale crackers

Leafy tops trimmed from vegetables

Dead bouquets

Buggy dried fruit

MOUNDED BEDS WITHOUT THE EROSION

Mounded garden beds give you the advantages of raised beds, without the considerable hassle of constructing a border to contain the soil. But these beds can fray around the edges, unless you take precautions.

Beds of mounded soil are easy to shovel and rake into place, but they tend to migrate—to erode with heavy rains, or to slump as the soil dries. Here are a few remedies.

- To keep the bed from losing its shape, mix in a good measure of thoroughly prepared compost; the larger compost particles will help to anchor the soil.
- Dry soil is vulnerable to slumping and simply blowing away, so take extra care to keep the mounded beds watered.
- Whenever heavy rains are forecast, cover the mounded beds with floating row covers. The soil will receive some moisture, but much of the excess will run off the fabric.
- Once plants are tall enough, add a layer of mulch to help keep rain from eroding the soil.

PEAT POLICY

Peat is harvested in Canada's vast bogs, as well as in more than a dozen states. And although it's true that bogs eventually regenerate, they do so extremely slowly, typically growing just ¼ inch a year.

Because bogs take so long to form—a thousand years or more—it's questionable whether they really can be called a renewable resource, according to Linda Chalker-Scott, PhD, an extension urban horticulturist and associate professor at Washington State University. "There is no economically realistic, environmentally friendly way to harvest peat moss," she writes. While mined bogs can be restored to resemble their original state, there is evidence that these engineered bogs release carbon dioxide into the atmosphere because their biological cycles have been altered. That's in contrast to normally functioning bogs, which serve worldwide as a vital storehouse of carbon.

So, what's an environmentally conscious gardener to do? Look into using amendments that have less impact. Your own finely sifted compost can play a bigger role, and commercially composted manure is another source. In the meantime, researchers are busy developing environmentally sound alternatives to peat moss.

SOIL, COMPOST, AND FERTILIZING

SOIL pH, SWEET AND SOUR

Even in the best of times, soil can still be improved. Part of improving the soil in your yard is minding the pH, as well as each plant's preferences.

Your garden may be plugging along well enough even if its pH balance is off. But why settle for so-so performance if all you need is a little adjustment in that department? The pH level can limit how well plants can pick up nutrients from the soil—even very good soil. A low pH reading may mean that calcium, phosphorus, and magnesium are less available. And at levels of 6.5 and above, plants may have trouble making use of phosphorus and many micronutrients.

pH PUSHERS

If a test reveals your soil is too sour or too sweet, ground sulfur and limestone are powerful amendments for setting things right. The amount of help your soil will need depends on both the pH level and the soil type. If you're shooting for a certain pH, it's best to apply the sulfur or limestone at least a year in advance of planting, then test again. And remember that achieving the level isn't a once-and-done chore. The surrounding soil may gradually bring the pH back toward its original reading, meaning that you'll have to continue adding amendments.

Here is what you'll need to do to *raise* the pH reading of 100 square feet by one point.

+ If the soil is especially sandy, add 3 to 5½ pounds of ground limestone.
+ If the soil is a sandy loam, add 5 to 7 pounds.
+ If the soil is loam, add 7 to 10 pounds.
+ If the soil is heavy clay, add 7 to 8 pounds.

And if your soil tests alkaline, here's how to *lower* the pH of 100 square feet by one point.

+ If the soil is sandy, add 1 pound of ground sulfur.
+ If the soil is heavy clay, add 2 pounds.

IF YOUR BLUEBERRIES HAVE THE BLUES

Blueberries are one of those plants that just won't thrive in ordinary garden soil, so either concentrate on other fruits or reconfigure the bed where they're to be planted.

Blueberries thrive on acid soils. While they may not collapse into a pile of dead sticks if this requirement isn't met, you won't get many berries and growth will be slow. If you have soil with a pH above 7, it's better to grow other things. Below that, it can be soured up sufficiently.

Sphagnum moss is the most frequently mentioned amendment for lowering the pH to the ideal blueberry range of 4.0 to 5.0. If your readings are coming in at from 5.5 to 7.0, add 4 to 6 inches of peat into the top 8 inches of soil. Other acidic ingredients include pine needles, composted oak and sumac leaves, and cottonseed meal. You also can buy commercial organic fertilizers formulated for acid-loving plants.

BLUEBERRIES IN A HOLE

Because so much work has to be done to an average garden soil to ready it for blueberries, you'll find it considerably easier to remedy only the soil in which they'll actually make contact with their root systems. Don't use up the family's savings to buy the sulfur and peat moss needed to redo an entire bed.

Dig individual holes for each plant. The size of the hole depends on the size of the bush you'll be planting, but plan on 15 inches deep and 24 inches in diameter for a variety of average size. You should also space the holes at intervals corresponding to the size of the plants when mature: 4 to 6 feet apart for highbush varieties, and a spacing of 3 to 4 feet for half-high blueberries. If the existing soil isn't that far from the ideal, you can shovel half of it back in the hole along with an equal amount of moistened sphagnum peat moss, mixing thoroughly.

BLUEBERRIES IN A BARREL

Another relatively quick fix if your soil is too high on the pH scale is to grow blueberries in a bottomless barrel or tub that's sunk in the ground. Fill it with a custom-made medium of 3 parts sand, 3 parts sphagnum peat, and 2 parts acidic leaf mold.

A SOUR TEST FOR LIMEY SOIL

It can be challenging to lower the pH of soil containing calcium carbonate in the form of limestone particles—what is known as a *calcareous* soil. Such a soil typically will have a pH of 7.3 to 8.5, and it can take a lot of sulfur to neutralize the calcium carbonate. To find out if you are dealing with a calcareous condition, put a sample of dry soil in a cup and pour a few drops of household vinegar on it. If you see and hear active fizzing, that suggests the soil contains a good deal of calcium carbonate. You would need to apply generous amounts of sulfur over time just to neutralize this mineral. On top of that, it would take more sulfur to bring the pH down to the blueberry range, and that means more sulfur than is good for the soil or for plants. So, if vinegar really sets the soil to fizzing, consider planting something other than blueberries—or grow them in pots containing an acidic medium.

A TEST FOR WHEN TO BEGIN DIGGING

You may be ready for your garden, but is your garden ready for you?

At the first signs of spring, most of us are eager to go out into the garden with a shovel and get busy. But until the weather really moderates, the soil is apt to be sodden, heavy, and uncooperative. As a quick check to see if the soil is ready to welcome you, dig up a clump, drop it on the ground, and give it a good smack with the back of the shovel. If the clump doesn't oblige you by breaking up, then you might want to put off turning the beds for a week or two. Another test is to grab a handful of soil and give it a squeeze. If water drips out, the garden beds could benefit from a drying-out period of several days.

STOP TIPTOEING THROUGH THE TULIPS

Walk the plank to keep from compacting good garden soil.

Once you've prepared garden beds to a nicely light and fluffy state, it feels just plain wrong to go galumphing over them. Instead of tiptoeing apologetically, or threatening your lower back by reaching over the beds to plant, cultivate, and harvest, keep a gangplank on hand—a 2-by-12-inch board of convenient length that you can lay down between rows. The board will distribute your weight, much like a pair of snowshoes. It also can be used to help plant seeds in arrow-straight lines; lightly press its narrow edge into the soil to make an indentation. To give sprouting seeds a break from the sun, support the board on a few bricks as a shade. When the board isn't in use, you can rest it across two or three stacks of cinderblocks as a garden bench.

A sturdy board or two can serve both as a handy bench and as a plank for distributing your weight when it's necessary to stand in a garden row.

DRIP IRRIGATION FOR FREE

Looking for a way to check out soil-level watering before investing in a system?

An old hose, plastic cider jug, or bucket is all you need to try out the benefits of drip irrigation without spending a dime.

A NEW USE FOR AN OLD HOSE

If you have a vintage garden hose that loves to kink and cause trouble, use an electric drill to make tiny holes in the last several feet of its length; install a screw-on cap at that end, and you have a drip irrigation system. For a low-tech timer, set your watch to beep when the watering period is up.

ONE-DRIP-AT-A-TIME IRRIGATION

You can use plastic jugs and weary buckets as individual plant waterers. Poke or drill small holes in the bottom, no more than $\frac{1}{8}$ inch in diameter, and place these dripping containers next to tomato plants or shrubs. Arrange a few of them in a circle around newly established trees, rather than applying a lot of water all at once and watching most of it run off. To keep the jugs and buckets from blowing away when empty (and to make them less conspicuous), you can set them in the ground. When you make daily rounds with a hose, stop by to give the containers a fill-up.

DRIP IRRIGATION: WATERING WITHOUT THE WORRY

Work saving? Time saving? Hassle free? Yes, all three! A drip system never forgets to water the lawn, and it can cut water use by 30 percent or more.

Next Year's Garden

Six Good Reasons to Drip Instead of Spray

Like any number of garden improvements, installing a drip irrigation system takes time initially but spares you considerable trouble in years to come. Here are a half-dozen reasons to switch from overhead sprinkling.

1. You'll use 30 to 70 percent less water.
2. You distribute water just where you want it, shutting out the weeds.
3. Foliar diseases are less apt to be a problem if leaves remain dry.
4. Any pesticide or fungicide you place on leaves will stay put longer, meaning you can use less of it.
5. Because the watering network is already in place, you don't have to lug sprinklers around or stand there with a hose.
6. There's just a subtle trickle, meaning you can work in the garden while watering!

Watering the garden is a time-honored task. It's also time consuming. As a result, plants may go thirsty when your summer schedule heats up. With a timed drip-irrigation system, you don't have to attend to sprinklers or stand around with a hose. The plants are apt to be happier, too, because they're spared the growth-slowing effects of water stress.

The system begins at the hose bib, and this is the nerve center of the whole works.

❖ Plan on installing a Y-connector at the faucet so that you can have a separate line for a garden hose.

❖ A simple timer will water plants for the optimum duration. A more sophisticated model can be set to do the watering at the best time each day. That means you can go on vacation feeling confident that your garden is getting enough moisture—not necessarily the case if you were to rely on a neighbor's kind offer to stop by and water while you're away. There even are gizmos that detect the moisture in the soil and adjust the watering schedule accordingly.

❖ A pressure regulator will probably be needed to lower the household water pressure to the manufacturer's recommendation.

❖ You may want to install a filter at the faucet, so that bits of debris don't clog the system. The usual sort of filter in a hose washer doesn't have a sufficiently fine mesh.

❖ If you understand how siphoning works, you'll understand why a backflow preventer is important. It keeps water in the irrigation lines from being drawn back into the home water supply.

SOIL, COMPOST, AND FERTILIZING

A Vacation Pot Sitter

It's not always possible to find a friend who'll happily water a few dozen potted plants while you're away on vacation. Instead, corral the plants in a spot with dappled sunlight and run a drip irrigation line to them. For each pot, make a hole in the main irrigation tube and insert a connection fitting with a ¼-inch feeder tube, snaking this tube over the rim of the pot and securing it with an inverted U-shaped piece of coat hanger wire.

A typical irrigation kit involves a plastic hose that extends aboveground to the garden, where it can branch into several lines as needed. The water is delivered in any of a few ways: through a slowly seeping soaker hose; through emitters that deliver water underground to plant roots; or through microsprays that operate much like tiny sprinklers. The timer can be operated by AC current or a battery.

Set the timer, turn the tap—and here's one less routine gardening task to clutter your summer.

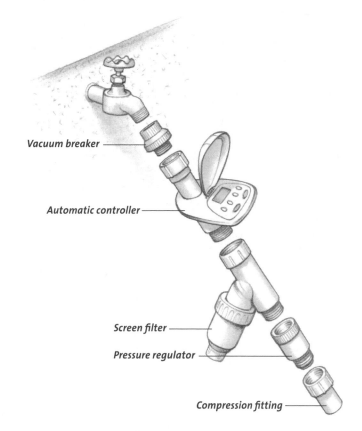

Vacuum breaker

Automatic controller

Screen filter

Pressure regulator

Compression fitting

The nerve center of a drip-irrigation system may look complicated, but the various parts twist together easily.

DON'T GET HOSED WHEN BUYING A HOSE

A cheap hose is satisfactory for washing the car and watering a few plants, but gardeners deserve better.

There are few things more frustrating than trying to water with a hose that likes to kink. Heavy-duty hoses have better couplings and resist kinking. The best (and most costly) are made of rubber instead of vinyl. They may come with a lifetime warranty and will stand up well to ultraviolet rays and cold weather.

No matter what you buy, avoid that first kink—a hose has a memory and will tend to bind in the same place. Once fall brings freezing temperatures, drain the hose, coil it, and bring it indoors.

GO WITH MORE FLOW

Skinny hoses cost less. They also deliver water more slowly, meaning that you are apt to spend more time standing around with a hose or keeping an eye on sprinkler attachments. Here's a table to suggest how much time you'd save by moving up to a hose with a larger diameter.

DIAMETER	GALLONS/MINUTE	MINUTES TO WATER 1,000 SQ. FT.
1/2"	10.5	63
5/8"	17	37
3/4"	31	24

A HOSE ISN'T A DRINKING FOUNTAIN!

You're standing there watering the garden on a sweltering day, and what could be more refreshing than to stick your mouth right in that stream of icy water?

Refreshing, maybe. But it also may not be good for you. Chemicals in a vinyl hose can leach into the water. Brass couplings may contain a smidgen of lead, a heavy metal known to be a neurotoxin. And bacteria tend to colonize in sun-warmed garden hoses. So resist the temptation and go inside for that sip.

COMPOSTING WITH RED WIGGLERS

Worms make short work of breaking down food scraps into excellent compost. But not just any worms!

All you need to get worms behind your gardening effort is some sort of bin to contain them (even an old dresser drawer with $\frac{1}{2}$-inch holes drilled in the bottom and sides will do for a start). You also need worms, of course—and not just any worms. The familiar earthworm won't perform well in a bin of compost. You have to buy redworms, either from a local source (try bait shops) or by mail order through the Internet. Once the worms get established, a bin measuring 1 foot high and 2-by-3 feet will be able to handle about 6 pounds of kitchen waste a week. The completed compost is harvested by shifting the material to one side of the bin, placing fresh garbage on the other side, and allowing the worms to migrate into the new stuff. Then the finished compost can be shoveled out for use in the garden.

STRESS A PEPPER FOR MORE HEAT

Angry, abused peppers will take it out on your tongue—if that's what you like.

For most of us, the pepper varieties available today are plenty hot enough, thank you. But if you want to coax more heat out of a favorite pepper, try stressing a couple of plants (not your entire crop, in case the experiment fails) by withholding water just a bit. You may have noticed that apples and berries seem to taste more flavorful when the growing season has been less than generous with rainfall, and the same principle can work with peppers. Just keep in mind that the yield may be less if plants are stressed.

KEEP SAND ON HAND

Read on for the top 15 uses for sand in your yard and garden (and not one of them is for filling sandboxes).

Sand is one of those basic gardening materials that is good to have around but that you might tend to overlook when stocking up on supplies. It's one of the three ingredients of a good, loamy soil, along with clay and silt. Keep in mind that sand comes in different particle sizes—fine, medium, and coarse. For most gardening purposes, coarse (or builder's sand) is the one to have. You can buy it in bags; or, for bigger gardens and more-ambitious projects, buy it loose and have it delivered or bring it home in your own truck. Store loose sand under a tarp, weighing down the perimeter so that cats can't dig in it.

- Add sand to garden soils for better drainage.
- Make your own potting mix out of equal parts garden soil, compost, and sand.
- Start cuttings in sand.
- Place sand around plants vulnerable to slugs.
- Mix tiny seeds with sand to make it easier to sow evenly.
- Store root crops and summer-flowering bulbs in sand in the basement.
- Set out a bowl of moist sand in the garden to attract sipping butterflies.
- Make a Japanese rock garden with raked sand.
- Scatter sand on walkways to cut down on slick and slippery surfaces.
- To clean garden tools, plunge them into a bucket filled with sand and some vegetable oil.
- Stir 1 cup of sand into exterior paint before painting porch floors or steps to improve traction.
- Mix sand, compost, and peat moss into soil from a planting hole when transplanting a container-grown plant.
- Level stepping-stones or stone walkways with sand.
- Keep a shallow, large basin of sand near the back door to rid boot soles of mud and soil clumps.
- Relax on the patio using sand-filled buckets for candleholders after a hard day of gardening.

A CROP THAT FEEDS THE GARDEN

To improve soil, grow a cover crop of rye while the garden sleeps.

Even in chilly northern winters, the garden can be sown with annual rye (*Lolium multiflora*) as a cover crop that will resist erosion, control weeds, and then lend its organic matter to the soil. If done over a few winters, the result will be improved structure and aeration, and more activity by a variety of beneficial subterranean life from earthworms to fungi. Rye also contributes some nutrients, although it isn't a nitrogen builder like leguminous cover crops.

1. At summer's end, rake the beds to smooth the soil and remove plant debris.
2. Hand-sow 2 to 3 ounces of annual rye seed per 100 square feet of garden area. This will go more easily if you mix the seed with sand or friable soil.
3. Rake the seedbed.
4. In spring, from 2 to 4 weeks before you put out seeds or plants, mow the rye and turn it under.

VERMICULITE AND YOUR LUNGS

Vermiculite can be described as a "natural" product, since it is made from a naturally occurring mineral. But that doesn't necessarily mean that using it as a potting mix ingredient is hazard-free.

In recent years there have been reports that some vermiculite products contain asbestos, a fibrous mineral identified as a potential cause of respiratory ailments that include lung cancer. According to the U.S. Environmental Protection Agency, "asbestos contamination in vermiculite and vermiculite products has become a national concern." And yet vermiculite continues to be used in widely available potting mixes.

What can you do to protect yourself? If you handle a mix containing vermiculite, do so outdoors and upwind from the product whenever possible. Indoors, provide good ventilation to minimize inhaling dust from the mix. A mix will produce less dust if it is kept moist, and you can wear a dust mask and gloves for more protection. Avoid handling straight vermiculite as an ingredient in your own potting mixes. Finally, consider skipping vermiculite altogether by using such alternatives as peat, sawdust, compost, perlite, and bark.

CHAPTER 4

Weeds and What to Do about Them

You know the old saying: A weed is just a plant growing out of place. Those words almost certainly weren't penned by a gardener. Weeds are a remarkable force of nature, with a vigor and adaptability that put crops to shame. They also are a thorn in the side of anyone who wants to determine what grows and what goes on a piece of land, whether it's a lawn, flower bed, or vegetable garden.

While the automatic response of some homeowners is to wage an all-out herbicide attack, there are many less-drastic control measures—strategies that worked efficiently in the centuries before synthetics existed and that still do the job. And there are a few new wrinkles in weed control, as well.

Weeds aren't completely without redeeming values. Many of them produce food, including nectar and seeds, for wildlife (the monarch butterfly couldn't manage its well-known migration without weeds). You can get an idea of a weed's worth by taking the time to observe a forgotten patch of wild plants. It's likely to be a lively spot on every level—high and low, from afar and when viewed through a magnifying lens. Hawks hover overhead. Songbirds flit from one seed-

head to another. Bees, butterflies, and many other insects flock to flowers no less attractive than those in carefully cultivated beds. Spiders spin their webs to harvest some of the bug life. Succulent plant growth is apt to be crawling with sap suckers of all sorts—not a sight to warm a gardener's heart, but these insects will help attract beneficial parasites and predators. There likely will be warm-blooded critters on the ground, as well.

The weeds you pull or mow can make an important contribution to the compost pile, so long as the temperature of your compost pile is high enough to inactivate seeds. And a healthy patch of weeds will even serve as a diagnostic tool, telling you something about the quality of your soil.

COMPOST YOUR WEEDS

Immature weeds make good compost fodder.

When you yank weeds or hoe them from the garden, the task will seem a little lighter if you see these unwanted plants as material for the compost pile. By only a slight stretch of the imagination, future crops will spring from the energy embodied in these unwanted visitors to the yard. You can even *encourage* certain weeds to grow for composting. Not every wild plant is a good candidate, but try permitting certain manageable annuals to leaf out—chickweed, lamb's-quarters, purslane, and ragweed are commonly seen choices. Just be sure to keep an eye on these weeds so that you harvest them for composting before they set seed. While a steaming-hot compost pile may inactivate weed seeds, it's best not to take a chance.

PICKLE YOUR WEEDS

Douse weeds with a dressing of pure vinegar for an effective natural control.

Vinegar may preserve pickles, but it's devilishly tough on garden weeds. Studies by the USDA's Agricultural Research Service found that vinegar containing 15 to 20 percent acetic acid could knock out 95 to 100 percent of the weeds in its trail. But before you rush into your pantry for a bottle of apple or distilled vinegar, note that household vinegars typically run from just 5 to 8 percent. While this concentration may work well enough on younger weeds, you'll need to buy supersour "horticultural vinegar" to get a near-complete kill. Check with local gardening centers. This natural herbicide is thought to work by breaking down cells in the leaves and desiccating the plant.

The vinegar is applied to foliage with an ordinary spray bottle. But do so with care. Horticultural vinegar can irritate the skin and eyes. It also is indiscriminate in what it kills, so make sure that the spray doesn't drift over to garden plants.

ANNUAL WEED BAKE-OFF

One clear plastic sheet + one weedy garden bed = Too-clever weed elimination trick!

You've felt the intensity of the midsummer sun on your back when gardening. Well, you can harness that energy to combat weeds, bacteria, fungi, and nematodes. All you need is a sheet of clear 1-mil plastic—and a good, long stretch of sunny weather. Also, keep in mind that while a bed is in the process of being *solarized* under that sheet, it will be out of commission for the 4 to 6 weeks that it takes the soil to cook. That may leave you enough time to plant early- and late-season crops.

1. Preceding the hottest 4 to 6 weeks of the growing season, groom the bed to be solarized, removing all garden waste and weeds.
2. Water the bed, soaking the soil well so that the sun's heat will penetrate deeper. (If the soil dries out in the weeks that follow, peel back the plastic in the early morning or evening, soak it again, then re-cover.)
3. Place the clear plastic over the bed. Use clear wrapping tape as necessary to seal any seams. Seal the perimeter of the area with a berm of soil.
4. You may need to leave the plastic on for the full 6 weeks, depending on your climate and also on how sunny the weather has been. Also, if this period has been unusually cloudy, temperatures under the plastic may be insufficient to do the job.

BRUSH HOGGING

There's an aggressive sound to the term "brush hogging," and this is a high-powered task as landscaping chores go. It involves taking on a patch of ground that has gone beyond the weedy stage and is host to shrubs and young trees. In many parts of the country, this is the natural fate of any area that's left to its own devices. Don't attempt to tame the woody stuff with your lawnmower. Instead, buy or rent a brush hog—either a dedicated walk-behind machine, or a self-powered unit that is towed behind a good-size lawn tractor. Some hogs can handle sapling trunks up to 2 inches in diameter.

EAT YOUR WEEDS

Graze your way to a cleaner garden!

A number of all-too-familiar garden weeds can be eaten fresh, steamed, or sautéed. That continues to be a tradition along the Mediterranean, with families going out to forage each spring. In the United States, we seem to have lost the knack, even though there's no shortage of wild edibles. You may find yourself fond enough of certain weeds that you dedicate a part of the garden to them, allowing your favorites to go to seed for the next year's crop. Try sautéing wild greens with garlic in olive oil. Add them to bean-and-pasta soup. Tuck them into calzones or layer them in lasagna.

✦ **Purslane (*Portulaca oleracea*).** A bright-colored variety, 'Goldberg', is marketed for its hue and its more generous size, but the wild version is also fine, holding up well with cooking.

✦ **Dandelion (*Taraxacum officinale*).** This is perhaps the best-known wild green, and some people go off into the countryside in spring to harvest them. Get them young, before they become bitter. A traditional recipe from the Campagna region of southern Italy combines wild dandelion greens, sausage, and cannellini beans.

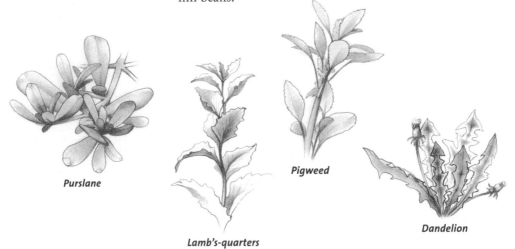

Purslane

Lamb's-quarters

Pigweed

Dandelion

There can be no greater victory over weeds than not only yanking them but also eating them.

- **Lamb's-quarters (*Chenopodium album*).** The somewhat spinachlike young shoots can be used in salads and soups.

- **Pigweed (*Amaranthus hybridus*).** A relative of the amaranth you see in seed catalogs, this wild cousin offers leaves that are good steamed.

- **Garlic mustard (*Alliaria petiolata*).** This spring visitor catches your eye with its white flowers and your nose with its garlicky scent. Garlic mustard is an invasive nonnative species, but you can keep it in check by processing the leaves and taproots in a blender to make pesto, a novel idea suggested by Steve Brill in *The Wild Vegetarian Cookbook* (Harvard Common Press, 2002). Or simply toss a few leaves in a salad to give your greens an edge.

- **Shepherd's purse (*Capsella bursa-pastoris*).** The young leaves of this common weed are mild enough to use in salads. Collect the heart-shaped seeds for use as a peppery addition to soups.

KNOW WHAT YOU'RE PICKING

Before taking advantage of this no-plant, no-till, no-mulch harvest, take a few precautions. First, be familiar with what you're about to put on your plate. Educate yourself with a field guide or accompany a knowledgeable forager. Second, avoid plants that may have been sprayed with an herbicide, particularly along roadsides. Third, be cautious about having children seeing you forage, or they may do the same on their own—and some weeds, wild berries, and fungi are poisonous.

WEED BARRIERS FOR WALKWAYS

Here are five fast, frugal, almost-fun fixes for weed-strewn garden paths.

There is no one perfect way to banish weeds from garden paths, except perhaps for laying down blacktop, and even paving can give way to certain aggressive growers. Most of us would prefer something soft and yielding underfoot, at any rate. A layer of mulch looks good, breaks down into a valuable soil amendment over time, and allows water to quickly perc through. But it won't be impervious to weeds, requiring a second out-of-sight layer to squelch them. Here are a few choices.

- Newspaper is free, if a bit lumpy. And unless you keep it well covered, it can be unsightly and—worse still—become airborne in a strong wind.
- A roll of plastic or landscape fabric goes down quickly, but it may not hold up more than one season and is not biodegradable.
- A roll of brown kraft paper, available at office and art supply stores, also goes down in a jiffy, and it will biodegrade.
- Corrugated cardboard, recycled from large boxes, is stouter stuff than paper, and it also biodegrades.
- Roofing paper, with its coating of tar, is rugged stuff, and you can roll out more than one thickness for lasting effect.

If you've been unhappy with past efforts to tame garden paths, you might convert those vulnerable strips of soil to lawn. That's not a magical solution. First, you've got to establish a healthy patch of turf if the grass is to stand up to frequent foot traffic. That requires watering as needed and cutting regularly with a mulching mower. And you'll need to keep the grass from turning the beds into lawn. For that, install strips of plastic edging that extend deeply enough that grass won't migrate. This edging can have the additional benefit of helping to shore up the sides of raised beds.

WEEDS AND WHAT TO DO ABOUT THEM

A ROCK-SOLID FIX FOR WEEDY FENCES

In this trickiest of places to yank weeds, the solution is right at your feet—lay down a "path" of flagstones.

ADVICE OVER THE FENCE

Weeds Take a Thyme Out

What about the cracks between the stones? Even a hairline space will allow weeds to get a purchase. Beat the weeds to it by tucking in a variety of creeping thyme that produces an attractive (if tiny) flower.

The most stubborn weeds of all must be those that grow along a garden fence, where they are all but immune to mowing, shoveling, and hoeing. Weeds are particularly infuriating if they weave their way up through a fence clad with chicken wire. An attractive, permanent cure is to lay a row of rectangular flagstones under the fence, using smaller pieces as necessary to bring this stone layer flush up against fence posts. You even can use a circular saw with a masonry blade to cut notches in stones for a good fit around the posts. If the fence abuts the lawn, the flagstone row will serve as a mow strip, making a crisp edge between garden and yard.

Slabs of stone make the mightiest mulch of all. Use flagstones to keep weeds from tangling with garden fences, cutting notches for a snug weed-defeating fit around posts.

HOLDING A TORCH FOR WEEDS

Try a scorched-earth policy if weeds are taking over the garden.

Flaming a Stale Bed

Creating a "stale bed" sounds like a bad idea, but it's a technique used by large-scale growers to make their soil relatively free of weeds. You begin by tilling the soil as you would normally but then allow the beds to sit idle during the predictable flush of new weeds. Some growers will even water the beds to encourage weeds to appear now, rather than later in the season when they will be intermingled with crops. The weeds are flamed before they go beyond the seedling stage, and the way is then clear for sowing seed or putting out transplants. You even can flame weeds that appear after sowing seed, as long as your seedlings haven't pushed aboveground.

A surefire way to kill weeds is with a *flamer,* a type of propane torch with an extended wand. The goal isn't to burn the unwanted plants, but to heat them to the point that their cell walls are destroyed, leading to a gradual death. Flamers of various sizes are sold by mail-order garden supply firms. The smallest are handheld, of the sort used for removing paint. To take out weeds on a large scale, you can buy a backpack flamer with a 3-gallon propane cylinder. At a weight of more than 30 pounds and a price over $200, this amounts to all-out weed warfare.

Flaming is particularly useful in killing stubborn weeds along brick paths and in clearing newly turned beds in which weed seedlings are just beginning to show their heads. To deflect heat from garden plants, hold the blade of a shovel alongside the flame. Keep the garden hose handy if there is combustible brush nearby.

Not all weeds are equally susceptible to flaming. Purslane resists it. So do grasses, because much of their activity is belowground and out of reach of the flames. Perennials that grow up from a fleshy root system may require repeated treatments.

Do as commercial growers do, and use a torch to efficiently kill weeds.

A SAVAGE LITTLE HOE

You'll think you're the caveman inventing the wheel when you try a swan's-neck hoe for nipping weeds. It's THAT good!

EASY DOES IT

The Weed-Zapping Two-Step

Most of the troublesome weeds in the garden have sprouted from seeds in the top 2 to 3 inches of soil. If you cultivate the beds, then take a break for at least a couple of weeks to allow these weeds to come to life, you can nip them in the bud with a second tilling. That will mean a relatively clean slate for your seedlings or transplants. The technique works best if the soil is warm enough for the weed seeds to sprout readily, so try it when preparing the garden for fall crops. And make that delayed tilling relatively shallow, to avoid stirring up more trouble.

ADVICE OVER THE FENCE

Have a Nice Decade!

Whenever the task of weeding becomes a drag, keep this in mind: By zapping a weed promptly, before it can scatter seed, you could be sparing yourself 10 years of trouble. That's because weed seed may lurk in the soil for many growing seasons, waiting for an opportune moment to sprout.

The hoe is such a simple tool that you might not be all that curious about various models. But a swan's-neck hoe really is something improved in the gardener's arsenal. That graceful crook in its neck positions the blade so that you can make weed-killing slices without killing your back. You can stand erect, rather than stoop. The blade's sharp edges are particularly suited to poking out stubborn weeds and getting into cracks between bricks and flagstones.

Standard hoes are fine for general-purpose tasks around the yard, but the swan's-neck version is especially nimble and gives you greater accuracy in pinpointing your attack on weeds.

HAY IS FOR HORSES, STRAW IS FOR GARDENS

It's important to get to know the difference between hay and straw.

To the uninitiated, a bale of hay doesn't look much different from a bale of straw. And while there is more nutritional value in hay, straw is the one you want as a weed-smothering mulch for the garden. It contains far fewer weed seeds than hay and also resists becoming a wet, moldy mass when spread over the ground.

Straw bales are awkward to bring home. If you're having mulch trucked in at the beginning of the growing season, try to include straw with the delivery. Then consider tarping the bales (as well as the mulch) to keep them from rotting prematurely.

Straw is valuable in other ways worth looking into.

- Fluff up a layer of loose straw over fall vegetables to help buffer them from freezing temperatures.
- Build a wall of bales around a chilly compost pile to help rev up the biological processes within.
- To prevent ingredients in a compost bin from becoming wet and heavy, keep a couple of bales of straw close by to add by the occasional handful.
- Don't have a compost bin? You can make a biodegradable one out of straw bales, leaving one side lower to facilitate adding to the pile.
- For a small single-season raised bed, poke the center out of a hay bale and fill the void with compost for planting vegetables.
- If you're putting in a new lawn, it's a challenge to keep the soil from drying and snuffing out the sensitive new grass. Take the time to scatter straw over the area to filter the sunlight and slow evaporation from the soil.
- When seedlings are brought outside to become acclimated to the elements, they are particularly vulnerable to strong spring winds. Stack up a wall of straw on the windward side of flats and pots to create a friendlier microenvironment.

Finally, keep in mind that by using straw instead of plastic, you're living a bit more lightly on the land. Each year, commercial vegetable growers in the United States roll out some *200 million pounds* of plastic mulch.

USE BIG-SHOULDERED VEGETABLES TO KEEP WEEDS IN THE DARK

Some vegetables cover a lot of real estate with their leaves, and they can help you shade out weeds.

You've probably noticed that there isn't a lot of weed activity beneath the jumbo leaves of squash, for example. Whenever possible, try to use vegetable foliage to block out weeds, both by choosing big-leaved crops and by planting on a tighter spacing. Fast-growing vegetables also can help by getting a jump on weeds. And you yourself can help the vegetables compete, by seeing to it that you've given them adequate water and nutrients. Here's a list of weed suppressors.

Beans

Cucumbers

Kale

Lettuce

Potatoes

Squash, pumpkins, and melons

Sweet corn

Sweet potatoes

Swiss chard

Tomatoes

LEAVE POISON IVY IN THE DARK

Even this annoying vine needs daylight to survive.

Poison ivy is tough to eradicate, even with chemicals. But it isn't immortal and requires daylight to grow. If you have a limited patch of it (and unlimited patience), try placing two layers of blue plastic tarp over the area (a single layer may not block enough light) and arrange bricks, stones, or concrete block all around the perimeter. Then keep an eye out for tendrils that the plants will send out to snare some daylight—as they appear, you'll have to sever them with a stab of a shovel, then bag and dispose of the cuttings. Otherwise, the ivy may simply spread to brighter pastures. Give this method a year or two to work. Once it's time to remove the tarps, roll them up while wearing gloves and clearly mark them as FOR POISON IVY ONLY with an indelible marker before storing them in case of another ivy incursion.

THE IMPORTANCE OF BEING SHALLOW

Deep cultivation may dig up trouble, in the form of a fresh crop of weeds.

A weed seed buried beneath a foot or so of dirt isn't able to cause you much grief. And the soil in your garden is likely teeming with these potential specks of trouble. That—and not laziness—is the reason stated by some gardeners for preferring to cultivate shallowly. You might experiment with letting sleeping weed seeds lie by doing the same. Over the next few growing seasons, the seeds in the top few inches of soil will sprout. Assuming you take care of them before they can set and broadcast seed of their own, you're then home free—or at least weed free, relatively speaking.

WORTHWHILE WEEDS

Set aside a small area for wild plants to attract beneficial insects.

EASY DOES IT

Butterfly Weeds

Weeds attract not only helpful insects, but also beautiful ones. The caterpillars that will turn into butterflies like to feed on clovers, milkweed, nettle, Queen Anne's lace, common sorrel—and butterfly weed itself (*Asclepias*). So allow a weed-prone edge of the lawn to go wild, and see what develops.

If your local government allows it, you might allow a patch of weeds to flourish somewhere in your yard. One nice thing about a weed patch is that it's zero maintenance—the weeds are growing there because they're happy, so there's no need for you to get involved. Second, these plants likely will provide meals and lodging to a number of beneficial insect species. Helpful predators and parasites are apt to be found in wild carrot, wild daisies, dandelions, stinging nettle, goldenrod, common sorrel, and tansy, among others. In a Michigan State University study, five or more beneficial insect species were found on shrubby cinquefoil, wild coriander, meadowsweet, evening primrose, yellow coneflower, buttonbush, hoary vervain, culver's root, and swamp milkweed.

You may find that neighbors feel threatened by the sight of wild things growing so close to their perfect putting-green lawns. If so, try calling the patch a wildflower meadow or a butterfly garden. It's all a matter of perspective.

GIVE YOUR WEEDS A VACATION, TOO

When you pack your bags for an extended summer trip, don't forget to mulch.

Gardeners return home from summer vacations greeted by a lot of mail, lawn grass long enough to bale, and weeds, weeds, weeds. To ensure that weeds take some time off, too, leave time while packing for your getaway to spread mulch in the yard's trouble spots. If your supply of bark mulch and straw is running low, lay down disassembled cardboard boxes as a stopgap and weigh them down with rocks or bricks. Mulching will not only keep the weeds at bay, but also help allow plants to get by with less watering.

A (NEARLY) WEED-FREE LAWN

If you can tolerate an occasional nongrass plant in your lawn, you should be able to handle weeds with cultural and mechanical controls.

The first step in establishing a good-looking lawn is to make sure it is a *healthy* lawn, with a dense and vigorous stand of turfgrass. Weeds will be less likely to move in if the ground is already occupied. There are a number of things you can do to keep the grass growing thick and green.

- Remove no more than one-third of the blade length when you mow, to avoid slowing plant growth.
- Keep weeds from spreading by mowing before they can set seed.
- Water deeply, rather than sprinkling often and only superficially.
- Allow mulched clippings to stay in place and fertilize the lawn.
- If necessary, periodically remove thatch either with a rake or a rented dethatcher.
- Make sure you are growing an appropriate mix of turfgrass species for your region, as well as for the light conditions of your own yard. For information, check with your county agricultural extension agent or your state's agriculture department Web site.

READING YOUR WEEDS

If your lawn has been looking shaggy, the weeds growing there may give you clues as to what needs fixing.

You don't necessarily need a soil test or rain gauge to diagnose the problems underlying a lousy lawn. The weeds may tell the story.

❖ Quackgrass does well on thin, poorly watered lawns.

❖ Ground ivy is apt to trouble lawns that get too little sunlight and have poor drainage.

❖ Knotweed shows up in lawns with compacted soil.

❖ Crabgrass suggests you've been mowing too short or watering too often.

❖ Clover is a sign that the lawn has insufficient fertility.

❖ If you spot chicory's sky blue blossoms, that's a sign that the soil is high in clay and also relatively fertile.

❖ Buttercups signal wet hardpan soils.

❖ Acid clay soils are apt to host a good crop of dandelions.

❖ Horsenettle flourishes in sandy soils high in nitrogen.

❖ Fumitory favors soil high in potassium.

❖ Eastern bracken tells you the soil likely is low in potassium and high in phosphorus.

❖ Wild mustard moves in to acidic hardpan soils.

❖ All (or a few) of the above? Then your lawn likely has a number of shortcomings that are preventing the grass from looking its best.

The Quickest Way to a Lawn You'll Love

A scattering of weeds in the lawn can cause you to invest your warm-weather weekends in trying to get rid of every last one. *Or,* you can try to accept them, no matter how pristine the other swards may be along your street. Even healthy lawns have some weeds, the University of Wisconsin–Extension reminds homeowners.

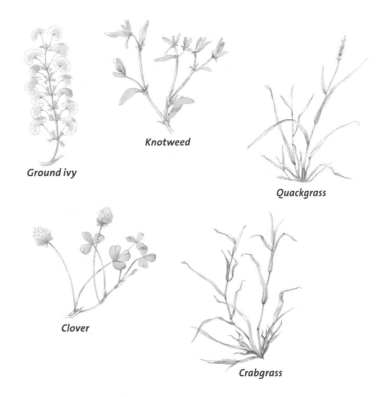

Ground ivy

Knotweed

Quackgrass

Clover

Crabgrass

Just like the plants you grow, weed species have their preferences when it comes to light, nutrients, water, and soil quality. The presence of a certain weed can tell you something about growing conditions in that spot.

LET SLEEPING SEEDS LIE

It seems that really working the soil to a good depth would have to be a good thing. But it ain't necessarily so. Some aggressive weeds just love having their belowground parts chopped up. Take quackgrass, for an infamous example. This weed is trouble, as suggested by its other names: devil's grass, witch grass, and dog grass. The underground rhizomes are mighty enough to grow right through asphalt, and just a single plant can send out 300 feet of them in a year. You only make matters worse by going over quackgrass with a rototiller, because this creates thousands of pieces that each can grow into a new plant. So disturb only the very top layer of soil. Take a sharp hoe to shoots that appear, and eventually the rhizomes will be starved.

HELP FOR PROBLEM LAWNS

One grass seed and one mowing technique won't fit all types of lawns in this climatically diverse country. Tailor your lawn to suit the site.

Water Just Enough and No More

A lawn typically requires about 1 inch of water each week when actively growing. That's from both nature's contribution and your own with a sprinkler. It's hard to judge that inch, so you may want to place an inexpensive rain gauge out on the lawn where it will be filled by your watering as well as by rainfall.

It's a rule of thumb that weak lawns lead to weed problems, and not the other way around. So, rather than focus angrily on the weeds that pop up, do what you can to make the turfgrasses thrive.

THE SHADY LAWN

Lawns can be burned and browned by the midsummer sun, but they do need light. If a Kentucky bluegrass lawn gets less than 6 hours of full sunlight in a typical day, the grass may be thin and weed prone. The telltale weeds in a sunlight-starved yard include ground ivy and chickweeds, along with patches of moss. You can overseed with shade-tolerant grasses such as fine fescue. It also may help to prune nearby shrubs and trees to admit more sunlight. Or, you could forget about turfgrass and switch over to shade-tolerant ground covers such as vinca and pachysandra. Another alternative is to investigate native woodland plants that flourish in your area.

MOW HIGH

If you raise the mower deck to 3 inches or so, you'll leave longer grass blades and cut down on the sunlight available to sprouting weeds. Come fall, however, it's best to lower the deck to about 2 inches for the last mowing in order to guard against snow mold.

WATER WELL

To discourage weeds, water less often but thoroughly, preferably early in the morning. Light and frequent watering tends to favor shallow-rooted weeds, as well as certain turf diseases.

FERTILIZE AS NEEDED

Fertilizer feeds the weeds as well as the grass, of course. But a proper level of fertilization helps the turfgrass to grow thickly and shut out most weeds. Too much fertilizer can be as bad as too little, reducing the lawn's vigor and giving weeds a better chance.

BE WARY OF THESE WILD ONES

Some weeds and wild plants can be worse than an annoyance if they are poisonous or are armed with itch-producing chemicals.

Even if you are sympathetic to weeds, there are several common species that shouldn't be welcomed to the yard because of their potential hazards to health. That's especially true if you have inquisitive children who like to roam the grounds. Here are several of most notorious weeds you're apt to encounter.

Poison ivy (*Toxicodendron radicans*). No surprise here. This vine supposedly was once imported to England as an ornamental—it does have glossy foliage and red berries, after all—but that sounds like horticultural folklore. If you can't eradicate the plant, teach your kids how to identify the leaves. Be cautious about embracing a pet that has been cruising an area rich in PI.

Deadly nightshade (*Solanum dulcamara*). This perennial woody vine attracts attention with small star-shaped purple flowers and berries that turn lipstick red when ripe. Its toxin is at its most concentrated in the unripe berries, and small children are particularly vulnerable because of their lower body weight.

Poison hemlock (*Conium maculatum*). Attractive enough to be mistaken for a garden plant, poison hemlock resembles anise or wild parsley. The entire plant is poisonous to humans: the leaves, the stems (children may become ill if they use them as straws), the roots, and especially the seeds.

Pokeweed (*Phytolacca americana*). This weed is a standout, sending up thick stems to a height of 5 feet or more. The inky berries ripen to a rich purple, and if digested they can bring on headache, abdominal pain, and severe diarrhea.

American bittersweet (*Celastrus scandens*). This woody vine finds its way into wreaths and dried flower arrangements, where it shows off its yellow-orange berries. The berries can cause stomach upset and diarrhea if ingested.

Holly (*Ilex* spp.). It's rarely thought of as an unwanted plant, but holly is worth mentioning for its attractive, yet poisonous berries. Eating them can lead to nausea, vomiting, and diarrhea.

A ROGUE'S GALLERY OF LAWN WEEDS

To have a nicer lawn next year, it helps to get to know the interlopers growing there.

Next Year's Garden

Preparing a Soft, Plush Lawn of Moss

Perhaps the most attractive no-mow alternative is to encourage moss to take over a part of the lawn. That won't work in a sunny area with soil that tends toward a high pH. The best candidate would be a shady spot were moss is already giving lawn grass a run for its money. There's no need to water or fertilize a moss lawn, and except for hot, dry spells, it should look good throughout the year. To quickly restore the green color to parched moss, sprinkle the area briefly with water. In autumn, it's a good idea to gently sweep away fallen leaves or collect them in netting, then roll them away. And that's about it for maintenance, unless you need to lower the pH.

The ideal range for moss is from 5.0 to 5.5. To prepare the ground for a moss carpet, spread aluminum sulfate or ferrous sulfate over the area. Lowering the pH also has the effect of keeping grass and weeds from moving in. The best time to establish the carpet is in fall, with some mosses needing up to 3 years.

By getting familiar with the growth habits of the more common weeds, you'll be better prepared to keep them in check. *Annual weeds* are spread by seeds and live just 1 year. They can be classified as either winter annuals that germinate in fall and complete their life cycle the following spring, or summer annuals, germinating in spring and growing until fall. Shepherd's purse is a winter annual; crabgrass is a summer annual.

Perennial weeds live at least 2 years and typically go dormant for a period in summer. The best-known perennial is the dandelion. Some perennials are classified as broadleaf weeds, with wide leaves marked by prominent veins. They often grow from a thick taproot. Grasses such as quackgrass have much narrower leaves, and spread primarily through underground root systems.

Here are general cultural controls for some of the most troublesome annuals and perennials.

❖ **Crabgrass** is an annual, dropping seeds in fall that lie dormant until warm weather returns in spring. To help the lawn resist this new crop of weeds, reseed the troubled areas in the fall and add fertilizer to get the grass off to a strong start. As with a number of other weeds, crabgrass is encouraged by shallow watering and mowing infrequently.

❖ **Quackgrass** is a perennial that spreads via underground rhizomes, so that dealing with it requires digging in order to get at these unseen stems. If an area is riddled with quackgrass, you should repeatedly hoe the shoots that appear. But you may be better off exhuming the entire patch and either putting sod in its place or adding soil and then seeding.

❖ Many broadleaf perennials can be controlled by digging. These include **dandelions, thistles, buckhorn and broadleaf plantain, chicory, spotted spurge, field sorrel, ground ivy, creeping jenny**, and **mouse-eared chickweed.** Go at them in spring, before they have a chance to store food in their roots. If you don't get around to digging until fall, you may have to face them again. Repeated digging will eventually deplete their energy reserves, if you're persistent enough.

- **Moss and algae** can be managed by improving growing conditions. That's because they will get a foothold only where the yard is acidic, wet, infertile, or compacted.

- **White clover** wasn't always regarded as an unwelcome addition to the lawn. The plants used to be valued for their texture, blossoms, and ability to add nitrogen to the soil. But sometime in the 1950s, an advertising campaign portrayed clover as a noxious weed and in need of chemical control. Whatever the merits of clover may be, if you would rather see a little less of it in your lawn, be careful to avoid applying high levels of potassium in fertilizer blends. Cut your grass higher to shade out the clover, and hoe, pull, or flame seedlings to prevent them from flowering and setting seed.

Perennial weeds with taproots are difficult to evict from lawns. You can dig them up, or gradually starve the plant by keeping the foliage from developing.

CHAPTER 5

Getting a Leg Up on Pests and Diseases

When trouble strikes the garden, a gardener's reflex is to do *something*—almost *anything*—to fix things. That's understandable, when you've gone through the work of digging and raking, seeding and watering. But experienced gardeners learn that benign neglect sometimes may be the way to go, for a couple of reasons. First, if nature is allowed to take its course, the situation may right itself. Beneficial insect predators and parasites, as well as naturally occurring diseases, may keep pest populations in check. And healthy soil harbors organisms that work to cancel out diseases. If you enter this environment with sprays or powders—even relatively mild ones—you are apt to upset an intricate, subtly operating mechanism.

Second, it's possible you really don't need that nibbled end of the lettuce row. Or your family may tolerate blemishes on apples that otherwise are fine for eating. If you aren't growing for market, you don't have to generate a huge quantity of produce or strive for aesthetic perfection. You got involved in gardening to have something good to eat, or pretty things to look at, of course. But if pest and disease control begins to dominate your gardening activities and makes you consider radical (and chemical) means, it may be time to step back and reassess matters. While a new pest management strategy may make your vegetable and flower beds spotless, it doesn't necessarily follow that you'll take more enjoyment out of gardening.

Third, we homeowners spray and spread billions of dollars worth of products on our yards each year, and the environmental impact of these interventions is still not fully understood. While it's true that a botanically based pesticide will biodegrade relatively quickly, that's not to say that it won't have some adverse effect on an ecosystem downstream.

So it may be that the best way to have an even better garden next year isn't to change the garden, but to change your relationship to the piece of the earth's surface entrusted to you. A more relaxed approach can feel sublime, allowing you to appreciate the home landscape rather than fret about it. And you'll feel good knowing that less is more.

A USEFUL COVER-UP

Suit up your garden with fabric row covers to protect it from common pests.

Lightweight spun fabric row covers have a few uses that make them an indispensable aid in many gardens. Among other services they perform is keeping bugs off the plants. It might seem that a roll of flimsy fabric couldn't be relied upon to deter determined bugs, but the benefits can be dramatic. The outlay in time is minimal, and you don't have to bother with toxic sprays and powders. Row covers are basically of two sorts—those that do indeed float on the tops of plants, and those supported by hoops. It's certainly less bother to skip the hoops and just let the fabric rest on the rows. But in windy conditions, a row cover may abrade the tender foliage on which it rests.

You should keep in mind that no row cover will exclude bugs that emerge from the soil or plant debris. Thorough cultivation and a good garden cleanup in fall are the way to prevent them from making trouble.

Not all row covers are made from plastic and destined to become a tattered blight on the home landscape. You now can buy covers made from cornstarch and tinted with a nonchemical pigment. The film lasts long enough to shepherd young plants through chilly weather and competition from weeds, then decomposes. Three months after you lay it over the garden rows, all but 5 percent of the cover will have merged unobtrusively with the soil, thanks to microbial action. One such product, Garden Bio-Film, is available from Back to Basics, P.O. Box 1189, Waynesville, NC 28786; www.backtobasicsnc.com.

LET IN THE POLLINATORS

Row covers are great, but they don't function as doorkeepers that exclude only potentially harmful bugs. They keep out beneficial insects as well. Winged pollinators will have a hard time visiting the flowers of fruiting plants—eggplant, cukes, melons, squash—unless you roll back the covers once the threat of a particular target pest is gone and the blossoms appear. Covers can interfere with pollination by the wind as well.

GETTING A LEG UP ON PESTS AND DISEASES

FASHION YOUR OWN FENCE

Come up with a fence design as distinctive as your garden.

Next Year's Garden
Creative Fence Posts

As you plan a garden fence, consider having at least a couple of posts extend higher than usual. These extra-tall posts can do double duty, providing a place to hang a birdhouse where you can enjoy the occupants (as they help you control plant-eating worms). Shy birds might not take to such a public spot, but wrens seem to put up with having humans nearby, even though they show their irritation by chattering a good deal. Or, string wire between a pair of tall posts for training sweet peas, runner beans, or honeysuckle.

You can buy all sorts of fencing material at a home and garden center, including preassembled panels in various woods or plastic. To set your garden apart, give some thought to designing your own pickets. The least expensive option is to saw them to length from bundles of 1 × 3s. You can even cut decorative top ends on each picket—a time-consuming project, but one that will set your garden apart. A few ideas are shown here. Make straight cuts with a circular saw or saber saw; a saber saw will negotiate any curves; and a drill will make the holes. To drill the half-circle cutouts in adjacent pieces, place them side to side in a simple jig that, along with a couple of clamps, will hold them securely. A *forstner bit* in an electric drill will make a neater bore. If you put a sharp point on the pickets, the fence will be that much more formidable to climbing and leaping animals.

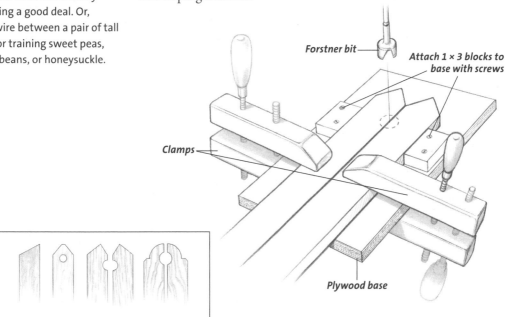

Forstner bit

Attach 1 × 3 blocks to base with screws

Clamps

Plywood base

For something different, try your hand at cutting or drilling ornamental tops for fence stakes.

OUTFOXING DEER

There are strategies for keeping these Olympian jumpers from doing the high hurdles over your fence.

One of the main reasons gardeners throw in the trowel is the devastation wrought by the cutest horticultural pests of all: deer. The changing American landscape has caused a population explosion of this animal, once a rarity in much of the region it now browses to nubbins. Wildflowers are scarce in many once-verdant forests and fields, thanks to deer. And few plantings in the home landscape are immune.

Deer can't very well dig under a garden fence, unlike other persistent mammal and rodent malefactors. But they are splendid jumpers, able to leap 6- and 7-foot fences in a single bound. They've even been observed vaulting across 14-foot-wide streams. But they have yet to evolve wings, and can't travel both high and wide. While you can go higher to keep them out, it is easier to go *wider*. By placing obstructions a good distance out from the fence, the deer can't get close enough to leap effectively. A relatively simple web of wires will keep them at a distance. You'll need fence posts sturdy enough to support 2 × 4 outriggers on which the wires are strung. An alternative that looks a little less like suburban warfare is a double fence—just two ordinary fences, 4 feet high and spaced 4 feet apart. Another alternative is 8-foot-high fencing of lightweight black plastic mesh. It goes up quickly, without the need for heavy-duty posts, and it isn't quite the eyesore created by other barriers.

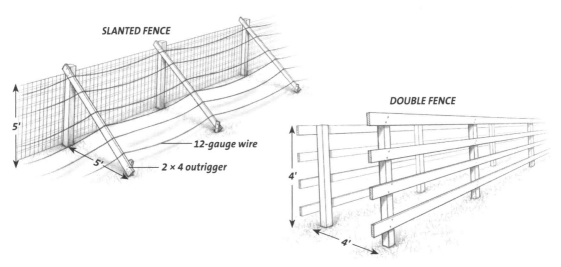

SLANTED FENCE

5'

5'

12-gauge wire

2 × 4 outrigger

DOUBLE FENCE

4'

4'

Deer can jump high, they can jump wide, but they can't manage both high and wide at the same time. So, you can foil them by building a barrier of modest height that also would require them to travel a good distance over the ground. Here are two solutions, one requiring more lumber and time to construct.

DEERPROOF, MAYBE

It seems there is no plant under the sun that deer won't nibble, but some vegetables, herbs, and shrubs are less delectable to them.

Here are a couple of dozen choices for a deer-beleaguered yard. Still, these plants aren't completely invulnerable, because hungry deer will sample just about anything.

ANNUALS, BIENNIALS

Anise (*Pimpinella anisum*)
Foxglove (*Digitalis purpurea*)
Goldenrods (*Solidago* spp.)
Larkspur (*Delphinium consolida*)
Poppies (*Papaver* spp.)
Pot marigold (*Calendula officinalis*)
Sweet alyssum (*Lobularia maritima*)

PERENNIALS

Ageratum (*Ageratum houstonianum*)
Autumn crocus (*Colchicum autumnale*)
Bleeding heart (*Dicentra spectabilis*)
Bugleweed (*Ajuga reptans*)
Butterflybush (*Buddleia davidii*)
Caryopteris (*Caryopteris clandonensis*)
Catmints (*Nepeta* spp.)
Coralbells (*Heuchera sanguinea*)
Corydalis (*Corydalis sempervirens*)
Daffodils (*Narcissus* spp.)
Dame's rocket (*Hesperis matronalis*)

Ferns (various species)
Flowering tobacco (*Nicotiana alata*)
Forget-me-nots (*Myosotis* spp.)
Fountain grass (*Pennisetum setaceum*)
Garden sage (*Salvia officinalis*)
Hardy geranium (*Geranium* species)
Hellebore (*Helleborus orientalis*)
Horseradish (*Armoracia rusticana*)
Hyssop (*Hyssopus officinalis*)
Irises (*Iris* spp.)
Jack-in-a-pulpit (*Arisaema triphyllum*)
Lamb's ear (*Stachys byzantina*)
Larkspur (*Delphinium* × *elatum*)
Lavenders (*Lavandula* spp.)
Lemon balm (*Melissa officinalis*)
Lily of the valley (*Convallaria majalis*)
Marjoram (*Origanum maiorana*)
Mints (*Mentha* spp.)
Oregano (*Origanum vulgare*)
Pampas grass (*Cortaderia selloana*)

Penstemons (*Penstemon* spp.)
Peonies (*Paeonia* spp.)
Rose campion (*Lychnis coronaria*)
Rosemary (*Rosmarinus officinalis*)
Rue (*Ruta graveolens*)
Russian sage (*Perovskia atriplicifolia*)
Siberian squill (*Scilla siberica*)
Snapdragon (*Antirrhinum majus*)
Solomon's seal (*Polygonatum biflorum*)
Spiderwort (*Tradescantia ohiensis*)
Sweet woodruff (*Galium odoratum*)
Thyme (*Thymus vulgaris*)

WOODY PLANTS

Allegheny spurge (*Pachysandra procumbens*)
American holly (*Ilex opaca*)
Barberries (*Berberis* spp.)
Daphnes (*Daphne* spp.)
Heaths (*Erica* spp.)
Heathers (*Calluna* spp.)
Pachysandra (*Pachysandra terminalis*)
Potentillas (*Potentilla* spp.)

VEXING VOLES

From the pages of Beatrix Potter they're not! Gear up for battle with voracious voles.

At first, you decide to share your bulbs and root vegetables with voles. How much could they possibly eat? Then, you realize you'll have to get out the armor to protect your investments.

A VOLE CAGE

Gardeners have been wildly clever in coming up with vole controls: putting up little windmills to generate annoying vibrations in the soil, placing broken glass and razor blades in the tunnels, and even piping car exhaust into these underground networks. None is effective. And electronic gadgets on the market are a waste of money as well, according to the Department of Entomology at Purdue University. A surer remedy is to keep them out in the same way that you keep flies out of the house—with screens. Try making a cage of sturdy screening and placing vulnerable plants in it.

For best results, use ¼-inch-mesh hardware cloth (see "Easy Does It" on page 127 for more on hardware cloth). Build the cage with four sides, or with only three if it will abut a wall of the house. Construct simple frames or panels with 1 × 3 lumber, driving 2-inch screws in pilot holes at the corners. There's no need to attach these frames to one another, because they can be held in place by the soil. If you plan a cage with long sides, use two or more panels in a row to avoid struggling with a single, large, flimsy one. Use a staple gun to attach the hardware cloth, ideally leaving a 3-inch flap along the bottom edges to fold outward as a further discouragement. Dig a trench and bury each frame on its long side, leaving 6 inches above the soil surface. Firm soil around the frame to keep it in place.

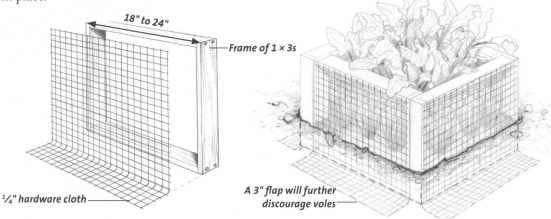

18" to 24"

Frame of 1 × 3s

¼" hardware cloth

A 3" flap will further discourage voles

To fence out voles, make panels with ¼-inch hardware cloth mesh and inset them around sensitive beds.

A GRITTY DEFENSE FOR BULB SNATCHERS

Interplant with Bad-Tasting Bulbs

The easiest way of protecting bulbs is also the prettiest. You may be able to discourage bulb-eating pests by mixing tulips with bulbs they shun, including daffodils, fritillaria, and alliums.

Voles apparently have sensitive snouts and can be put off if you include sharp particles of some sort when you plant vulnerable bulbs. You can toss in crushed gravel (not rounded pebbles), or try a commercial product formulated for the purpose, VoleBloc, made from pieces of slate. Make the hole 2 or 3 inches deeper than otherwise necessary, line it with a 2- or 3-inch layer of gravel or VoleBloc, then put the bulb in place and cover with more of the particles. To further discourage pests, you can fill in the hole with a mix of soil and the particles you are using.

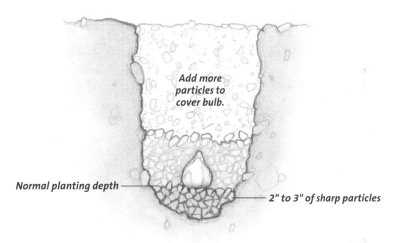

Add more particles to cover bulb.

Normal planting depth

2" to 3" of sharp particles

Sharp particulate matter can discourage voles from nosing their way to your precious spring bulbs.

PROTECTING BULBS

Flower bulbs are plump, juicy morsels just sitting there asking to be eaten by squirrels. It's worth the effort to protect your investment in time and money.

Spring-blooming bulbs are a glorious addition to the yard. But these perennials can turn into annuals if hungry animals catch on to what's lurking underground. When planting, come up with a control strategy to protect them.

If squirrels have been digging up your flower bulbs season after season, try burying a barrier of chicken wire. Begin by excavating the flower bed to the depth at which the bulbs are to go. Lay out the bulbs, then spread roughly half the soil over them and tamp lightly. Place chicken wire over the bed, followed by the remainder of the soil. The squirrels will be frustrated, while the flowers will easily find their way up through the barrier mesh.

PRIVATE SCREENING FOR PESTS

The simplest controls are often the best, and a roll of hardware cloth may go a long way to excluding a variety of nibblers.

A garden that's vulnerable to animals with big appetites will be a headache, year in and year out. A sturdy, good-looking fence may be your best gardening investment.

While it takes little effort to put up a roll of chicken wire on a row of metal stakes, a well-thought-out fence will bring piece of mind and can also be an attractive addition to the yard. If you decide on a traditional-looking fence of wood stakes, couple it with a band of chicken wire or hardware cloth along its lower edge to discourage animals from gnawing their way through.

A SUBTERRANEAN STRATEGY

Depending on what's out there in the yard waiting to share your crops, you may want a fence that not only goes up, but down and out as well.

A conventional fence blocks would-be crawlers, leapers, and climbers, of course. And by extending wire mesh belowground, you can foil tunneling animals as well. That involves a good deal of work, in that you have to dig a trench in order to install the fence.

Chicken wire is inexpensive and relatively easy to work with, making it a familiar sight. But for a considerably sturdier choice, go with hardware cloth. If you buy it with ¼-inch spacing, this material also will exclude smaller animals that might slip through the holes in chicken wire.

To stop burrowing rabbits, surround the garden with a 6-inch-deep, 6-inch-wide trench, then run the fencing to the bottom of the trench and out another 6 inches, as shown. Then fill in the trench with soil or, better yet, with sharp gravel. Groundhogs are another matter. You'll need to dig a trench big enough to allow going down at least 12 inches and 24 to 36 inches out from the fence. Even then, these accomplished diggers may undo your hard work by going deeper still. Filling in the holes they make with soil or rocks won't necessarily deter them. Instead, soak rags in household ammonia, place them in the hole, and keep them in place with rocks.

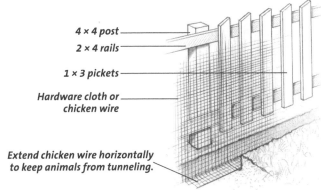

4 × 4 post

2 × 4 rails

1 × 3 pickets

Hardware cloth or chicken wire

Extend chicken wire horizontally to keep animals from tunneling.

Using hardware cloth or chicken wire, you can turn a conventional wood fence into a far more formidable barrier to rabbits and woodchucks.

COLLAR THAT CUTWORM

Surface cutworms can leave a garden in ruins overnight. Protect your plants with cardboard armor.

Cutworms emerge at night to nibble (and destroy) the tender stems of seedlings. They wrap themselves around a stem and chew through it. Outwit these destructive pests by creating a barrier around plants so cutworms can't get close. Cut 2-inch-high rings from cardboard juice cans, cardboard paper towel rolls or cardboard toilet paper rolls. Place the rings over seedlings when you transplant, then push the rings into the soil about 1 inch deep. The rings will eventually decompose and your plants should be hearty enough by then to withstand a cutworm attack.

PLANTS THAT PROTECT

Familiar garden plants have evolved all sorts of strategies to protect themselves from insect pests.

You can enlist many plants to help keep neighboring crops from harm. As a general rule of thumb, plants with a strong, sharp scent can work by confusing the olfactory clues that guide many pests to their dinners. Freely interplant the vegetable garden with these fragrant wonders.

While this is hardly an exhaustive list, it will get you started in this chemical-free (and fascinating) way of managing bug behavior.

PLANT	INSECT REPELLED
Basil	Tomato hornworm
Chives	Aphids
Dahlia	Nematodes
Marigold	Mexican bean beetle
Mints	Cabbageworm
Rue	Japanese beetle
Tansy	Cucumber beetle
White geranium	Japanese beetle

BUG SUCKERS

If squashing bugs grosses you out, a battery-powered bug vacuum may be just what you need.

To dispose of troublesome insects tidily, inside or out in the yard, try a bug vacuum. Its extendable wand allows you to reach across rows and snuff up pests. Snuff them *out,* too, if you buy a model that also electrocutes the bugs with a minute charge once inside the device. You can then simply empty the storage container into the trash without worrying that anything is going to crawl or fly back out. A rechargeable vacuum will spare you the bother, expense, and waste of using throwaway batteries. Note that delicate foliage may be harmed by the suction. In that case, first dislodge the insects so that they fall onto a sheet of cardboard, and then go after them with the tool.

PEST CONTROL BY THE CALENDAR

The life cycles of insect pests are programmed so that they appear when their favorite plants are around. So try breaking your date with these bugs to minimize damage.

EASY DOES IT

Ants on Peony Buds: Do Not Disturb

When peonies are just about to blossom, those full buds are likely to be visited by ants, and you may be tempted to do something about it. But this is a fine example of symbiosis at work. The buds secrete a sweet, nutritious nectar to lure the ants. The ants, in return, will do battle with any insect pests that come along. Contrary to a popular (and charming) bit of folklore, the licking of ants is not necessary for the blossoms to open.

By planting certain crops earlier or later, you can foil insects that emerge at the usual time and find the garden larder is empty.

- Cabbage loopers will cause less trouble if you plant cabbage 4 to 5 weeks before the last frost, for harvesting in late spring.
- Corn borers may miss the boat if you plant corn 2 weeks after your last frost date.
- Carrot maggots are hardest on early crops, so try delaying your planting until spring is well underway.
- If leafhoppers have been the bane of your potatoes, plant your potato crop as early as the ground can be worked in spring.

GUARDING THE GARDEN WITH BENEFICIAL BUGS

Often unseen and underappreciated, insect predators and parasites help keep plant feeders in check.

Next Year's Garden
Don't Pull All the Parsley

Or all the carrots and celery, for that matter. Leave a few in the ground over the winter, and next year they will develop the kind of flowers that are magnets for beneficial insects.

You have to be observant to notice it, but there are biological controls in progress all over the garden—and even under it, with microorganisms in good soil working to check plant diseases. A host of predators and parasites help to keep a balance of bugs—both plant eaters and the bugs that prey on them. And *balance* implies that there will always be at least a few pests around the yard. You won't get the complete kill that a chemical insecticide might provide, because as the natural enemies reduce the population of pests, their own population either dwindles or moves to buggier pastures. So, next time you see a few spider mites on your roses or whiteflies on your tomatoes, remember that you won't have beneficials in residence unless there's something for them to prey on.

BIODIVERSITY IN THE GARDEN

The best way to attract natural predators and parasites to your yard is to have a diverse array of plants and habitats. Flowering plants, both cultivated and wild, will provide pollen and nectar, as well as shelter and a place to overwinter. On the other hand, a broad expanse of lawn with a few foundation plantings isn't likely to draw them in.

You can add some plantings specifically with beneficials in mind. Rosemary and mint offer shelter for predatory ground beetles. Predatory wasps, hover flies (also known as syrphid flies), and robber flies are attracted to composite flowers such as daisy and chamomile, as well as mints. One mint in particular, horehound, is best known as an old-time flavoring for candy, but it also happens to be a favorite of important beneficial insect species. The flowers are highly attractive to braconid and ichneumonid wasps, as well as tachinid and syrphid flies.

PLANT A BANQUET FOR BENEFICIALS

Growing plants that attract beneficials—natural enemies of pest insects—is another way to help you garden without chemicals.

PLANT	BENEFICIAL INSECTS ATTRACTED
Coriander (cilantro)	Braconid wasps, hover flies, lacewings
Cosmos	Hover flies, lacewings, ladybugs, spiders
Fennel	Braconid wasps, hover flies, lacewings, ladybird beetles
Flowering buckwheat	Hover flies, lacewings, ladybugs, minute pirate bugs, predatory wasps, tachinid flies
Mint	Hover flies, spiders
Queen Anne's lace	Hover flies, ladybugs, spiders
Sweet alyssum	Braconid wasps, chalcids, hover flies
Tansy	Insidious flower flies, lacewings, ladybugs, parasitic wasps
Yarrow	Bees, hover flies, ladybugs, parasitic wasps

EASY DOES IT

Don't Shoo Away This Bee Mimic

Syrphid flies (or hover flies) are curious in that they mimic the appearance of hovering bees so that they are less likely to be preyed upon. They can't defend themselves by stinging and also are different from bees in that they do their hovering on just two wings, not four. Their larvae are blind, slow-moving maggots that drain the innards of aphids at a clip of one a minute.

It looks like a bee, but it doesn't sting like one. In fact, this is a syrphid fly, a beneficial garden visitor whose larval form feeds on aphids.

BUYING BENEFICIALS

As interest in natural controls has grown, so has the list of beneficial species you can buy for use in the garden.

There now are some 50 of them, including ladybugs, lacewings, ground beetles, predatory stink bugs, spiders, wasps, dragonflies, damselflies, fireflies, praying mantises, predatory mites, minute pirate bugs, assassin bugs, and for belowground defenses, predatory nematodes.

Making use of beneficials is a bit more involved than broadcasting a pesticide. These are living creatures and as such will perform only when there are bugs to prey on and a favorable climate.

A release of beneficials can work in a couple of ways. They may clear out the pests, then die off or go elsewhere. Or, better for you, they may settle in your immediate area, to respond the next time there's a population spike of the target pests.

- **Wasps.** The *encarsia* wasp is a parasite of whiteflies, used primarily in greenhouses but also effective outside. For the wasps to do their work, your minimum average temperatures should be at least 72°F, going no lower than 62°F at night. You can use an insecticidal soap spray at the same time without significantly bothering the wasps. *Trichogramma* wasps can help you battle cabbageworms, tomato hornworms, and corn earworms. They lay their eggs in the eggs of these caterpillars, which kills them.

- **Lacewings.** Lacewing larvae are also known as aphid lions, for good reason. They help control thrips and certain smaller caterpillars as well. If you purchase lacewings, it's better to get them as eggs or larvae, rather than the adult form. Or, attract the adult lacewings with an artificial version of the sweet insect exudates on which they feed. If you spot an invasion of aphids or thrips, mix up a solution of an insect food such as Pred-Feed or Bug-Chow and sprinkle it on the foliage of the affected plants.

- **Beetles.** The lady beetle or ladybug is perhaps the best known beneficial on the market. They eat aphids, scale, and spider mites, among other pests. And they're cute to boot. It's best to buy *preconditioned* ladybugs, which will be ready to lay eggs in the area. But if they

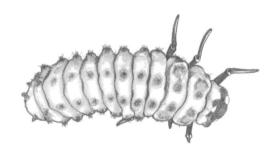

The larval form of the cute little ladybug is this rather terrifying-looking creature.

have been collected in a different part of the country, they may simply take wing and go elsewhere. You may have better luck with locals, attracting ladybugs by using the food mix described on the opposite page for lacewings. Another product you can distribute over plants is Wheast, made from whey and yeast. It also helps to grow plants that serve as food sources, such as angelica and dill, and to allow dandelion, wild carrot, and wild yarrow to grow nearby. You might even try to collect local ladybugs that have gathered in hay and grain fields and bring them home.

✦ **Predatory mites.** Several species of mites are commercially available for the control of spider mites and thrips. While these are used primarily for indoor and greenhouse plants, they also can be called upon for outdoor control on roses, strawberries, fruit trees, and eggplant. Lay off pesticides, including mild soap sprays, when using predatory mites.

✦ **Predatory nematodes.** You may not have noticed them, but nematodes are tiny worms commonly found in the soil. Most of them dine on microorganisms and are no trouble, and some species feed on plant roots. Still others are helpful, preying on a host of pests that includes armyworms, Colorado potato beetle larvae, cutworms, Japanese beetle grubs, onion maggots, and strawberry root weevils. They infect these hosts with bacterial diseases before consuming them. Beneficial nematodes typically are distributed in a soil drench.

✦ **Toads.** Before you throw out a chipped terra-cotta pot, or break it into smithereens to put in the bottom of other pots to promote drainage, consider setting it upside down in a shady part of the garden as a toad house. Wearing work gloves, you can use a pair of pliers to break away enough of the rim to make an entrance. Before long, if you're lucky, a toad may take up residence and begin eating the several thousand insects it needs each year.

A broken terra-cotta pot can make a good home for a toad. Place it in a shady spot that's surrounded by vegetation. Toads will need a nearby semipermanent pool of water in order to reproduce.

EDUCATE, THEN DISPOSE OF, EARWIGS

Let those nasty-looking earwigs spend a few moments reading the evening news, then upend your newspaper trap to get rid of them.

European earwigs aren't all bad—they eat decaying matter in the garden and dine on aphids and mites. They can be particularly bothersome to favorite plants, though, such as hollyhocks, strawberries, lettuce, and potatoes. They feed at night, then crawl into cool, moist places during the day. Make a trap by rolling up a newspaper and placing a rubber band around it. Tape one end of the roll closed, then lay the roll's open end near your plant stems. In the morning, quickly shake the open end of the roll over a bucket of soapy water; the earwigs will come wiggling out of the newspaper, fall in the bucket, and drown.

CAT-PROOFING POTTED PLANTS

Here's a pointed method for keeping felines from mistaking potting soil for a potty. All it takes is a little needling.

What's the difference between a pot full of dirt and a litter box full of something that looks like dirt? It's a riddle that apparently stumps cats. To fend off felines, insert a few dark-colored knitting needles into the potting medium so that they project by 2 to 3 inches. The needles won't be obviously visible against the soil to humans viewing the plant, and yet they will keep cats away without hurting them.

YOU AREN'T ALONE IN BATTLING CABBAGE PESTS

Before you go to great lengths, give nature a chance to help control cabbage crawlers.

Too Much Fertilizer Brings On the Bugs

Take it easy when fertilizing to avoid giving plants more nitrogen than they can make use of. It causes trouble, encouraging them to promote vegetative growth that may lead to a population explosion of aphids and mites.

If cabbage loopers and imported cabbageworms threaten to make mincemeat of the tender heads of their namesake crop, think before you spray—even with a homemade repellent. All sorts of natural controls may be ready to kick in, if given the chance, including such predators as stink bugs (yes, they really are good for something), ground beetles, spiders, yellow jackets, and the larvae of lacewings and syrphid flies, as well as parasitic wasps and tachinid flies. Cabbage pests are susceptible to viruses and bacterial diseases, too. This isn't a plea for passive resistance (see the controls described below); just be observant of any free help you may be getting from nature.

Naturally occurring diseases can be harnessed to help control the imported cabbageworm. All it takes is identifying worms infected with granulosis virus, then yucking up a kitchen blender. The diseased worms appear sluggish, they don't eat, and you may see them hanging off the plant. Collect a few sick worms and process them in the blender with water. Use this microbial insecticide as a spray, applying it on the cabbage late in the day so that ultraviolet rays won't degrade it.

CATERPILLAR WATCHING

Worms in the garden can be an occasion of wonder, not worry.

Many gardeners count bird-watching as one of the great fringe benefits of being out there in the beds. You can get still more pleasure by expanding your field of interest to caterpillars—and you don't need binoculars! The more you learn about these colorful, often downright odd creatures, the less you'll be apt to instinctively kill them. Most do relatively little damage to crops. For example, the parsleyworm certainly *sounds* like it's made for mischief in the garden, and this gorgeously patterned larva does feed on parsnip, carrots, celery, dill, and caraway, as well as the namesake crop. But chances are they won't cause significant damage. You can simply remove them from the garden to another part of the yard. And don't forget that if given the chance, these slow-moving, avaricious worms will metamorphose into beautiful swallowtail butterflies. The Monarch caterpillar is another highly visible visitor to the yard, but it is a picky eater and eats only the foliage of milkweed.

A first step to caterpillar appreciation is to buy or borrow an illustrated field guide. Excellent choices are *Caterpillars of Eastern North America* by David L. Wagner (Princeton University Press, 2005) and *Caterpillars in the Field and Garden: A Field Guide to the Butterfly Caterpillars of North America* by Thomas J. Allen, James P. Brock, and Jeffrey Glassberg (Oxford University Press, 2005). You may find that you're charmed, rather than disgusted, by their fascinating life cycles and clever mimicry, imitating twigs, buds, and flowers, bird droppings, and even dead leaves that wag convincingly as if in the wind. One species squeaks when disturbed. Your eyes will be that much more open to wonders of the natural world.

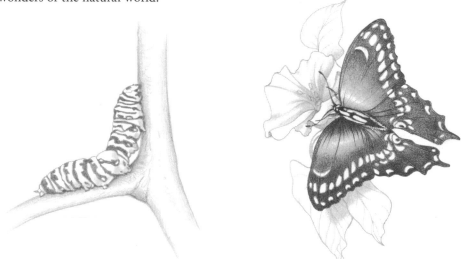

When is an insect a pest, and when is it a remarkable creature? The two can overlap, as with this parsleyworm caterpillar, which metamorphoses into a beautiful swallowtail butterfly.

GETTING A LEG UP ON PESTS AND DISEASES

A COOL LIGHT SHOW

Lightning bugs offer pest control as well as a dazzling light display. Here are ideas on encouraging them to visit your place each summer.

Adult lightning bugs seem to exist only for their own pleasure, and perhaps ours. They float about on warm summer nights, winking mysterious codes with their phosphorescent glow. In fact, they only have sex on their minds, eating only a bit of nectar. The blinking lights serve to guide males and females to one another, as well as to warn predators that lightning bugs aren't very palatable. The glowing eggs are laid in the soil, and hatch to larvae known as glowworms.

These wingless larvae are a very different sort of bug from their placid parents. They look like miniature monsters and aggressively go after slugs and snails, following their slime trails and then injecting them with an immobilizing poison. Among their prey are snails and slugs that might be garden pests.

Unfortunately, there is evidence that the populations of some firefly species are declining, with the possible causes including climate change, pollution, and loss of habitat. There are steps you can take to get them to take up residence on your property. A patch of shrubs or trees will provide shelter. It helps to eliminate or reduce the use of chemicals in the garden and on the lawn. Consider turning off unnecessary outdoor lighting, so that the mating adults can better see their signals. If artificial light levels are bright enough, some species won't even bother flashing, and the adults only live for a matter of days.

SWEET 'N' SOUR CODLING MOTH TRAP

Codling moths are infamous pests of the orchard, and they can be lured to their deaths with a homemade attractant.

ADVICE OVER THE FENCE

A Bitter Pill for Cabbageworms

Some gardeners swear by tansy, a bitter herb long used medicinally as a vermifuge. Tansy has fallen out of popularity as a human tonic, but studies have shown that it also can cause imported cabbageworms to lay fewer eggs and to develop more slowly. Process 1 cup of tansy in 3 cups of water in a blender, filter through cheesecloth, and then spray on vulnerable plants.

For a nontoxic way of catching codling moths around fruit trees, mix up a brew of household ingredients.

1. Pour 1 cup of cider vinegar, ⅓ cup of dark molasses, ⅛ teaspoon of ammonia, and 5 cups of water into a plastic gallon jug. Put on the cap and shake well to mix.
2. Cut two or three 2-inch holes just below the shoulders of the jug.
3. Hang the jug from a fruit tree, passing a strip of cloth through the handle so that the holes are canted downward and won't admit rainwater.
4. Monitor the trap and replace the brew from time to time.

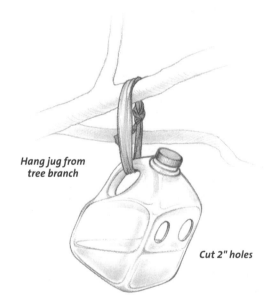

Hang jug from tree branch

Cut 2" holes

You can mix up your own attractant to lure codling moths to their deaths in this trap.

HOT WATER TO THE RESCUE

It's difficult to think of an herbicide or pesticide that has less environmental impact than hot water.

Here are a few ways to use plain water to handle garden problems, with no residual effect.

COOK YOUR WEEDS

The next time you boil too much water for tea, try pouring what's left in the pot on weeds growing between stones in a garden path or under a fence. Cities are now using a more sophisticated version of this technique to control weeds, with steam injectors that deliver superheated water. There's no harmful residue, although you should keep in mind that nearby plants may be damaged.

COOK YOUR FIRE ANTS

Should you be unlucky enough to be plagued by fire ants in your yard, try pouring 2 to 3 gallons of near-boiling water in the nests. Researchers report that this simple technique can destroy some 60 percent of their mounds.

COOK YOUR PLANTS' PESTS

Researchers have found that some plants can be treated with hot water at temperatures that kill pests without damaging plant tissues. In one study, a temperature of 120°F for between 1 and 10 minutes proved effective in controlling aphids, scale, mealybugs, and mites on nursery plant cuttings. Not all plants take to hot water baths. For example, tarragon was effectively cooked at temps above 110°F—not steamy enough to eradicate pests—while rosemary came through its 10-minute immersion at 120°F.

YELLOW JACKETS AT GROUND ZERO

Looking for nonchemical ways to rid your yard of ground-dwelling yellow jackets?

If you've ever stumbled upon an underground yellow jacket nest, you know about their remarkably aggressive behavior. They rally in seconds to meet a perceived threat, stabbing repeatedly with their barbless stingers. And if you should smash one in self-defense—bad idea. Its body will release an attack pheromone that sounds the alarm for other wasps within 15 feet.

The most common control is to spray the nest opening from a distance with a wasp-and-hornet aerosol. But if you'd rather not douse your yard with a chemical, there are alternatives you might try. Do so cautiously. Work after dark, when most yellow jackets will be in the nest. A chilly night is best, because the insects will be less active. Wear long pants and a long-sleeved shirt of heavy fabric, and use tape to close the cuffs. You should have sneakers on so that you can make a speedy exit. Find the nest using a flashlight with red cellophane attached over the lens—yellow jackets can't see red objects.

❖ Put a couple of quarts of household ammonia into a bucket with a lip for easy pouring. After sundown, dump the ammonia down the hole of the nest.

❖ Another approach is to drizzle honey in and around the opening, then let a raccoon or skunk dig up the nest in search of more sweetness.

❖ Place a clear glass baking dish over the hole, upside down, to confound the critters.

❖ And then there's the defensive approach. Preassemble a large round cage of chicken wire or hardware cloth and roll or carry it to the site of the nest. This will act as a fence to keep children away from harm, and also serves as a reminder to you that a hazard lurks in the grass. Come winter, the nest will become inactive and you can fill it in with soil.

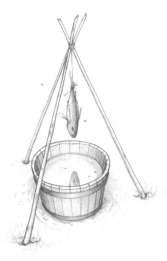

It seems that yellow jackets like raw fish a little too much for their own good. They'll tend to break off a chunk, then plummet to the washtub below.

❖ Here's a folk remedy that will have your neighbors wondering if you've lost touch with reality. Lash a tripod from three stakes, and suspend a raw fish over a washtub with soapy water. Here's how it works: Yellow jackets will cut out a piece of the fish for food, but they characteristically bite off more than they can carry and will drop into the water and drown. Of course, you also may attract dogs, cats, and other wildlife. Keep them away by putting up a temporary chicken wire fence. And change the bait every few days—yellow jackets won't come around if the fish has spoiled.

PLANT TOMATOES IN GOOD COMPANY

Folklore or not—many gardeners rely on companion planting to ensure that tomatoes have a friendly environment.

ADVICE OVER THE FENCE
Flour Power

Rye flour not only makes pumpernickel bread but also can be used to turn cabbageworms into tiny immobile bread nuggets. Early in the morning when there still is dew on the forming cabbage heads, sprinkle them lightly with the flour and any crawling larvae will be gummed up and then eventually harden in the sun.

For many of us, tomatoes are the jewel of the garden and the one crop we most want to succeed. You can help guarantee a good harvest by surrounding tomatoes with plants that seem to have a positive effect.

❖ Basil will help repel pests, while improving the growth and flavor of tomatoes.

❖ Bee balm, chives, and various mints will improve the plants' overall health.

❖ Pot marigolds repel tomato hornworms and other pests.

❖ Dill and borage may also deter hornworms.

DUNK YOUR HOUSEPLANTS

Same idea—new outcome! If you have trouble spraying soapy water on the foliage, do the opposite. Try sticking the foliage in the soapy water.

When spraying an ailing houseplant with an insecticidal soap, the directions usually say that you should saturate the foliage. Easier said than done. To ensure that you really get the job done right, you can completely immerse the top end of the plant in a bucket of lukewarm water with 1 teaspoon or so of mild dishwashing detergent per gallon. The only trick is keeping the plant and its soil from dropping out of the pot. Cut halfway into a disk of cardboard, then slide this collar over the top of the pot and around the stem of the plant. Holding the collar in place, upend the foliage into the drink and gently agitate the plant to help rinse away bugs, dirt, and dust. Follow with an upside-down rinse in clear water.

Cardboard disk with slot cutout

When giving potted plants a bath, use a simple cardboard disk to keep the soil and plant from falling out.

A BOTANICAL ARSENAL

In the garden, "organic" doesn't equal "toothless" when battling pests.

Organic growers can draw on a number of reliable plant-based sprays and dusts. Just keep in mind that their natural origins don't mean that they're entirely safe—to the plants and the beneficial insects that may be crawling or hovering about, or to you and your pets. Protect yourself with a respirator when applying in any quantity. Follow the manufacturer's directions to the letter. Finally, use them only when necessary to salvage an important crop or plant. You can learn more about substances allowed in organic production from the Organic Materials Review Institute (OMRI) at www.omri.org or 541-343-7600.

❖ **Rotenone.** This pesticide is nonselective, which means it isn't used to target certain insect pests. Generally, rotenone is lethal to beetles and other insects with chewing mouthparts. As for non-target species, rotenone can do in beneficial insects, as well as birds and fish in the area. And some people may be highly sensitive to the product, with severe allergic reactions. Because the pesticide can remain on plants for at least a week, allow at least 2 weeks between treating plants and harvesting. Rotenone is particularly toxic to fish and has a "restricted" designation from OMRI.

❖ **Pyrethrum.** It's hard to believe that flower blossoms could kill on contact, but this daisy, grown in Africa and South America, is the source of a potent toxin. It's effective for killing a host of chewing and sucking insects, and the Environmental Protection Agency (EPA) has approved it for more uses than any other pesticide. Pyrethrum can cause people to have allergic skin reactions. The active principle has been synthesized; the natural form of pyrethrum has a "restricted" designation from OMRI.

❖ **Sabadilla.** Made from the seeds of a South African lilylike plant, sabadilla is a contact and stomach poison. It is useful against caterpillars, leafhoppers, thrips, stink bugs, and squash bugs. Honeybees are extremely vulnerable, so lay off the sabadilla when these beneficial insects are buzzing about. Some people may have a severe allergic reaction to sabadilla. Sabadilla also has a "restricted" designation from OMRI.

❖ **Neem.** Neem has long been used in India as both a pesticide and a fungicide. It has a relatively milder effect on target insects as well as beneficials, and can be used to control leaf miners, gypsy moths, caterpillars, and aphids. Neem works as a growth inhibitor, keeping insects stuck in an immature state so that they can't reproduce. OMRI has given neem extract and its derivatives a "restricted" designation and states that it can be used as a pest lure or repellant, as part of a trap, or as a disease control.

WASH TROUBLE AWAY

Out of the kitchen and straight to the garden, homemade sprays come to the rescue.

A number of household ingredients can be whipped up into pest-repellent sprays, without resorting to those commercial insecticides with dire warnings all over the label. Here are a few sprays that researchers have found to be effective. Just keep in mind that nearby beneficial insects may be reeling as well, so use any spray discriminately.

- **Flea beetles.** You'll know you have them by the tiny perforations on the leaves of broccoli, cabbage, eggplant, potato, and spinach, among other crops. Shoo them away with a garlic spray when plants are young and especially vulnerable. Place several cloves in a blender with water, give it a whirl, and then strain the product into a spray bottle.

- **Mites.** A forceful spray of plain water may be all it takes to dislodge mites. This also helps by washing away dust on foliage, which gets in the way of potentially helpful mite predators. Also, the spray can work to destroy pests' webs, which interferes with egg laying. Your mite roundup might also benefit from an uncomplicated soap spray. Place 1 teaspoon of dishwashing liquid in a pint of water and stir well.

- **Squirrels.** To keep squirrels and other rodents from nosing around plants, try the tactic used to keep muggers at bay—a spray of hot pepper. Chop up habaneros or jalapeños and simmer them in a pot of water. (Use disposable gloves for this, lest you make the memorably painful mistake of rubbing your eyes with peppery fingers.) Strain off the liquid and spray it around and on vulnerable plants.

- **Aphids.** Stinging nettle (*Urtica dioica*) is a wild perennial that can cause painful stings when touched. It also has been used to discourage plant pests. Harvest the leaves while wearing gloves and steep in enough water to cover, allowing the brew to sit for at least a couple of weeks. Filter the liquid and use it as a plant spray.

- **Cutworms, armyworms.** Spray a solution of neem extract on plants. It works best in humid weather.

- **Fungus.** Here's a tidy treatment for a disease that may trouble orchids. Mist the leaves with water, then lightly sprinkle the diseased area with powdered cinnamon.

- **Powdery mildew.** Got milk? Then try combating this disease by spraying with a solution of 1 part milk in 9 parts water.

- **Black spot.** If this disease shows up on roses, spray foliage with ½ cup of baking soda mixed well in 4 gallons of water.

TERRIFY THEM WITH TECHNOLOGY

Transform an ordinary garden hose into a garden guardian.

The surest weapon for scaring off the animals that prey on the garden is you, the gardener. But you can't be out there waving your arms at all hours of the day and night. And while the folksy form of a scarecrow is a quaint sight, it's not apt to be intimidating to animals for long. Instead, consider buying a Scarecrow, a clever battery-powered device that's attached to the end of a garden hose. It detects movement (caution: *any creature's movement,* gardener included) and directs a blast of water in that direction.

TUNE IN THIS PEST-CONTROL DEVICE

It was reported that U.S. forces attempted to drive out at least one Central American dictator by blasting him with loud rock music. If your nearest neighbor lives way down the pike, you might try the same technique in the garden.

Seed-plucking birds and other garden visitors can be scared away by simply clapping your hands. But these animals quickly become accustomed to repetitive sounds, even from ear-splitting explosive scares. Instead, put a boom box in the garden, tune in a station with the most raucous rock you can find, then crank up the volume.

FLOATING SCARECROWS AND FLASHING TAPE

Scaring off bird pests might be easier than you think. A couple of alternatives to the traditional scarecrow may help keep birds on guard.

Research has shown that a simple hawk kite—a helium-filled balloon with the image of a hawk on its underside—can be more effective than loud propane exploders in keeping blackbirds from cornfields. (The kite would be a lot less apt to annoy your next-door neighbors, as well!) Simpler still are strips of Mylar bird-scaring tape. To work well, they should be supported by stakes at both ends of each row between the plants—not over the plants themselves. And the strips have to be free to spin in the breeze, which causes them to flash alarmingly. The Washington State University Cooperative Extension suggests that you attach a loop of strong packing tape to both ends of the strip; pass a loop of string through the tape loop; give the tape a few twists so that it will spin in a breeze; and then place the string loop around a stake. Allow enough slack so that the tape can spin freely without allowing it to drag on the ground. You may have to adjust the stakes periodically to keep the tape relatively taut.

BANISHING BIRDS WITH LASERS AND INFLATING DUMMIES

The technology for frightening agricultural pests has become remarkably sophisticated. For example, around $7,000 will buy you a rifle complete with scope that fires a laser beam to disorient birds from up to a mile and a half away; the birds aren't harmed but will be seriously freaked out. More practical for the gadget-minded gardener might be Scarey Man, at about a tenth the price. This human-size inflatable scarecrow will dramatically puff up to full height while sounding a siren and setting off a flashing light. It is battery powered and can be made to inflate and collapse at intervals controlled by a timer. As with many other bird banishers, this one may lose some effectiveness if birds make repeat visits and become habituated to the show.

GETTING A LEG UP ON PESTS AND DISEASES

CHAPTER 6

The Vegetable Plot

When planning next year's garden, consider yourself as well as the plants. What would make this part of the yard more welcoming to you? Vegetable gardens are high-maintenance endeavors, and you'll do a better job of tilling, planting, weeding, and harvesting if you enjoy entering the place. That may mean being more generous with the paths, so that you can walk freely about the garden, with or without a garden cart in front of you or long-handled tools in your arms. You may find that cushioned paths feel a lot better underfoot than those paved with brick or stone. A mulched garden walk, like a thickly carpeted floor, will be less jarring to your joints—and chances are your joints are already being put to the test by yard chores.

While you're giving some thought to wider paths, how about setting aside a small area for a bench? That will encourage you to indulge in a pleasure that gardeners all too seldom allow themselves—looking up from their work to enjoy the birds, the sky, or even the prim topography of the garden beds themselves. You might choose a spot that gets a bit of afternoon shade from a nearby tree. Or attach a canvas beach umbrella to a fence post next to the bench. The only trick is to remind yourself to take a break every hour or so. One way to do that is to keep an inexpensive nonelectric kitchen timer under the bench. Give it a twist to 60 minutes before you get to work, and wait for the recess bell.

All gardening and no play may not be the best way to approach your hobby. Consider setting aside a corner of the garden, and a few minutes, to enjoy the sights and sounds of your yard.

PLAN A ROOT-FRIENDLY BED

If your garden soil is at all heavy, root crops may turn up their noses and fail to perform for you.

Carrots, parsnips, beets, potatoes, and turnips thrive in a deep, sandy loam. If you want to be successful with them, it's important to modify heavy soil with sand and lots of organic matter—if you have access to it, 10 pounds of compost for a 10-foot-square bed. Vigorously double-digging a clay-rich soil will also help to aerate and break it up.

All of this is easier written about than done. It may seem like a Herculean task to convert the entire garden to being root-crop friendly, so concentrate on just one bed and dedicate it to deep growers. Either improve the existing soil, or build up a raised bed to establish a better growing medium from scratch. Take care to avoid walking on the bed, or you run the risk of compacting the soil. A footstep exerts between 6 and 10 pounds per square inch—and tiptoeing across the beds won't help.

A broadfork allows you to aerate the soil without bringing up slumbering weed seeds from below.

GARDENING BY THE COMPASS

The vegetable garden is a solar-powered machine, taking the sun's energy and converting it to food. Keeping that in mind, it makes sense to orient the garden in a way that delivers the optimum levels of sunlight to various crops.

Full sunlight is recommended for most plants, as the informative blurbs on seed packets so often remind us. All-day, blazing sunshine will bring out the best in tomatoes and peppers and corn. Vegetables will reap the most solar benefit if growing in east-to-west rows. Alternately, you can moderate light levels by planting north-to-south and arranging to have taller plants provide shade from the south end of the bed. If you are encircling the garden with a picket fence, it's also possible to use it as a light filter for lettuce and other plants that don't take to hot conditions. Grow them in the row running parallel to the south-facing side. Another such crop can be grown *outside* the north-facing side if it isn't vulnerable to the animal pests that caused you to put up the fence in the first place.

Next Year's Garden

Map the Sun

When you plan what's to go where in your garden, it's important to know how the sun travels throughout the day, in each month of the growing season. The sun makes a much lower arc through the sky for the months on either side of the vernal equinox, casting long shadows. By making a map of the yard, you can note the sunniest areas at various times of year and choose your plants accordingly.

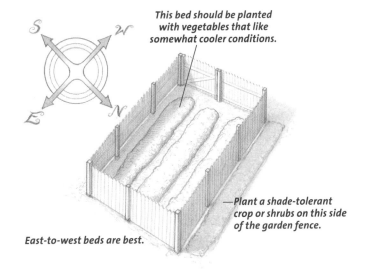

This bed should be planted with vegetables that like somewhat cooler conditions.

Plant a shade-tolerant crop or shrubs on this side of the garden fence.

East-to-west beds are best.

Most yards have different levels of sunlight and shade, at different times of day. Try to position your plants to take best advantage of what the sun has to offer, keeping in mind the shade cast by fences and taller crops.

GARDENING IN SHADY PLACES

Even "full sun" requirements don't mean full sun every minute of the day. Look on the sunny side—you can be a little more relaxed about daylight requirements.

If there are few places in your yard that offer the "full sun" requirement given for many plants, be assured that this condition isn't necessarily meant to be taken literally. After all, only desert dwellers and beachcombers are likely to be entirely free of shadows from hills and trees. Eight to 10 hours of sunlight should be sufficient, even for lumen-loving tomatoes and peppers. And if your garden is blessed with just 5 hours of sun a day, you're in great shape to grow outstanding salad greens, as well as arugula, broccoli raab, chard, collards, kale, parsley, spinach, and an enormous variety of Asian greens. You might also tuck in a few shade-tolerant shrubs for fruit, such as gooseberry, currant, and blueberry.

FORECASTING A FREEZE

If you like to stretch your gardening year into the cooler months, it's good to know the signs of an impending frost.

Even the best computer model used by professional weather forecasters can't predict just what a cold night might hold for your garden. Learn to look for signs of frost, in the sky and on the ground.

- Look up. A clear sky means there's no cloud cover, which can serve as an insulating blanket to help keep the earth's warmth from escaping to the heavens.
- Wet a finger. If you don't detect a breeze, that favors a frost.
- Feel the lawn. If the grass is relatively dry, not dewy, frost will be more likely.
- Read the thermometers, plural—not just one, but a few placed around the property.

The temperature on your back porch may be significantly different from the reading you'd find in the garden.

- If you get a 10:00 p.m. reading of lower than 45°F and the above signs indicate trouble, cover up crops in the ground and bring in potted plants.

FOILING THE FROSTS OF FALL

There are all sorts of tricks you can use to get a couple more weeks out of the growing season.

When the air gets nippy on fall nights, don't give up on your garden without trying a couple of easy ways of protecting the plants. After all, you've already done the hard labor of preparing the soil and pampering the garden.

EVENING DRESS FOR THE GARDEN

As any hibernating animal or insect could tell you, the ground remains warmer than the air as night comes on. You can take advantage of the soil's warmth by placing covers over plants in the evening. Just about anything you have hanging about the house or garage will work: old sheets and blankets, plastic tarps, newspaper, and even overturned cardboard boxes. The results aren't pretty, and you have to remember to remove the covers the following morning. Or, you can buy lightweight floating row covers of spun polyester and bump up the plant's micro-environment from 2° to 5°F. They're easy to lay down, and can be rolled up in a jiffy.

WATERING FOR WARMTH

Your neighbors might think it strange to see you out watering the garden on a cool, dark fall evening. If so, reassure them by explaining that crops can be protected from an early frost by putting more moisture in the air around them. Wet soil also is potentially able to hold considerably more heat than when it is dry.

CHEER UP CHILLY PLANTS WITH CHRISTMAS LIGHTS

The Colorado State University Cooperative Extension suggests that as fall turns frosty, you get out the Christmas lights a little early. Suspend a string of lights from the hoops of a hoop house and turn them on at dusk. Not only will the structure take on an unearthly beauty, but plants will benefit from the gentle, evenly dispersed source of heat.

CATCH THIS WINTER FLUE

Drop root crops down a chimney to keep them at their best.

Next Year's Garden

Focus on Fresh

When it comes time to order seeds and buy plants for next spring, consider planting the garden with crops that will be a clear cut above what you'd find in the supermarket. Vegetable gardens have traditionally been serious places, cultivated to generate basic foods—cabbages, carrots, potatoes, beans, winter squash. And many of us are still in the habit of growing these stalwart crops. But think about giving over more of the garden to the most perishable crops—the ones that inevitably arrive at the supermarket in less than perfect condition, such as salad greens, peas, tomatoes, and herbs. Chances are a commercial grower can produce a butternut squash that's the equal of homegrown, as satisfying as it may be to grow your own.

It used to be that gardeners routinely stored root crops in their cool basements. But that option is out if you keep this level of the home nice and cozy through the winter. If so, try sinking a section of terra-cotta flue liner in the garden and using that for storage. To ensure good drainage, place a few inches of gravel in the bottom of the hole you dig, followed by a couple of handfuls of loose straw to keep the crops clean. Then put the flue in place and carefully lower vegetables into it—beets, cabbage, carrots, kohlrabi, parsnips, potatoes, rutabagas, and turnips. Add more loose straw to fill the air space. Top off the flue with a lid of wood or Styrofoam insulation, weighted with bricks or a flat stone. When temperatures drop well below freezing, you can replace the bricks or stone with a bale of straw for better insulation.

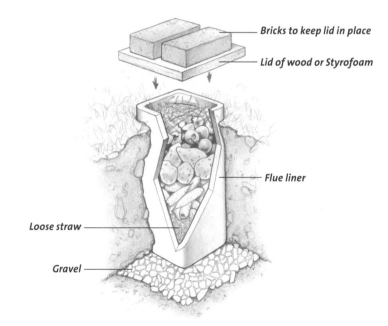

Bricks to keep lid in place

Lid of wood or Styrofoam

Flue liner

Loose straw

Gravel

Root crops take form underground, and after harvest you can preserve their goodness by returning them to the soil. A sunken length of terra-cotta flue liner acts as a mini root cellar, keeping vegetables at a nearly steady temperature into the winter months.

PLAN A FROSTBITE BED

Plan ahead and reserve a corner of the garden for plants that will overwinter.

Give Beds a Winter Coat

To help vegetables make it through wintery weather, keep a few straw bales on hand and scatter beds with a mulch of loose straw. That layer of insulation may make all the difference, retaining just enough of the earth's heat to ward off killing temperatures.

Nothing gladdens a gardener's heart more than crops that sail right through the frosts of fall. Kale, spinach, Swiss chard, beets, carrots, potatoes, turnips, radishes, broccoli, cauliflower, Asian greens, and some lettuces—these may come into their own when the rest of the natural world is settling down for its winter-long snooze. Come spring, you'll find it easier to cultivate and plant for the new season's crops if these over-winterers are growing in their own dedicated part of the garden. So place them with a view to the year ahead.

GROWING BETTER WITH AGE

It's easy to overlook that some crops improve with storage.

Here is a rundown of vegetables that go against the rule that fresh is best.

- Some winter squashes will develop their full flavor in the weeks after harvest, including butternut and buttercup.

- Carrots and parsnips may benefit from a light frost.

- Freezing temperatures may bring out the full character of many brassicas: kale, cauliflower, Brussels sprouts, kohlrabi, cabbage, turnips, and rutabagas.

- Garlic right out of the garden will taste like garlic. But if the heads are cured and stored for a time, their full flavor will have a chance to develop. (For more on curing garlic, see "Let Garlic Rest for Full Flavor" on page 168.)

A HOOP SKIRT KEEPS GARDENS GROWING IN GOOD FASHION

Hoops really help! A simple system of row cover fabric and wire hoops can improve your garden's yield throughout the year.

While a floating cover will indeed rest lightly on the plants below, you can trap more warm air within a row cover that's elevated by hoops. And just about the easiest hoops to erect are lengths of 9-gauge wire. You can buy coils of it from home and garden centers, as well as mail-order seed and vineyard supply companies. To size hoops for a bed's particular width, experiment with how long a curving piece of wire you'll need, including enough to sink the ends firmly in the soil. Keep the cover in place with anchors made for the purpose or simple U-shaped pieces cut from coat hangers.

Row covers offer a number of benefits.

❖ By trapping heat from both the sun and soil, they can protect plants from frost, elevating temperatures by 2° to 7°F.

❖ They warm the soil and the air in spring, getting plants off to a quicker start, which means faster germination, better root growth, and an earlier-maturing crop (beating the performance of black plastic mulch by 1 to 3 weeks).

❖ You may get a better yield from a number of crops, especially cukes, squash, and melons.

❖ The covers serve as a barrier to flying insect pests. Not only will the plants be nibbled less, but you can spare them from diseases commonly spread by bugs. Expect to have good results against such pests as cabbage moths and the cabbage root maggot fly; various flea beetle species on several vegetables; spinach leaf miner; striped cucumber beetle on melons, summer and winter squash, and pumpkins, as well as cukes; European corn borer; Colorado potato beetle on potatoes and eggplant; and potato leafhoppers.

Note that in some circumstances, a row cover can aggravate pest problems, if an insect pest manages to find its way under the cover and then reproduces freely without interference from beneficial insects on the outside. If you see this happening, consider removing the cover temporarily to admit the good bugs. A row cover may also protect pests that have overwintered in the soil below. Again, you may need to pull back the row cover for a time. And consider rotating crops each year so that when pests come out of dormancy, they'll find a barrier between themselves and their target vegetable.

There's another sort of pest to consider when using row covers—mice. If you don't take the trouble to store the fabric at the end of the growing season, you're apt to find that mice have made good use of it for making nests.

❖ By placing 50-percent shade cloth over the hoops in hot weather, you may be able to grow lettuce right through the dog days of summer; the green cloth can lower temperatures by 3° to 6°F.

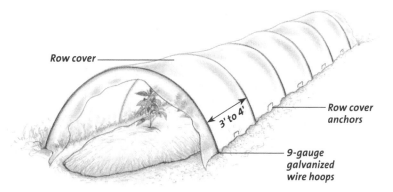

Row cover

Row cover anchors

3' to 4'

9-gauge galvanized wire hoops

There's nothing much to this plant-protecting system—just wires and lightweight spun fabric—but the climate change within the covering is significant.

DOUBLE YOUR INSULATION

You can give plants an extra layer of protection from chilly temperatures by insulating them with both a hoop house and covers on top of the rows below. If you garden in zone 5, your plants will think they're luxuriating in Zone 7. You'll be raising temperatures by from 2° to 4°F. But stop at two layers—you won't get much more insulative value by piling on more row covers, and a third would cut down light transmission by 12 to 14 percent.

A STURDIER HOOP HOUSE

To keep the wind from making havoc with row covers supported by wire hoops, try making the frame out of concrete reinforcing screening instead.

For a hoop house that gusty weather won't topple, buy a roll of concrete reinforcing screening. It's available through companies that sell concrete supplies; consult the commercial pages of your phone book. The wire is tough stuff, and you'll need bolt cutters to snip through it. Cut pieces to bend into tunnel-like sections, leaving protruding wires so that you can anchor the sections in the soil. Place the sections side by side, to cover rows of any length. Then drape floating row covers over this hoop house. Tomatoes and peppers will flourish in this environment. Coddle them for up to a month, at which point they'll be outgrowing their house. Then remove the screening and cloth and set them aside for use as a late-season coverup.

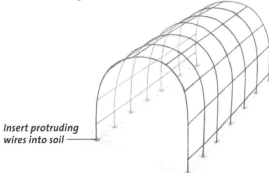

Insert protruding wires into soil

To make a simple hoop house, cut sections of concrete reinforcing wire and form it into a series of anchors.

SPACE BLANKETS TO THE RESCUE

Aluminum space blankets may come in handy in protecting plants from a killing frost. They work something like the traditional practice of placing old quilts over vulnerable beds, but with an important twist. By draping them over hoop houses, metallic side down, they will reflect back most of the soil's radiating heat. You can find the blankets at camping supply stores.

GROW YOUR OWN CALCIUM

Got rhubarb? You can get your calcium from this vegetable, as well as other familiar garden favorites.

Garden vegetables might not look like good sources of calcium—they don't lactate, after all. But a number of crops can deliver a considerable measure of this nutrient. That's a particular plus for people with lactose intolerance. Here's a look at what a 1-cup serving of these cooked vegetables will contain. (To put these numbers in perspective, 1 cup of milk contains 300 milligrams of calcium, and 1 cup of low-fat yogurt contains approximately 400 milligrams.)

VEGETABLE	MILLIGRAMS OF CALCIUM PER 1 CUP (COOKED)
Rhubarb	348
Collards	266
Turnip greens	197
Kale	179
Okra	177
Beet greens	164
Pak choi	158
Dandelion	147

PLANT SELF-TUCKING CAULIFLOWER

Look into cauliflower varieties that cover up without your help.

To spare yourself the ritual of tying leaves around the developing curd of cauliflower, you can plant self-blanching varieties that tuck themselves away as they grow. Check the descriptions in seed catalogs and on seed packets and seedling tags.

A BODY-BUILDING PROTEIN GARDEN

Vegetables aren't just about fiber and vitamins; they actually have protein, too!

ADVICE OVER THE FENCE

Measure Freshness with a Stopwatch

One advantage you have as a gardener is that your produce is as fresh as can be. But even with your own backyard source of vegetables, getting them promptly to the table can be important. For example, USDA research suggests that the flavor of a tomato peaks within *3 minutes* of being picked.

For many people (gardeners included), vegetables still have the reputation of being a "good-for-you" food to be eaten dutifully along with *real* food—meat and dairy products, which are good sources of protein. In fact, a number of crops can pump you up with substantial amounts of that nutrient. Vegetables should figure importantly in a well-rounded, healthful diet. And as a gardener, you are guaranteed a fresh and unadulterated source.

The big surprise in this chart, unless you are a nutritionist, may be that some leafy greens pack a protein punch. All of this is good news for people who are trying to lower their intake of cholesterol-rich foods. By the way, to put the numbers in perspective, 100 grams of broiled beefsteak would give you about 22 grams of protein.

VEGETABLE	GRAMS OF PROTEIN PER 100-GRAM SERVING
Pumpkin seeds	29.0
Peanuts (raw, without skins)	26.3
Adzuki beans (raw)	20.0
Soybeans (dried, cooked)	11.0
Soybeans (green, cooked)	9.8
Lentils (cooked)	9.0
Fava beans (green, raw)	8.5
Peas (green, cooked)	5.4
Kale (cooked, no stems or midribs)	4.5
Brussels sprouts	4.2
Collards (cooked, without stems)	3.6
Spinach (raw)	3.2
Broccoli (cooked)	3.1

FOUL AIR IN THE FRIDGE

The old wives' tale is true—don't store onions with potatoes. And watch what you store in the refrigerator because vegetables can exchange flavors.

The whole idea of storing vegetables and fruits in the fridge is to keep them tasting fresh, but foods in close juxtaposition may taint each other. Peter A. Ferretti, PhD, a Penn State professor of vegetable crops, has identified the most prevalent cases of flavor swapping. He suggests storing apples and potatoes in a cool garage rather than refrigerating them. Keep sensitive items as far as you can from whatever bothers them. Use up older stock first, before it can take on off flavors. And place a box of baking soda in the refrigerator to absorb odors. From time to time, skim off the top layer of powder to expose the fresher product below.

* Carrots affect celery.
* Green peppers affect pineapple.
* Onions affect apples, celery, and potatoes.
* Potatoes affect apples and pears.
* Apples affect cabbage, carrots, onions, and dairy.
* Pears affect cabbage, carrots, celery, onions, and potatoes.

SOME VEGETABLES LIKE IT WARMER

Most vegetables you bring in from the garden will have a longer storage life if kept in the refrigerator just above freezing, or from 34° to 40°F. This slows the enzyme action that results in a loss of flavor and change in texture. By the way, the chilliest section of most refrigerators is at the back of the uppermost shelf. Still, there are important exceptions to the colder-is-better rule. Crops that originated in tropical or subtropical climates don't take to being stored below 50°F, including cucumbers, squash, tomatoes, peppers, eggplant, snap beans, and potatoes. Store them in a *cool* place rather than the coldest part of the fridge.

ARTICHOKES FOR COOL CLIMES

Give these edible thistles a try even if your growing season is short.

Unless you live in California, chances are you get your globe artichokes at the supermarket rather than from your backyard. But with some care, they can be grown over much of the United States. Even if the crop isn't overwhelmingly generous, there is no disputing the majesty of the plants, which can reach a height of 4 feet and will form big thistlelike blossoms if allowed to.

Globe artichokes are cultivated as perennials in warm areas, but they will be done in by winter temperatures below 20°F. If you will be growing artichokes as an annual, 'Imperial Star' is a good variety. Start plants indoors about 8 weeks before your last frost-free date. They will produce better if subjected to a bit of *vernalization,* or exposure to cool temperatures. Bring the plants out to the garden soon enough that they will spend at least a week in temperatures around 50°F. Although artichokes tend to get off to a slow start once transplanted, they'll need plenty of space before long; allow 30 inches between plants. By July, you can expect to begin harvesting the small buds—small, but more tender than the big commercial ones.

If you have spare room in your vegetable or flower beds, try growing a couple of globe artichokes from seed. They'll be visually outstanding, as well as producing tender, flavorful 'chokes.

BASIL RESCUE MISSION

Nip a few cuttings before frost nips the plants.

Root for This Hormone

Many plants can be started readily from cuttings, but some will do better if you stimulate them to send out roots with a commercial rooting hormone. These products are available in powdered or liquid form, and you should be able to find them at well-stocked nurseries and gardening centers. Before dipping stems in the hormone, put as much of it as you expect to need in a separate container; don't place unused hormone back in the package or you may contaminate its contents. Cuttings are apt to respond better if you keep them reasonably warm, from 65° to 75°F. If you have a heating mat or cable, it can be used to maintain a steady temperature.

There's no grimmer harbinger of winter's approach than a row of frost-blackened basil. To enjoy this highly aromatic cook's friend through the winter, you might try to dig up a few of the busy plants and wrestle them into pots. But it's easier to take cuttings toward the end of summer. Remove the leaves from the lower end of the cuttings to prevent dehydration. Place the cuttings in a glass of water, then stick them in pots once they've grown roots. The clove-like scent will take you back to summer every time you touch the plants. Next spring, take cuttings from these windowsill basils and repeat the rooting process to have plants you can set out as soon as warm weather returns.

Remove lower leaves.

By taking cuttings, you can make clonal copies of your favorite plants, including those about to be done in by freezing weather.

STRING CLIMBERS ALONG WITH A MAYPOLE

Beans and other vines will be happy scaling this simple maypole.

Next Year's Garden

A Fresh Look at Beans and Peas

Here's a slightly different twist on a couple of familiar garden standards that you might try when planting time comes around again.

- **Elegant green beans?** Yes, if you grow varieties meant to be picked when slender and tender. All too often green beans are assigned the role of the obligatory vegetable alongside the main dish. But filet beans, a French specialty, are a cut above the standard-issue green bean. They comprise distinct varieties intended to be picked young, slim—and remarkably delicate and sweet. The trick is to pick them daily and eat them promptly.

- **Edible pods and edible leaves?** Visit an Asian grocery store, and you are apt to see fresh pea plants, minus the pods. The tender top leaves and tips of sugar pea plants are widely used in stir-fries and as salad ingredients. To grow your own, try planting 'Dwarf Grey Sugar', an old variety that has particularly tasty tops.

Surround this pole with climbing edibles, flowering vines, or a mixture of both. To make it easier to remove the pole at summer's end and return it to the yard in spring, you can bury a length of pipe with a diameter just large enough to accommodate it, so that the top of the pipe is at ground level. Then all you have to do is slip the pole down the pipe, without needing to hammer while balanced on a stepladder.

1. While standing on a stepladder held firmly by a helper, pound a 6- or 8-foot-long 2 × 2 wooden stake into good garden soil. To prevent mashing the stake, you can cut an X in a tennis ball and slip it over the top before hammering.

2. Drill a pilot hole in the top of the stake and twist in a threaded eye.

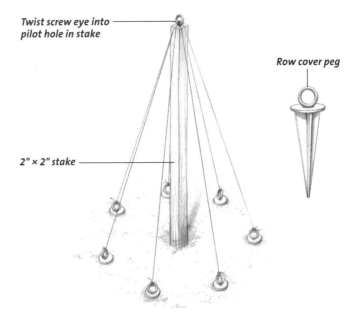

Twist screw eye into pilot hole in stake

Row cover peg

2" × 2" stake

To make the most of garden real estate, think vertical. This simple pole arrangement will encourage climbers to clamber up the twines radiating down to the ground.

3. Run lengths of twine from the eye to pegs placed 2 to 3 feet out from the pole's base. You can make pegs by cutting U-shaped hoops from coat hangers, but you'll be less likely to trip over or lose the brightly colored plastic pegs used for row covers.

4. Sow seeds or set out plants next to each peg.

AN EDIBLE ORNAMENTAL BEAN

Scarlet runner beans are a standout in the vegetable garden, producing showy blossoms that act as magnets for hummingbirds and butterflies. The large, shiny beans themselves are every bit as handsome in their own way, and they happen to taste good as well, with a flavor something like chestnuts. Even the flowers are edible, making an attractive addition to salads.

The vines need something to climb on—a maypole, trellis, arbor, or teepee of branches. Or you can snake them horizontally along a picket fence. Some gardeners even send them up tall-growing sweet corn.

STUBBY CARROTS FOR STUBBORN SOIL

If you can't beat 'em, join 'em. Instead of making your garden hospitable to carrots by changing the soil, change the carrot.

If carrots don't care for the density of your soil, try planting short varieties that won't stick their toes in very deep. 'Parmex' is a chubby ball-type variety that's just 1½ inches long at maturity. 'Kinko' is somewhat more conventional in shape, reaching a modest length of 4 inches by the time they're ready to pull. Short, stout 'Royal Chantenay' carrots will burrow their way down into heavy soil.

If you're stuck with unyielding soil, you can skip it altogether and grow short carrot varieties in pots. While you might be able to get away with as small as a 2-gallon pot, this crop will fare better if treated to a container holding 3 or even 6 gallons of soil. Remember that potted vegetables may need more frequent watering, especially if the pots are of clay and wick moisture.

TRY THIS ARTICHOKE COUSIN

Looking like a giant bunch of celery, cardoon is a vegetable with a visual harvest.

Cardoon is an odd-sounding and remarkable-looking relative of the globe artichoke. Preparing it for harvest is an unusual process as well. The stalks of the long, jagged leaves are the edible feature, not the flower buds. To keep the stalks tender, you blanch them once they reach a length of 18 inches or so. Tie the leaves at the top to bundle them, then wrap first with newspaper and then a layer of black plastic, or with burlap. After a month or so, remove this covering and cut the stalks below the crown. Strip off the outer leaves to reveal the blanched center of the plant.

Try sautéing stalks in butter to enjoy them as Italians do. Some cooks suggest simmering cardoons first in water with a bit of vinegar to bring out their best flavor. If you allow some of the plants to mature, they will display lavender flowers that are excellent for fresh or dried arrangements. Don't allow flowers to set seed and be scattered about, or you may have a nuisance on your hands.

Cardoon has a third use, beyond being attractive and tasty. It produces an enzyme that has been used by traditional cheesemakers in Portugal as a coagulant. To try it yourself, pick the flowers, dry them, weigh out about 1 ounce, and steep in a cup of warm water. Use 1 teaspoon per quart of milk to begin with, or more if needed to cause the milk to coagulate.

A CENTERPIECE FOR THE GARDEN

Most vegetable gardens are practical affairs laid out like tiny farm fields, with parallel rows and little thought to visual drama. For something different, try arranging the beds around a central feature. A cluster of three or so tall, commanding plants will do. Cardoon is a likely candidate, spreading its jagged-edged arms over a good area as it tops off at 6 feet or so. Other handsome edibles include globe artichoke and bronze fennel. Or, you can lash together a few 8-foot-long stakes, place them right in the middle of the central bed, and train runner beans up them. Shorter plants can make a bold statement, too, if grown in a super-size urn or pot set on a stump or other base to raise it up enough to stand out.

MORE CUKES, BETTER CUKES

You've been growing them for years but you can still pick up a tip or two for a better harvest. Here are a few clues for coaxing the best from cucumbers.

~ Next Year's Garden
Cucumbers without the Bite

If bitterness has been a problem for you, read catalog descriptions to identify sweeter varieties for next year's garden. In the meantime, you can somewhat salvage a bitter cucumber by salting it. Sprinkle slices or spears with salt and allow the cucumber to sit for an hour or so. You'll lose some crispness in exchange for a more agreeable taste. It may also help to cut off the stem end and remove the peel, where the bitterness tends to be concentrated.

Cucumbers aren't a very demanding crop, but they appreciate adequate watering and prompt picking.

DON'T PLUG UP CUCUMBER PRODUCTION

It's important to keep a close eye on the cucumber patch to make sure that you harvest the cukes at their peak. If you spot a yellow one that has gone past its prime, pick it promptly. Otherwise, the vine will tend to stall, putting no more energy into growing more fruits. Another reason to pick sooner rather than later is that plants harvested late in the season tend to yield bitter cukes.

AVOIDING BITTERNESS

Cucumbers react to stress by developing a bitter personality. There can be any of a few causes, including a run of hot days, insufficient moisture, low fertility, or foliar diseases. The off-putting taste is the work of compounds known as cucurbitacins; under difficult growing conditions, they migrate from other plant parts to the fruits. Make sure you water regularly in dry, hot spells. And look into resistant varieties; more than a half-dozen diseases can be dealt with by selecting cucumbers bred for resistance. Cucumber beetles spread pathogens as well as exercising their appetites, and they can be discouraged with a floating row cover. If you find that a particular plant is yielding bitter fruit, pull it, because its cukes won't get any milder; if the leaves show the white coating characteristic of powdery mildew, don't compost the rogued plant.

CORN: SWEET, SWEETER, SWEETEST

To choose the best sweet corn variety for your garden, take a moment to get familiar with corn lingo.

Buying seed for sweet corn isn't quite as simple as picking up a packet of, say, Deer Tongue lettuce. That's because plant breeders have been fiddling with the genetic makeup of regular old corn, with very sweet results. These newer hybrids are classified as *normal sugary* (SU), *sugary enhanced* (SE), or *super sweet* (Sh2) varieties, as well as *synergistic,* which sounds frightening but only means that some kernels on each ear are SE and others are Sh2. Here are the characteristics of each group.

❧ Traditional sweet corn is open pollinated, meaning that you can collect seed for planting the following year—an option you don't have with the hybrids. Gardeners continue to grow old-fashioned varieties for the "corny" taste and substantial, chewy texture.

❧ The SUs are moderately sweet, compared to those described below. Because their sugars begin to turn into starch soon after picking, they must be eaten within a very short time. Ears have what can be called a traditional corn flavor, harkening back to a time before all these abbreviations appeared.

❧ Sugary enhanced varieties have a gene that raises the sugar content above that of SUs, with an excellent tenderness and a creamy texture. The ears are slower to convert sugars into starch. Small wonder that SEs are highly popular with home gardeners.

❧ Super sweet varieties are in fact the sweetest you can grow, and they have a crisp texture with the kernels popping as you bite into an ear. The lack of a traditional corn flavor may be a shortcoming to some people. Plantings should be isolated from other varieties that are tasseling at the same time because super sweets have weak pollen and may turn starchy and tough if pollinated by other types. A distance of at least 500 feet is necessary, because the pollen is carried by the wind.

❖ Each ear of a synergistic variety will have a mix of sugary enhanced and super sweet kernels to bite into, for a good blend of sweetness and tenderness. The sweetness comes on only as ears reach full maturity; otherwise they will taste watery. You can grow this variety alongside sugary and sugar enhanced rows, but quality will suffer if synergistics exchange pollen with super sweets.

OTHER CORN CODES

When sorting through the many varieties of sweet corn, you also should be familiar with other abbreviations. *F1* means that the variety is a hybrid and it won't grow true from seed you collect from dried ears. Then there's resistance to common diseases: *NCLB* signifies resistance to northern corn leaf blight; *SCLB*, to southern corn leaf blight; *SM*, to smut; *SW*, to Stewart's Wilt; and *R*, to common rust.

BABY CORN FOR STIR-FRIES

Make your own babies rather than buying waterlogged ones out of a can.

Baby corn is a novel sight in East Asian dishes—and not all that flavorful if it has been languishing in a tin can. Fortunately, it's not that difficult to grow your own. Begin with a variety that yields especially good, tender premature ears, including 'Baby', 'Bonus', 'Candystick', 'Delectable', and 'Jubilee'. Plant at a tighter spacing, from 2 to 4 inches apart, and keep a close eye on the developing ears to make sure you harvest them before they become too big. Allow no more than a couple of days after the silks first appear. By picking promptly, you also encourage the stalk to produce more ears. Keep the husks on the harvested babies until you're ready to cook them.

GROW YOUR OWN GARLIC

Why settle for generic (often empty shells or even sprouted) garlic in the grocery store?

ADVICE OVER THE FENCE
Let Garlic Rest for Full Flavor

Garlic takes anywhere from 4 to 6 weeks to cure thoroughly. Then trim the roots and tops, and they're ready for storage in a cool, dry place. Unlike most vegetables, garlic improves with time, with each variety developing a characteristic flavor that's missing when it's fresh out of the ground.

ADVICE OVER THE FENCE
A Different Sort of Garlic Pesto

Unless you want garlic plants to make seed heads, you can harvest the curly flower stalks early, while they're still tender, and pulverize them into pesto. A simple recipe uses 3 cups of the tops, compressed a bit; ⅔ cup grated Parmigiano-Reggiano cheese; and ⅔ cup olive oil. Process in a blender.

Garlic is undergoing a modest rediscovery, as people find out that not all varieties taste alike. Not that there's anything wrong with supermarket garlic. It's cheap. It tastes garlicky, too. But it is only one color in a spectrum of garlics. Have a look at the offerings of seed catalogs for varieties that have become favorites around the world. Some are mild, some assertive. Some keep especially well. Some are a good choice for roasting into a sweet pulp. Some are quite pretty, in rosy or purple hues.

Come next fall, tuck two or three varieties in the garden for the next year's crop, allow them to cure and then rest in storage for a while, and then compare their qualities and culinary talents. Choose from between softneck varieties for good storage and braiding, or hardneck for outstanding flavor.

Chinese Pink. For an early harvest, try this relatively mild-tasting softneck. Stick the cloves in the ground in fall, and you may have fresh-from-the-garden garlic by the following May.

Inchelium Red. Discovered on an Indian reservation in northern Washington State, this softneck garlic has a mild, highly rated flavor. It's particularly suited to baking into a soft pulp.

Polish Softneck. This heirloom has been grown in the United States for a century, remaining popular because of its winter hardiness, large cloves, and sharp taste.

Chesnok Red. Originally from the former Soviet republic of Georgia, Chesnok has a flavor that stands up well when cooked. Try baking this hardneck to make a spread for crackers.

Purple Glazer. Both the bulb and cloves of this lovely hardneck variety are a rich purple embellished with gold or silver. Like Chesnok, it's from the Republic of Georgia and is a good choice for baking.

Spanish Roja. This heirloom is described as having a definitive garlic flavor, which helps to explain why it remains popular year after year.

GETTING TO KNOW EAST ASIAN GREENS

If you haven't yet made the acquaintance of the many East Asian greens now available in seed racks and catalogs, you're in for a gratifying new wrinkle in gardening.

Asian greens come in many shapes and sizes, with tastes ranging from mild and sweet to pungent. These varieties grow quickly with little trouble, and they may keep producing well after hard frosts have sent other vegetables reeling. Many can be harvested either early for salad ingredients and braising mixes, or when full size for steaming and sautéing in a wok. Even the flowers, characteristically a cheerful yellow, make a pretty, edible addition to salads. The only potential problem is the confusing mix of names—English, Japanese, Thai, Chinese, Indian, and more, with a riot of different spellings. You can always go by the photos in catalogs and on seed packets.

Generally, these vegetables are sown directly into the garden from early spring into midsummer, with a second sowing when cool weather returns in early fall.

Pak choi. Also known as bok choy, this is a relatively familiar green, similar in appearance to chard, with a thick white stalk and mild flavor.

Autumn Poem. This is a flowering variety, similar to pac choi but with thick, flavorful stems and attractive flower buds.

Tatsoi. The dark green, spoon-shaped leaves grow in tidy, low-growing rosettes. You can sow this form of pac choi right into fall.

Red Giant and Osaka Purple. Grown for both salads and stir-fries, these mustards have spicy, colorful leaves. They may self-seed and reappear here and there in the garden.

Mizuna. Mizuna is a striking-looking mustard, with deeply toothed leaves and a relatively mild flavor.

Komatsuna. Sometimes listed as spinach mustard, it matures quickly, with harvesting possible just 35 days after sowing.

Gai lon. Also called Chinese broccoli, gai lon has thick, flavorful stems. Cut the main stem, and others will branch out.

Hon tsai tai. This one is worth growing for its remarkable color as well as its mildly mustardlike zip. The stems are purple, becoming more vivid in cooler weather; the leaves are dark green; and the flowers bright yellow.

EGGPLANTS IN EASTER EGG COLORS

If big, spongy, dark supermarket eggplants are the only eggplants you know, you're in for a pleasant surprise.

Try growing slim and modest-size East Asian or Italian varieties. They come in cheerful lavender and cream colors, in solids and stripes. The fruits and the plants themselves are attractive enough to earn a place in flower beds. The taste is agreeable, too: mild, with no hint of the bitterness we associate with the familiar big boys of the produce section. And because they're slim rather than rotund, they cook up quickly in a stir-fry without sopping up a lot of oil.

GO WILD WITH KALE

It can be fascinating to grow "unstable" wild varieties of kale—you never know just what's going to spring up!

Seed companies take pains to provide you with packets that will yield dependable results. Most of the time, that is. Some mail-order firms sell seed for open-pollinated kale that hasn't been stabilized. It's a treat to see the varied forms and colors that spring up out of those apparently identical seeds. Frilly or plain edges, smooth or crinkly, big or small, green or multicolored—it's like looking at a little forest of different trees. Pick them young to add to salads, and you'll better be able to enjoy their distinctive looks than if they're cooked. If you have a favorite couple of kales, allow them to flower and go to seed, and save the seed for the following year. When you label the seed containers, don't be shy about coming up with a fanciful name for your rare variety.

A LETTUCE EXPLOSION

Iceberg lettuce is no longer the lettuce of choice on salad plates. There's a whole world of lettuce just waiting to be sown.

There's no explaining taste, in art or in lettuce. Profound changes in the use of lettuce and other salad crops have been taking place in the United States, western Europe, and several other parts of the world. The most surprising change has been the adoption of crisphead lettuce (also known as iceberg) in countries where it was hardly used before. In England, for example, people consumed mostly butterhead lettuce until the late 1970s. At that time, only about 3 percent of the lettuce used was of the iceberg type. Then, the British discovered iceberg lettuce, and it now composes about 80 percent of the lettuce consumed in Britain. Similar changes have occurred in the Scandinavian countries and are beginning in other countries as well.

On the other hand, we in the United States have rediscovered that not all lettuce heads are round, crisp, and hard and once again are eating romaine, butterhead, and leaf lettuces, not to mention endive and escarole (*Cichorium endivia*) and spinach (*Spinacia oleracea*). In addition, we have discovered 'Little Gem', a Latin-type lettuce, part romaine and part butterhead, which is small, crisp, and sweet. We have also discovered radicchio, a red Italian chicory (*C. intybus* L.); mizuna, a leafy vegetable from Japan (*Brassica japonica* L.); and rocket (*Eruca sativa* Mill.), formerly found in the wild, but now known in the cultivated form as arugula. Mizuna, arugula, and spinach are often found in a salad mixture called mesclun, which is made up of tiny lettuce leaves of various shapes and colors and other salad greens.

A CHILL PILL FOR BITTER LETTUCE

When lettuce is subjected to hot summer weather or begins to bolt, the leaves are apt to take on a bitter edge. You can sweeten lettuce somewhat by rinsing it and storing it in the refrigerator for a couple of days.

JUMP-START A SALAD

Next year, expand your salad bowl spectrum by growing sprightly greens.

Next Year's Garden

Plant a Palette of Cherry Tomatoes

The past several years have seen a surge of interest in cherry tomatoes, with all sorts of shapes and sizes now readily available to gardeners. Because they're bite size, these varieties are perfect for dropping into a salad or into a lunch box. And if you grow a range of colors, they can be a visual standout on an hors d'oeuvre tray. In addition to the familiar reds, try the remarkably productive and flavorful Sun Gold; Yellow Pear, an heirloom with a distinctive pear-like shape; cheerful-looking 'Gold Nugget'; the distinctive 'Green Grape'; the eerily white 'Dr. Carolyn'; and the richly flavored near-black 'Black Cherry'.

The reputation of iceberg lettuce has taken a hit lately because of its famous blandness. But most lettuces are relatively mild-tasting; fortunately, you can perk up a salad by including homegrown greens from the genus *Cichorium*.

- **Chicory.** These full-flavored greens look a lot like the common dandelion and are sometimes referred to as Italian dandelion. Snip them young for salads, or later in the season for braising. If you allow a few to bolt, you'll be rewarded with the familiar sky blue chicory flower seen along roadsides.

- **Belgian endive.** Also known as witloof, this unusual vegetable has a double season. It starts out in the garden, developing a root. Then it is dug up and brought into a cool basement (from 50° to 60°F) for forcing in the winter. The traditional method is to stick them in a bucket of moistened sand, leaving the crowns exposed. A lid is placed over the bucket to exclude light, which would turn the forced leaves green and cause them to be bitter. The *chicons*, as the tight pale heads are known, are ready for harvesting after 3 to 5 weeks. If given a month or two to recover, the roots may produce a second harvest. Newer varieties can be forced without this ritual.

- **Radicchio.** Similar in appearance to a small head of lettuce, the heading radicchios are bright in color and spirited in flavor. Unlike most leafy greens, they can be grilled or roasted.

- **Escarole.** This European salad green has a somewhat bitter flavor. It will taste milder if blanched for a few days or a week before harvest; cover plants with overturned bushel baskets or pots, or simple A-frames of plywood. Or, with a bit of twine, you can tie up the outer leaves to shield those within from the sun. Escarole not only adds oomph and texture to salads, but can be braised with olive oil and a splash of balsamic vinegar.

- ❖ **Endive.** Distinct from Belgian endive (see above), this leafy green looks like a frilly lettuce but has a touch of the bitterness characteristic of this group and a more substantial texture. Those with deeply dissected leaves may be listed as *frisée* in catalogs.

A DRESSING FOR SUCCESS

If you like the assertive edge of greens in the chicory group but want to tone the flavor down a bit, use a dressing with slightly more salt or tamari than you might otherwise. According to Harold McGee in *On Food and Cooking: The Science and Lore of the Kitchen* (Scribner, 2004), salt works to make our tongues a little less sensitive to bitterness.

PURPLES AND GOLDS TO GO WITH YOUR GREENS

Please do eat the violets and the lavender and the dianthus. Try adding blossoms to salads for unusual color and flavor.

To visually spike a salad of greens, toss in edible flower blossoms. Some contribute mainly color, while others add a novel taste. Pick the blossoms just before using them, and either include them in the mix or scatter them over the top of the heap. Soups are famously bland-looking and also will benefit from a garnish of pretty petals. Here is a crayon box of possibilities.

EDIBLE PLANT	COLOR
Borage	Blue
Calendula	Gold
Chives	Purple
Dianthus	Pink
Lavender	Purple
Nasturtium	Yellow, orange
Violet	Purple, yellow, white

LETTUCE AS AN ORNAMENTAL

It's interesting, sassy, and fun to go geometric with a multicolored bed of lettuce.

Plant concentric rectangles with lettuces of contrasting colors.

For crisp lines between each area, place boards along the edges as you sow.

You may be the sort of no-nonsense person who views the garden as a source of good food. Period. But the range of colors and shapes now available in many crops suggests laying out beds with an eye to design. Lettuces, as an example, come in cool and hot colors, and in all sorts of shapes. Instead of sowing separate blocks of this or that variety, try alternating reds and greens, or tall lettuces and round ones. Another approach is to sow a pattern, perhaps a border of 'Red Sails' or 'Outredgeous' lettuce surrounding cool green 'Deer Tongue', which in turn forms a border around a speckled variety such as 'Freckles' or 'Forellenschuss'. For another pattern, divide a bed into equal-size diamonds. To keep the lines sharp between varieties, place boards along the edges of an area as you scatter seed. There's no practical benefit to planting this way—except that you may have the incentive to take more pleasure (and more care) in weeding and watering to maintain that bit of artful design.

A KINDER, GENTLER JALAPEÑO

You might be happy to know that not all jalapeños are created equal, when it comes to heat.

If past experiences with hot peppers have scared you off, try growing a jalapeño with good flavor but less heat, such as Numex Primavera (supposed to pack just one-tenth the wallop), or the intriguingly named Fooled You, an F1 hybrid that looks like culinary dynamite but is devoid of heat.

And here's a tip if you've learned to be cautious around horticultural hotties. Grow truly hot varieties and milder ones in separate areas of the garden. It's all too easy to confuse the two once you have them on the kitchen counter.

SMOKING JALAPEÑOS

By curing peppers over a smoldering fire, you can both preserve them and add a haunting flavor.

No, the idea isn't to light them up like ruby red cigars, but to preserve these peppers by drying gradually over a smoky, smoldering fire. The dried result is known as a chipotle. You can use a barbecue with a snugly fitting lid, starting with charcoal briquettes. Then switch to branches or chips of a hardwood such as hickory, ash, oak, or pecan, or a fruit wood such as apple. The wood can be soaked in water to help keep the fire at the moderate temperature necessary to avoid burning the peppers. Also make use of the vents to control the amount of air reaching the fire.

Rake the coals over to one side of the barbecue and place the stemmed peppers on the other side of the grill. Turn the peppers from time to time, and add wood as needed to maintain the fire. It's a slow process, taking at least several hours for the peppers to dry, so you are better off beginning early in the day. Store the cooled peppers in zippered plastic bags.

A SIMPLE RISTRA

Try this easy (and traditional) way to put up and display peppers.

Ornamental strings of red pepper ristras are a common sight around Southwestern and Mexican households. They're practical as well, allowing the peppers to air dry with little danger of mold forming. You'll need a lot of peppers—5 to 20 pounds of them if you want to make a 3-foot-long ristra, depending on the size of the variety. Possibilities include Anaheim, Cascabel, Cayenne, De Arbol, and Mirasol. The traditional method of stringing peppers involves tying them in bunches and then braiding individual strings along a length of twine. This version is a lot simpler: Just thread sturdy fishing line through the stems, tying the stem of the first pepper so that it will secure those above it. Make a loop at the top of the line so that you can hang the ristra. When you want to use a pepper, remove the uppermost one, rinse off any accumulated dust, and reconstitute it by dropping it in simmering water, then turning off the heat and allowing the pepper to sit for 10 minutes or so.

PUMPKINS, BIG AND FAST

No vegetable is more rooted in North American history and tradition than the pumpkin. But we'll bet there's a few fun facts you didn't know!

ADVICE OVER ⛏️THE⛏️ FENCE
Pumpkin Pie from Winter Squash

If making pumpkin pie (or cookies or ice cream) is a tradition in your household, try using winter squash instead of the familiar jolly, round fixture of Halloween. Some cooks prefer squash, with its excellent flavor and less fibrous texture. Winter squashes come in all shapes and sizes. If your household doesn't have the appetite to handle the familiar Waltham Butternut or Blue Hubbard squashes, for example, you now can find smaller varieties of these longtime favorites.

You can buy pumpkins for a song when fall comes around. But if you grow your own, the crop will lend a cheerful presence to the garden at a time of year when most plants have given up. When selecting varieties, keep in mind that some are grown primarily for their looks—color, shape, and size. Others are renowned for cooking, with sweet and flavorful flesh.

BUILDING A BIGGER PUMPKIN

Gardeners like to brag about huge tomatoes and moan about huge zucchinis. And there's a particular fascination with pumpkins the size of Cinderella's coach. Here are a few tips for growing the biggest pumpkin on the block.

❖ Select a variety known for size. A couple of favorites are 'Prizewinner', a hybrid; and bigger still, Dill's 'Atlantic Giant', which is a different species from the familiar *Cucurbit pepo*. The largest pumpkin on record is an Atlantic Giant weighing in at 1,469 pounds, but chances are your best effort will be in the range of 200 to 300 pounds. To order seeds right from the developer of Dill's himself, contact him at www.howarddill.com.

❖ Start early, sowing seed indoors 2 weeks before planting them in the garden.

❖ Give them plenty of room to roam, at least an area measuring 25 feet square. A jumbo may carpet more than 2,000 square feet with its foliage.

❖ Anchor them. Growing vines are vulnerable to strong winds. Pile up soil at nodes along the vines; this also has the benefit of encouraging the plant to put down secondary roots. Consider putting up a length of snow fence on the side of the pumpkin patch from which prevailing winds tend to blow.

- Focus the plant's energy by cutting off all but one of the developing fruits.

- To prevent the outer skin of the developing pumpkin from hardening before it reaches full size, put up a board or a section of fence covered with fabric to block the full force of the sun.

- Position them. As a big pumpkin grows, the stem tends to meet it at an increasingly narrow angle. Gently and gradually move the fruit so that the stem remains nearly perpendicular.

- Feed and water them. It stands to reason that a living thing this big has to have a good appetite. Continue to fertilize through the season. Trickle irrigation and soaker hoses are a good approach to watering because they will be less likely than overhead sprinkling to cause mildew problems.

TOWARD A MORE PERFECT PUMPKIN

For a rounder pumpkin, rotate weekly.

Pumpkins may become somewhat misshapen if allowed to just park in one place and get huge. To help ensure that they'll develop a pleasing round shape, get into the routine of rotating them about a quarter of a turn every week or so. And if you would like the pumpkins to be really big as well as really round, plan ahead for their need to sprawl by placing the hills 25 feet apart.

PUNKIN' CHUNKIN'?

Fall is that time of year when people feel like picking up a pumpkin and seeing how far they can hurl it. Or, at least *some* people do. Delaware hosts the annual Punkin' Chunkin' competition in which contestants use all manner of contraptions to all but put that plump orange fruit into orbit. The record now stands at an astounding 4,331 feet, accomplished with an air cannon. According to contest rules, the pumpkins must weigh between 8 and 10 pounds—no Baby Boos allowed. Pumpkins don't always fly straight and true; if it strays in flight, the competitors who fired it have 3 hours to locate it.

EDIBLE ORNAMENTAL WINTER SQUASHES

Instead of the basic varieties, try growing one of these handsome varieties. Then enjoy the new flavors you'll discover.

ADVICE OVER 🏠T🏠H🏠E🏠 FENCE
Wrestling with Squash

You may have noticed that supermarkets now sell winter squash in ready-to-use chunks, sparing you the physical contest required to prepare thick-skinned varieties. But if you grow your own, you'll have to do the work.

Use a heavy-duty chef's knife or cleaver, or even a small (and scrupulously clean) hatchet if you have one handy. You and your kitchen may be safer if you perform the operation on the floor, rather than struggling at countertop height. Place the squash on a sturdy cutting board, align the blade down its length, and apply weight. You may need to administer a few taps with a mallet or block of wood in order to get the blade started. While you can continue to hack the squash in smaller chunks, it's easier to put the halves in a large covered pot on the stove, or in a baking dish covered with foil; then add an inch or so of water and put the pot on the stove or the dish in the oven. The squash will be softened to the point that you can spoon out the flesh.

These brilliantly colored squashes make excellent autumn decorations—forget the fake colored leaves and the phony Halloween cobweb effect. Here's a rundown of the prettiest.

- ✦ 'Sweet Dumpling' has a brilliant patterning of dark green against warm white. Each squash has enough scrumptious flesh for one serving.

- ✦ 'Carnival' is a harlequin among dumpling-type squashes, with a riot of color. A cooler summer will help bring out the school-bus-yellow coloring. The flavor is considered to be not quite up to the par of 'Sweet Dumpling'.

- ✦ 'Cream of the Crop' acorn squash not only is an attractive cream color on the outside but also offers creamy textured flesh within.

- ✦ 'Table Gold' acorn is a diverting golden color.

- ✦ 'Turk's Cap' is more of a novelty than a culinary favorite, but it works well in soups.

- ✦ 'Sunshine' is a Scarlet Kabocha that does seem to bring rays of sunlight into the garden and onto the windowsill.

- ✦ 'Orangetti' is a new, brightly colored version of the standard spaghetti squash. As its color suggests, this variety delivers far more beta-carotene. It also has a sweeter flavor and cooks in less time.

You don't need to buy seeds to have an interesting array of winter squashes in the garden. Supermarkets often carry a colorful selection, and you can choose the most attractive, then taste-test them at home before committing the considerable garden space that they require. Scoop out the seeds, spread them out on a few thicknesses of paper towel to dry, then store in sandwich bags on which you label the variety.

OVEN-DRIED TOMATOES

Make your own dried tomatoes even when the sun doesn't shine.

Rather than stand over a hot stove stirring tomatoes down into a sauce for canning, you can let the oven do most of the work of preserving them, by drying. Choose a meaty paste tomato, such as the widely grown San Marzano. Slice them in half the long way, remove the seeds, and place the halves on cake racks set on baking sheets. Sprinkle with salt. Place them in the oven, using just the pilot light if you use gas or a setting of about 150°F for an electric oven. The tomatoes will need anywhere from 8 to 24 hours to dry to a pliable state. Pack the dried halves in glass jars, pouring in olive oil to displace the air as you do so. Tuck in garlic cloves, basil, or oregano if you wish.

FIGHT ANTHRACNOSE ON TOMATOES

To protect against anthracnose and other water-driven diseases, spread a thin layer of newspaper around tomato plants.

Anthracnose is a soil-borne disease that causes round, sunken spots on tomatoes. These indentations eventually turn black at the center as fungal fruiting bodies are formed. Plants are especially prone to the affliction if you haven't been regularly rotating tomatoes and peppers with other crops.

Although anthracnose can be bothersome to home gardeners, you can stay a step ahead of it with a simple barrier technique. Lay two or three sheets of newspaper on the soil around tomato plants. Lightly moisten the paper, then top with 2 or 3 inches of grass clippings. This traps the disease spores in the soil and prevents them from splashing onto plant leaves during irrigation or rain.

SPAGHETTI SAUCE SHORTCUTS

Standing over a hot stove, waiting for fresh tomatoes to turn into sauce, is nobody's idea of a good time.

Here are a few ideas to take some of the time (and steam) out of the job.

❖ It's not necessary to have special-purpose sauce or paste tomato varieties to simmer down a great-tasting sauce. But it helps. That's because San Marzano, Roma, and other sauce favorites contain relatively less moisture. That means you spend less time standing over a hot stove at summer's end, waiting for the water in juicier tomatoes to go off as steam.

❖ You don't have to convert the entire harvest into hot-packed sauce for use months later. Enjoy fresh sauce right now. Begin by getting a start on dinner early enough to allow at least an hour of simmering with the lid off to thicken the sauce. You can speed things up by spooning off clear liquid from the top; reserve this liquid for use in soup stock.

❖ Why not do your sauce simmering when the weather isn't simmering? Run tomatoes through a strainer as you would normally, then place them in plastic containers and freeze. Label the containers as tomato *juice,* rather than *sauce,* so that you'll know they still need to be cooked down before ladling them over pasta. When the weather turns cooler and you won't mind the added heat and humidity, take the containers out of the freezer for further processing.

TOMATOES ALL THROUGH THE WINTER

Tomatoes can be the largest and most unruly plants in the garden, but pint-size varieties can be grown indoors in pots.

ADVICE OVER THE FENCE
Shake Your Tomatoes

On hot, still summer days when you don't feel like moving an inch, tomato pollen also may stay put, meaning that fewer of those yellow blossoms will turn into fruits. To get the pollen in motion, grasp the plants and give them a gentle jostle.

A 6-inch pot will be large enough to grow a plant, although a bigger pot will need watering less frequently and you may see more-vigorous growth. Varieties to try include 'Healani', 'Pixie', 'Small Fry', and 'Tiny Tim'. Although the plants will be small, they still may need to be staked when fruits appear. Don't forget to rotate the plants so that all sides will benefit from direct sunlight.

You may have to play the role of pollinating insect once the plants develop their yellow blossoms. Just give the branches a gentle tap with your finger to help broadcast the pollen. Look for this dust around blossoms as you jiggle the plant.

WINDOWSILL TOMATOES

All you need to grow tomatoes next winter is a sunny window.

ADVICE OVER THE FENCE
Accelerating Tomatoes

Determinate tomato varieties can take their own sweet time to ripen their fruit and often are caught by the first frost of fall. To speed up the ripening process at the end of the season, try stressing the plants. Jab a spade down through the roots—about 8 inches should do it—making a circle 12 inches out from the plant's base.

You're better off with a small variety such as 'Pixie', 'Small Fry', or 'Tiny Tim'. Start seeds, transplant seedlings to pots placed in the window, and fertilize moderately. When watering, make sure the full depth of the pot is moist. As plants develop, support them with sticks poked into the growing medium. A fluorescent light fixture, placed just above the plants, will help to ensure that you get a crop. Rotate the plants so that all sides are treated to a sun bath. Once blossoms appear, tap the plants to help distribute the pollen.

BE WARY OF WALNUTS

Walnut trees have evolved an effective way of warding off competition from nearby plants. In a strategy known as allelopathy, their roots put off a chemical in the soil that is toxic to many other species. Tomatoes afflicted with walnut poisoning may wilt on warm afternoons, a symptom like that caused by wilt diseases. The cure? Next year, plant the tomatoes elsewhere.

TRY THESE MEMBERS OF THE TOMATO FAMILY

Time to expand your horizons! Ground cherries and tomatillos are easy to grow, and they can be cooked down into excellent salsas.

Here are a couple of members of the tomato family that are easy to grow, are fun to look at, and have a hint of the flavor of their better-known relative. Their flavor is part vegetable, part fruit, and you can use them in both savory sauces and desserts.

GROUND CHERRIES

For something completely different, experiment with ground cherries, also known as husk tomatoes and Cossack pineapple. Whatever you call them, these old-time treasures offer a novel appearance, with a husk concealing the "cherry," which is in fact a tomato relative. The berry may be yellow, orange, or red, and it's edible, with a distinctive flavor that varies from one variety to another. You might notice a suggestion of pineapple, tangerine, or even vanilla. Start them indoors a week or so before you sow tomatoes. Pick the berries when they develop full color for eating fresh or cooking down into a salsa, jam, pie filling, or ice cream topping.

TOMATILLOS

You may associate them with Latin American cooking, but chances are that tomatillos will thrive in your garden. They aren't very demanding, and cook down quickly into delicious homemade salsas that will put supermarket versions to shame. Start them in flats a week or two after you do tomatoes. When the husks turn thin and papery, harvest the fruits. Chop them up and simmer with onions, sauce tomatoes, bell pepper, and cilantro to make a simple sauce for use as salsa or pasta topping. You can grow familiar green varieties, or try purple ones for a special fruitlike flavor.

PERSONAL-SIZE WATERMELONS

The new mini melons hog less space in the garden (and in the refrigerator).

A big monster of a watermelon is great for a picnic or backyard party, but there may be just too much juicy goodness for a small household. Try growing one of the new modest-size melons, weighing in as low as 2 pounds and closer in size to a softball than a bread box. They not only take up less space in the refrigerator, but also hog less real estate in the garden. Pint-size varieties are available with brilliantly colored flesh in yellow, orange, even a sherbet-colored mix of yellow and pink. The rind is apt to be thinner, meaning a greater percentage of the watermelon is edible.

With tomatoes, it seems bigger is better, but that's not necessarily the case with melons. Plant breeders have come up with mini-melons that are cute, flavorful, and easy to stash in the refrigerator.

HOT HARVEST TIP: COOL IT!

Did you pay attention in science class? It might be time for a refresher when it comes to freshness.

Snip a head of broccoli or pick a snow pea, and this disconnected plant part continues to live and breathe—but not in a way that improves its quality as something to eat. Enzymes convert sugars to starch. Cells lose moisture, so that crisp becomes flaccid. The plants put off ethylene gas, which hastens the ripening of nearby harvested crops. Flavors and scents depart, too. You can't arrest these natural processes, but you can slow them down by chilling vegetables and fruit as soon as they are picked. That doesn't mean sprinting back to the house to toss your haul into the fridge. But if you'll be in the garden for any length of time, you can place a picnic cooler in a garden cart with a bit of ice, and trail that with you while harvesting. Or harvest early in the morning, before the day heats up and drying winds begin to blow. Here's how cooling helps maintain food quality.

- Slows respiration rate
- Inhibits growth of molds and bacteria responsible for decay
- Slows production of ethylene, and lowers sensitivity to ethylene's ripening effects
- Slows enzyme action
- Reduces wilting from water loss

Freezing further slows the enzyme activity in foods, but it doesn't stop the process. That's why most vegetables will hold up better in the freezer if they are first partially cooked (or *blanched*) to help inactivate the enzymes. This helps preserve color, texture, and flavor. Generally speaking, frozen food will maintain its quality if the blanching is at a relatively high temperature and of short duration, rather than using low heat over a longer period.

ZUCCHINI FLOWERS FOR THE TABLE

The large, dramatic blossoms of the zucchini can be enjoyed just for the color they bring to the garden, or as fodder for fritters.

Just about every gardener grows zucchinis, and too many zucchinis at that. For something different, try dipping these big blossoms in a light, eggy batter and frying them in ¼ inch or so of olive oil until they turn golden brown. Just make sure you sacrifice the male blossoms, unless you don't mind reducing the yield. The females will have the telltale bulge of a developing zuke. (The males aren't useless, however; you need a few of them around to pollinate the female blossoms in order to have squash.) You'll have to go out into the garden in the early morning soon after they've opened. Unless you plan on using them right away, you can keep the blossoms perky for a few hours by refrigerating them with the base in a jar of water.

EARLY PICKINGS

Did you know that there are good reasons for picking a few tomatoes and peppers prematurely? Read on!

While it's standard operating procedure to pick tomatoes and peppers only when they've developed their full color and sweetest flavor, you may want to try harvesting part of the crop earlier in the season. Some roadside markets sell green tomatoes well before the end of the season to suit customers who like to fry or pickle them in that immature state. Green cherry tomatoes are great when pickled. And even though peppers will turn a rich red, yellow, or chocolate brown if given the chance, you may want to pick some when green for the color contrast. Jalapeños heading for a pickling jar typically are picked when dark green and crisp in texture, and green serranos are usually the choice for making green salsa.

And of course if a frost is in the offing, you'll want to get out there and pick whatever you can, no matter what the color. Both green tomatoes and green peppers may warm up in color after you've rescued them.

HARVEST TIME HOW-TO

Let's get back to basics. Even experienced gardeners can benefit from Veggie Harvesting 101.

GREENS FROM UNEXPECTED SOURCES

You don't plant broccoli, Brussels sprouts, and cabbage for their leaves, but they are nutritious and flavorful when cooked up as you would collards or kale. Pick undamaged and relatively young leaves, only when it won't compromise the main crop.

HARVEST BEANS WHEN THEY PASS THE SNAP TEST

If beans are rubbery and won't snap when you bend them, give a little more time before picking. But don't let them go until they show bulges from bean seeds developing within, or you'll be eating fibrous beans.

CATCH CUKES AT THE OPTIMAL TIME

Harvest cucumbers before their seeds become half their full size. Pickling varieties should be dropped into ice water soon after picking to maintain their crispness.

WITH EGGPLANTS, BIGGER MAY BE BITTER, NOT BETTER

Many of us grew up knowing only the big black eggplants of supermarkets. With the bigness often comes a bitter taste that cooks routinely try to remove by treating with salt, but there is no compensating for an eggplant that has become spongy and seedy. To test an eggplant, press it lightly with your thumbnail. If the dent springs back, the fruit is ready to be picked; if not, you've let it go too long. Pick East Asian varieties when much smaller, still brightly colored, and glossy.

HARVESTING LIMAS TWO WAYS

How do you like limas, tender or somewhat meaty? For the most tender beans, wait for the pods to fill out but pick before they are fully mature, when they will take on a more substantial texture.

THE CABBAGE HEAD TWIST

Left to their own devices, certain cabbage varieties may mature and then crack toward the end of the season. To put off the harvest, try the old trick of grasping the head and giving it a gentle root-snapping twist, being careful to avoid uprooting it. With fewer functional roots, the plant may not pick up excess water from the soil.

REFRIGERATE MELONS ONLY AFTER CUTTING

Melons should be kept at room temperature until you cut into them, when they will keep better in the refrigerator.

PINCH BROCCOLI TO GET A BETTER YIELD

Most gardeners begin to harvest broccoli by cutting the main, central head when it is full size, which then stimulates the development of the side shoots. You may be able to get more heads from each plant if you try a different approach: Earlier in the season, when the plants have grown three leaves, pinch off the growing point that would develop into the main head. This causes the broccoli to form larger side shoots than you'd expect to find.

CORN POINTERS

Kernels should be plump and tender, producing milky juice when pierced with your thumbnail. The silks will be dry.

POTATOES DON'T BENEFIT FROM SWEETENING

Once harvested, potatoes don't react well in cold temperatures. Storing them in the refrigerator may cause some of their starch content to be converted to sugars. And while restoring them to a cool room or garage will partially reverse this process, there will be enough residual sugar to cause browning in fried potatoes.

KNOCKING WATERMELONS

It's difficult to know just when a great big watermelon is ready to eat. There are visual cues: The shaded underside will have warmed in color from whitish to a yellow tinge. If the tendril where the fruit stem meets the vine has died, that's a sign the fruit is ready to harvest. And then there's the old thumping test: An immature melon will give a metallic ring, but you'll get a dull thud if the melon is ripe.

Don't let a good garden hole go to waste. When you dig up potatoes at the end of summer, tuck two or three cloves of garlic in each hole for harvesting next summer. And next spring, follow good crop rotation practices by preparing a potato bed elsewhere on your property to discourage the development of plant diseases.

GREAT FLAVOR FROM GREEN TOMATOES

Unripe doesn't mean unfit to eat. Pick those green tomatoes before frost claims them.

For any number of reasons, you may find yourself at season's end with a bounty of grass-green tomatoes. Rather than toss those green tomatoes of fall into the compost bin, harvest them before the first frost and make good use of them, as gardeners have been doing for generations. Possibly because unripe tomatoes don't have the assertive taste of those that are mature, they can be used in a wider variety of recipes. Here are a few ways to convert your disappointment into good eating.

Chow-chow. Make this old-time pickled salad by chopping up green tomatoes (along with red ones, if you have them), onions, and bell peppers (green ones are just fine), and marinating in a mixture of sweetened vinegar spiced with cloves, dried mustard, allspice, and perhaps ground horseradish. Process in jars in a hot-water bath.

Dilled tomato pickles. Follow a recipe for making pickles from pickling cucumbers. Dilled green *cherry* tomatoes are an interesting variation on the traditional cocktail olive.

Green tomato pie filling. Combine chopped green tomatoes with chopped apples, and simmer with raisins, sugar, vinegar and lemon juice, cinnamon, nutmeg, and cloves.

Fried green tomatoes. To make this traditional favorite, dip tomato slices in a batter of flour, cornmeal, and egg before frying in oil.

Stewed green tomatoes. Sauté minced onions and sliced green tomatoes in butter, then add curry powder and salt to taste.

TOWARD BETTER TOMATOES

Even if you've been harvesting tomatoes for decades, you may be surprised to learn that there's a bit more to picking tomatoes than seeing red and giving a tug.

Next Year's Garden

The Most Popular Tomatoes

There never will be an agreement on the best tomato, but Cornell University has been keeping tabs on the most popular varieties as judged by the number of ratings received by the school's department of horticulture.

Sungold. A hybrid cherry tomato of an unusual yellow-orange color and strikingly flavorful.

Brandywine. A pinkish red heirloom that scores at or near the top of taste tests.

Early Girl. This hybrid is the most popular garden variety in some parts of the country.

Stupice. A relative newcomer to American gardens, Stupice is from Central Europe. The tomatoes are relatively small but richly flavored, and plants are productive.

Celebrity. A hybrid offering good disease resistance.

Cherokee Purple. "Dusty pinkish brown" might be closer to the color. In the 1990s a member of Seed Savers Exchange rescued the variety, said to have originated with the Cherokees, from obscurity.

Raise the quality of your own homegrown fruits a notch or two with these worthwhile tricks.

COOL (NOT COLD) RIPENING

Tomatoes ripen best when their very last stage of ripening occurs at a moderate temperature. That's because a hot summer day can cause sugars in the fruits to turn starchy. On sweltering days, tomatoes may benefit from being picked a little early, while still somewhat pink, and then brought indoors for ripening. That's assuming your home is cooler than its surroundings. If not, then it's best to allow the fruits to remain on the vine. Whatever you do, keep tomatoes out of the refrigerator: Just 40 minutes of chilling can spoil their texture and flavor, researchers have found.

POST-HARVEST TOMATOES DON'T LIKE SUNLIGHT

You probably have heard that tomatoes don't hold up well when refrigerated. Another curious piece of their personality is that once an immature tomato is harvested, you can't speed its ripening by placing it in sunlight, as pretty as the fruits might look on a windowsill. Instead, wrap them in newsprint and place them in unsealed paper bags. Keep the bags in a cool spot where you can check on them frequently.

DECK THE RAFTERS WITH TOMATOES

Determinate varieties are likely to have a not-quite-ripe crop of tomatoes at the end of the growing season. You can pick the green fruit and cook with them. Or pull up the plants and hang them upside down from the rafters in the garage or the joists in the basement. In time, the fruits should redden up. According to the New York State Agricultural Station at Cornell University, you aren't likely to confuse this late crop with your sun-ripened tomatoes, but they'll taste better than the supermarket's off-season fare.

CHAPTER 7

Flowers in Beds and Pots

A gardening book shouldn't have to say much to promote the growing of flowers. They are their own best spokespeople, representing themselves quietly and elegantly. And gardeners are perennially curious about new and improved varieties—or, considering the recent interest in cottage and heirloom blossoms, about old and *un*improved flowers with their simple blossoms, attractive scents, and cheerful dispositions. Gardeners also are always looking for better ways to arrange flower beds for best effect. Even when dealing with beautiful products of nature, there is a potential for clashing colors and a mismatch of sizes in beds that could be described as a horticultural hodgepodge.

It's important to keep in mind the larger role that flowers play in the home landscape. A diverse mix of varieties can have what seems like a magnetic draw for insects and birds. These garden visitors are more than just a diversion, because their numbers will include species beneficial to the gardeners. Among the insects will be beneficial predators and parasites. And birds, with their high-powered metabolisms and big appetites, help to keep bug populations in check.

So it is that flowers welcome the natural world, as well as our neighbors and friends.

The second part of this chapter moves indoors, with ideas for growing flowers in the home—a sheltered but relatively dark place, compared with the great outdoors, favoring some plants while challenging others. As a bridge between outdoors and in, there are tips on window boxes and even a window-mounted greenhouse.

DIVIDE AND CONQUER, BY ROOT DIVISION

An often-overlooked source of free plants is the garden itself, where perennials are apt to be elbowing each other in crowded beds.

You want perennials to be stalwart players in the home landscape, returning reliably each year. But a number of species may become overgrown, as evidenced by fewer blossoms or the woody, lifeless center in a clump of undersize plants. Instead of giving a dose of fertilizer in hopes of restoring youthful vigor, try dividing them. You're apt to get better performance as well as more plants.

There's no firm rule about what time of year you should divide the roots, but the plants will have a better chance of coming through the operation in great shape if you go about it either early or late in the season. In spring, get to work when you see the very first signs of them coming to life. Or, if you're too busy with readying beds and planting, wait until the return of cool temperatures in fall, particularly for low-growing *Phlox* species and lilies. Just make sure that the plants will have 4 to 6 weeks of growing before the ground freezes up for the winter. Generally, you want to divide plants when they are not flowering; in that way, the divisions will put more energy into growing roots and foliage.

By dividing perennials, you not only get free plants but also can revitalize a plant that has become ingrown.

The season for dividing may matter less than daily conditions. Cloudy days are best, particularly after a rainy spell. Water the soil around the plants a day in advance. To protect divisions from drying out, either drop them into a bucket of water or fold them up in a damp towel. Also have a plan in place—know where the new plants will go.

Here is a list of perennials to check on every 2 to 4 years.

Yarrows (*Achillea* spp.)

Asters (*Aster* spp.))

Chrysanthemums (*Chrysanthemum* spp.)

Tickseeds (*Coreopsis* spp.)

Purple coneflowers (*Echinacea* spp.)

Cranesbills (*Geranium* spp.)

Daylilies (*Hemerocallis* spp.)

Bearded irises (*Iris* spp.)

Loosestrifes (*Lysimachia* spp.)

Bee balm (*Monarda didyma*)

Obedient plant (*Physostegia virginiana*)

Black-eyed Susans and coneflowers (*Rudbeckia* spp.

Goldenrods (*Solidago* spp.)

HOW TO TAME A MONSTER ROOT MASS

If you unearth the underground portion of a gnarly old perennial and the thing is intimidatingly huge, what do you do? Put it in a garden cart, wheel it to a sidewalk or patio, pick it up as high as you can, and hurl it down onto the hard surface. With a little luck and a lot of force, you may break up the clump and dislodge much of the clinging soil.

REVIVING AN OLD PEONY

Although peonies seem to chug along year after year without any attention, they eventually will benefit from being dug up and divided.

A row of peonies brings drama and fragrance to the yard each spring, and the big plants seem to be remarkably self-sufficient. But you may have long-established plants that no longer pump out the blossoms the way they used to. To rejuvenate peonies, dig them up in September or October, before hard freezes. Shake off clinging topsoil from the roots. Divide each clump into sections with at least three or four eyes (buds) and part of the root system. Replant them in a spot with plenty of sunlight and well-drained soil.

This is a good time to make sure that the soil tests at a pH level that suits peonies. The ideal is from 6.5 to 7, and you may need to mix in limestone with the soil to bump the pH up to that range. Make sure you set the plant at the proper depth; the eyes (or buds) should be no deeper than 2 inches below the surface or they may not bloom. Fill the hole with soil amended with compost. To protect the divisions from freezing temperatures, spread a generous layer of mulch—straw, leaves, or shredded bark—around the plant in late fall. Remember to rake away the mulch in early spring before the plant stirs to life. And then you'll have to wait; the divisions won't blossom fully for 3 or 4 years.

DO NOT DISTURB!

Some perennials would rather you didn't dig them up, because they have deep or fragile taproots. If you want to propagate more, you're better off gathering their seed or taking cuttings. Here are several of the untouchables.

Monkshood (*Aconitum*)

Columbine (*Aquilegia*)

Butterfly weed (*Asclepias*)

Delphinium (*Delphinium*)

Garden pinks (*Dianthus*)

Gas plant (*Dictamnus albus*)

Euphorbia (*Euphorbia*)

Baby's breath (*Gypsophila paniculata*)

Lavender (*Lavandula*)

Oriental poppy (*Papaver orientale*)

Penstemon (*Penstemon*)

Russian sage (*Perovskia*)

Balloon flower (*Platycodon grandiflorus*)

PRUNING FOR REBLOOMING

Don't overlook an opportunity for color. Some plants will put on a second show if pruned back after their first flush of blossoms.

ADVICE OVER THE FENCE

Debudding for Monster Blossoms

To coax a plant into making extravagantly large blooms, try the old trick of snipping off the secondary buds along a stem and leaving only the lead bud to develop. This can work with many flowers, particularly roses, peonies, and mums.

You can double your pleasure by pruning some perennial flowers and shrubs after their first blossoms are spent. Not every cultivar will perform for you in every season, so approach this mid-season pruning experimentally.

- **Brugmansia.** In spring, when you bring potted plants out of your home, prune for a second blooming.

- **Catmint (*Nepeta*).** After the initial display, chop them back to half their height.

- **Clematis.** A light after-bloom pruning will benefit Nelly Moser and other varieties that flower on the previous year's growth.

- **Dianthus.** To produce another flush of these pretty little flowers, snip flower stems.

- **Hydrangea.** Check plant labels for the term *remontant,* which is a fancy way of saying "reblooming." Generally, candidates for a second bloom are to be found among *H. paniculata* and *H. arborescens* cultivars.

- **Roses.** Prune repeat-flowering hybrid teas and floribundas below the blossom at the first outward-facing leaf that has five leaflets; for hardy roses, cut back to the bract just below the flower. You may be able to encourage three or four flushes of blossoming by these successive light prunings.

- **Spirea.** This won't work for every shrub in this group, but you can try pruning after the blooms are shot.

IS YOUR YARD BUTTERFLY FRIENDLY?

Grow flowers or just a weedy patch of native plants to welcome winged wonders.

Butterflies are having a hard time cutting it in a nation with a population that recently topped 300 million. As people demand homes and stores and highways, butterflies lose the habitat they need to survive (and in the case of Monarchs, to undertake their famous Mexican migration).

To help the adult butterflies, plant any brilliantly colored, fragrant flowers that *you* like. As long as they produce a good supply of nectar, there's a good chance that butterflies will flutter by. The larvae that hatch from the eggs laid by adults will have a different appetite. Many species are very particular about what they'll eat.

PLANTS FOR BUTTERFLY LARVAE

Hollyhock (*Alcea rosea*)

Snapdragon (*Antirrhinum majus*)

Milkweed (*Asclepias syriaca*)

Asters (*Aster* spp.)

Turtleheads (*Chelone* spp.)

Bermuda grass (*Cynodon dactylon*)

Mallow (*Lavatera trimestris*)

Lupines (*Lupinus* spp.)

Passionflowers (*Passiflora* spp.)

Parsley (*Petroselinum crispum*)

Plantain (*Plantago major*)

Sorrel (*Rumex acetosa*)

St. Augustine grass (*Stenotaphrum secundatum*)

Marigolds (*Tagetes* spp.)

Clover (*Trifolium repens*)

Nettles (*Urtica dioica*)

Violets (*Viola* spp.)

PLANTS FOR BUTTERFLY ADULTS

Butterfly weeds (*Asclepias* spp.)

Asters (*Aster* spp.)

Coreopsis (*Coreopsis* spp.)

Purple coneflower (*Echinacea purpurea*)

Joe-Pye weed (*Eupatorium purpureum*)

Lantanas (*Lantana* spp.)

Liatris (*Liatris spicata*)

Black-eyed Susan (*Rudbeckia hirta*)

PLANT A MONARCH BUTTERFLY NURSERY

Do your part! Put out a floral welcome mat for these champion migrators.

Monarch butterflies are among the most amazing creatures on earth, managing to navigate a migration to a particular forested part of Mexico from thousands of miles to the north. Scientists can only theorize how that's possible, but one thing is for certain: Monarchs are dependent on milkweed, the only food source for their brilliantly striped larvae. Milkweed contains a toxin that the insects are able to store in their bodies, both as caterpillars and as winged adults, making them unpalatable to predators.

If you have a field or hedgerow in which milkweed is growing, you already are helping to ensure that these butterflies will be able to breed. Also, various attractive milkweed species can be started from seed or purchased as plants. Keep an eye out for the caterpillars, the beautiful gold-spotted chrysalis, and of course the adult butterflies themselves.

Do you ever find yourself wondering just where the Monarchs visiting your yard will eventually end up? Assuming you don't have wings of your own, the only way to find out is by purchasing a butterfly net and ordering a tagging kit from Monarch Watch at the University of Kansas (www.monarchwatch.org). You'll receive lightweight polypropylene tags to put on the wings of Monarchs that pass through on their southward migration to Mexico. The Monarchs die in forests there after giving rise to another generation. If someone retrieves the tag from one of your butterflies and mails it in to Monarch Watch, you'll be notified of the discovery. To date, more than 11,000 tags have been recovered, yielding valuable information about the migration of this fascinating insect.

Grow milkweed on your property, either allowing wild plants to flourish or placing cultivated varieties in flower beds, to welcome the monarch butterfly.

HUMMINGBIRDS IN THE GARDEN

Feeders are nice, but flowers give twice—to you and the hummers. It's easy to establish a hummingbird garden, if you pick the right blooms.

Hummingbirds have a terrifically fast metabolism, requiring them to take frequent high-carbohydrate sips all through the day. And not only through the day, but through the season that they spend in this part of the world. To be a good host to hummers, you should try to ensure that tubular, bright, nectar-producing plants be in bloom in a dependable succession. It's thought that these birds coevolved with certain flowers, such as *Penstemon* and *Salvia,* with each changing over the eons to serve the other—the flowers providing food, the hummingbirds providing pollination. In addition to the flowers listed below, you might also plant a willow tree. It provides both nectar and nest-building material in the form of the filaments attached to willow seeds.

Why not just hang up a bright red hummingbird feeder? For a couple of reasons. First, the birds need nutrients that are missing in a simple solution of sugar water. (Note that the coloring in red hummingbird food mixes is suspected to be harmful.) Second, it's less work to plant nectar-providing perennials—a one-time operation—than to repeatedly fill and clean a feeder with sticky liquid. And feeders must be kept clean to avoid sickening the birds, which means emptying and washing every few days.

Insecticides and hummingbirds don't mix, although the reason might not be obvious at first. These birds *do* snap up insects as well as sip nectar, because their nestlings need bugs in their diets. The toxins may end up in the baby food.

Here is a list of nectar plants, from spring to fall.

BEGINNING IN SPRING

Ajugas (*Ajuga* spp.)
Hollyhock (*Alcea rosea*)
Columbines (*Aquilegia* spp.)
Butterfly weeds (*Asclepias* spp.)

Hibiscus (*Hibiscus* spp.)

Honeysuckles (*Lonicera* spp.)

Currants and gooseberries (*Ribes* spp.)

BEGINNING IN SUMMER

Agastachias (*Agastachia* spp.)

Alstroemerias (*Alstroemeria* spp.)

Trumpet vine (*Campsis radicans*)

Fuschias (*Fuschia* spp.)

Jewelweed (*Impatiens capensis*)

Turk's cap lily (*Lilium superbum*)

Blue lobelia (*Lobelia siphilitica*)

Beebalm (*Monarda didyma*)

Penstemons (*Penstemon* spp.)

Salvias (*Salvia* spp.)

Weigelas (*Weigela* spp.)

BEGINNING IN FALL

Butterfly weeds (*Asclepias* spp.)

Asters (*Aster* spp.)

Jewelweed (*Impatiens capensis*)

Lion's tail (*Leonotis leonurus*)

Cardinal flower (*Lobelia cardinalis*)

A SODA FOUNTAIN FOR BUTTERFLIES

So-called root beer plant is a member of the wonderfully fragrant *Agastache* genus, and worth getting to know. It also goes by the name of anise hyssop (*A. foeniculum*). Plant it or the anise-scented Mexican hyssop (*A. rupestris*) for a long season of lovely flowers and lots of winged visitors. Nurseries carry a number of hybrids offering a range of inviting shades—salmon, a warm orange, pink, a pale blue.

DARE TO FLAUNT FLORAL FASHION

Regarded by some as the botanical equivalent of pink flamingo statuettes, gladioli and dahlias nevertheless deserve a second look.

Here and there you can find hints of a revival for glads and dahlias, a couple of lavishly brilliant flowers that can come across as a little *too* lavish and brilliant. Gladiolus carries the added burden of being associated with funeral bouquets. But fashions change, and what was tacky yesterday will predictably become presentable again. It helps that subtler cultivars are now becoming available. Try introducing these flowers into perennial beds, rather than growing them in isolated patches or sticking them with visually incompatible annuals.

GLADIOLUS

Look for species selections, many of which are being brought here from South Africa, rather than the showiest hybrids. When setting out glads, try mixing them with other company; use them with plants that can stand up to their appearance, such as ornamental grasses and larger perennials. You don't have to grow these flowers in a riot of colors. Instead, you might stick to all-white varieties for their calm beauty.

As with dahlias, one reason for the decline in the gladiolus's popularity is that the corms have to be dug up each fall in cooler areas, but this isn't by any means a big chore. With mulching, glads may make it through Zone 6 winters, and even Zone 5 with some luck.

1. Grow gladioli in fertile, well-drained soil in full sun. Plant the corms after the last frost, just 2 to 6 inches deep to get them off to a good start. You may want to hill soil around the stems once they are under way for more support.

2. After the first frost of autumn, dig up the corms, shake off the soil, and allow them to cure for 2 to 3 weeks.

3. Snap off and discard the past season's shriveled corms and save the new ones that have formed. You also can save the smaller

cormels for planting, although they will take 2 years to produce mature, blossoming plants. Place the corms and cormels in mesh bags to allow good air circulation. Store over winter in a dry, shaded place with temperatures between 45° and 55°F.

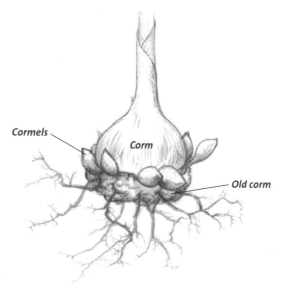

You can grow plants from both the gladiolus corm and the cormels that ring it.

DAHLIA

The golden age of the dahlia came to a close some 80 years ago, and all but a few of the 10,000 named varieties disappeared along with it. But there is a modest revival going on, and you can find dahlias with a surprisingly understated appearance in such sources as the catalog from Old House Gardens; these include 'Bonne Esperance', 'Clair DeLune', and 'White Fawn'. Most dahlias are hardy only to Zone 8, and either the tubers are dug up for the winter or the plants are abandoned, but 'Fannie Williams' can be left in the ground in Zone 6.

Planting and tending dahlias is a bit of extra work, but fans of the flower appreciate its late summer display, as well as the way the plants seem to reward your snipping them for bouquets by producing more blossoms.

(continued)

Next Year's Garden

Landscaping with Cool Blues

For a cooling effect in the yard, plant a backdrop of blue or blue-green evergreens. Candidates among the cedars include the deodars (*Cedrus deodara*) 'Glacier Blue' and 'Glacier'. From the cryptomeria you might choose Taiwan cryptomeria (*Taiwania cryptomerioides*) or Compacta cryptomeria (*Cryptomeria japonica* 'Compacta'). Blue or bluish cypresses include Wichita blue (*Cupressus sempervirens* 'Wichita Blue') and Blue Italian (*Cupressus sempervirens* 'Glauca'). Among the firs are the subalpine (*Abies lasiocarpa*) and the Candicans white (*Abies concolor* 'Candicans').

There is no shortage of junipers in the species *Juniperus scopulorum*, including 'Wichita Blue' and 'Blue Heaven.' Also have a look at the Blue Mountain juniper (*Juniperus virginiana* 'Blue Mountain'). As for pines, cool hues can be found with the Compact Korean pine (*Pinus koraiensis* 'Compact Glauca'), Vanderwolf's Pyramid Limber Pine (*Pinus flexis* 'Vanderwolf's Pyramid'), and Japanese White Pine (*Pinus parviflora* 'Glauca'). And if you're after spruces, check out Bakeri blue spruce (*Picea pungens* 'Bakeri') and Sander's spruce (*Picea glauca* 'Sander's Blue').

Follow these steps to have dahlias year after year.

1. Choose a spot that gets at least 6 hours of sun a day, and preferably 8 or more. The soil should be fertile and well drained. Plant the tubers after all danger of frost is past, or start them indoors 4 to 6 weeks early and transfer them to the garden.

2. Place the tubers on their sides, eyes up, in a 6-inch-deep hole, and then fill only halfway to the surface. Once the plant begins to grow, add more soil to fill in the hole. Place a stake alongside each plant and attach the stalk to it with twine.

3. If your winter is warm enough to allow leaving the tubers in the ground, cut back the plants to the ground at the end of the season. If you will be bringing the tubers inside, wait until frost turns the foliage black, wait 2 weeks or so, then carefully exhume the tubers.

4. Allow the tubers to dry inside for a couple of days. Place them in plastic bags along with slightly dampened peat moss or vermiculite and seal them. Store the bags in a cool, dry place and check on them occasionally through the winter. If the tubers appear shriveled, sprinkle a bit of water on the medium; if you see droplets of condensation on the inside of the bag, leave it open for a day and then reseal.

5. Dahlia tubers will have grown in size in their first year and can be divided to make more plants the following spring. Use a sharp knife, and make sure that each piece has at least one eye from which a new plant will grow. On the other hand, a piece with a lot of eyes will send up plenty of foliage but relatively few blossoms.

A ROSE BY ANY NAME?

Here's a brief guide to rosarian nomenclature that deals with the frequency of blooming.

Catalog descriptions for roses and other flowers may suggest how long in the growing season you can expect to see blossoms. The terms are a bit confusing.

- **Everblooming.** Sounds good, and in fact these plants will produce an ongoing display over much (but not necessarily all, by any means) of the spring-to-fall period.
- **Repeat bloom.** This bit of vagueness can be used instead of the following two terms. Note that in colder climates, these repeaters may bloom only once a year.
- **Recurring.** This suggests that blossoms come on in waves, with the display diminishing and then coming back strong.
- **Remontant.** It looks and sounds French, and it is. The term applies to flowers that make a showing, then disappear, then return for an encore.
- **Nonrecurrent, once-blooming.** These are the traditional roses that put on one good show. Why bother with them? Because they tend to have unsurpassed fragrance, subtle beauty, and a form that makes them count for something in the home landscape even after the blossoms are history, by cloaking arbors, pergolas, and arches.

VACATION-MINDING PATIO PLANTS

No need to think your beautiful patio won't be abloom when you return home. Try these tricks.

If you have a neighbor who is delighted with the job of stopping over to water your potted plants while you're away, fine. If not, you can help prevent the soil in terra-cotta pots from drying out by wrapping the pots in plastic produce bags. Leave the top of the bags open to catch the rain. It's not a pretty solution, of course, but you can remove the bags once you get home.

For medium and small pots, buy dollar-store buckets, add a few inches of water, and set potted plants down in the buckets. This will help to stave off drought conditions for quite a few days.

SNITCH A ROSE CUTTING

Cool weather is a good time to start new roses from a snippet of stem.

Chances are you've coveted a splendid, lavishly growing rose in a neighbor's yard, in a cemetery, or even growing wild along the road. You could enjoy growing that gorgeous shrub with only an insignificant bit of stem. No flowers, just a stem. You stick the cutting in a bit of potting mixture, and there you are—a few patient years later, that is.

You should always ask the owner of the property for permission to snip a cutting. The best time to do so is from fall through early spring. Take 6 to 8 inches of a stem that has had blossoms that season. To encourage the cutting to flourish, you can wet the stem, then dip the lower half in a rooting hormone. Or, take advantage of the hormones in willow trees by steeping several 1-inch pieces of branch from that tree in simmering water, then allowing this brew to sit for a day. Soak the cutting in it for a few hours. Whichever method you choose, prepare a damp rooting medium of half sand and half peat moss. Simply stick in the willow-prepared cutting; or, if you've dipped the cutting in hormone powder, first poke a pencil in the medium to make a hole, then stick in the cutting and gently firm the medium around it. Keep the medium moist, and use a plastic bag to maintain a high level of humidity around the cutting. In time, there should be signs of new growth. The cutting may be ready for transplanting to the garden after 6 months to a year.

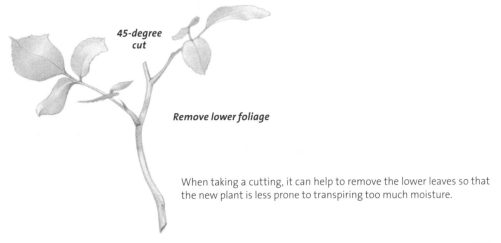

45-degree cut

Remove lower foliage

When taking a cutting, it can help to remove the lower leaves so that the new plant is less prone to transpiring too much moisture.

DIVIDING WITH DUAL SPADING FORKS

You've probably done your share of shovel pruning and now it's time to try something different. Two spading forks, placed back to back, can make easy work of dividing a clump of iris.

A bonus of growing iris is that the plants tend to multiply eagerly. But this boon can become a bane if you don't take the time to divide the rhizomes every 3 to 5 years. The flowers lose vigor as things become crowded underground. A good way to wrestle with the rhizome clumps is to use a pair of spading forks, as shown. (The method works for dividing many shrubs as well.) The handles give you plenty of leverage to pry the clumps apart into two or more pieces. Each piece can then be planted for a fresh start.

1. Begin by giving the iris bed a good watering at least a day before you dig.
2. To slow the loss of water, cut back the foliage to no more than half its length.
3. Carefully lift the clump with a fork. Shake off the clinging soil.
4. Divide the clump into two or more pieces by jabbing it with two spading forks, back to back, then pushing back on the handles.
5. Use a knife to cut away old, diseased, or insect-riddled rhizomes.
6. Place the pieces in a shaded spot to allow the cut ends to seal themselves.
7. Plant the pieces in good soil, burying them so that just the top of the rhizome shows. Water well.

A single person can summon a lot of leverage with a pair of spading forks, dividing stubborn clumps of iris and other plants.

FLUMMOXED BY MILDEWED PHLOX?

If mildew is making a mess of phlox foliage, it's time to give up the ghost of battling it. Let resistant varieties come to the rescue.

Phloxes offer a long blooming period and pleasant fragrance, but the foliage is apt to be marred by powdery mildew. While the disease is mainly a visual blight rather than a plant killer, the fungus does invade the leaf to extract nutrients, and that can depress the phlox's overall vigor. It helps to water early in the day rather than later, and to promote air circulation by allowing space around plants. If you really feel you need to take action to try and save the plants you have, mix 1 tablespoon of baking soda and 3 tablespoons of horticultural oil for a spray to drench the leaves. If you'd like a fresh start, though, check catalog listings and plant tags to find varieties that have some resistance; see the partial list below.

VARIETY	BLOSSOM COLOR
'David'	White, lavender
'Robert Poore'	Magenta
'Laura'	Pink-purple
'Prime Minister'	White with red eye
'Orange Perfection'	Salmon
'Speed Limit 45'	Pink
'Natasha'	White with pink

KEEP IT IN THE FAMILY (OF COLORS)

Looking for a way to avoid clashes in the flower garden? Think in terms of a color wheel. And don't assume that it's too hard for the average gardener.

Butterflies may zero in on a flower bed with an outlandish mishmash of hues. But they're only around for a few fleeting days, whereas you have to look at that garish combination all summer long. As a guarantee against straying too far from harmony, try keeping adjacent blossoms within an area of the spectrum: blue through violet, violet shading into cool reds, hot reds melding with orange. If the result looks a little sleepy or too predictable, toss in a few flowers from the other side of the color wheel: for example, a warm yellow will spike indigo.

When choosing colors for a bed, look *behind* the area to be planted and consider the colors of adjacent buildings and fences. One landscaping no-no is to plunk down plants with vivid pink or magenta blossoms near a brick wall with warm tones. (Magenta often proves problematic in the garden, a color conundrum that has preoccupied gardeners for generations.) As long as you're planting flowers and not large balled-root trees, you have the advantage of being able to freely shift your palette. The process will take at least a year, as you make note which plants are in bloom at any particular time. If their blooming seasons don't overlap, there's no chance of a color clash—unless you're dealing with brightly hued foliage, that is.

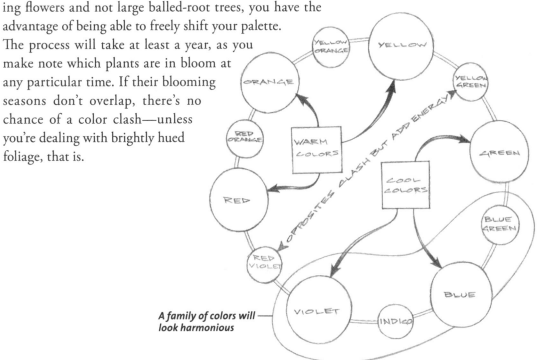

A family of colors will look harmonious

A color wheel can help you predict how flowers of various hues will relate to one another in the garden.

FLOWERS FOR SUN-SHY SPOTS

Instead of reflexively blanketing the darker areas of the yard with low-light ground covers, lighten things up with flowers that can thrive without the blessing of direct sunshine.

Give some thought to planting *flowers* in the forgotten shady niches of the yard. There is a special charm about flowers that bloom in the shade. They seem to bring light into their situation, rather than merely reflecting the sun's brilliance. You may face a couple of challenges in establishing flowers in shady areas, problems that have nothing to do with shade itself but rather with the reason for that shade—overshadowing trees and shrubs. They are apt to soak up both moisture and nutrients from the soil, impoverishing the smaller plants nearby. That means paying special attention to watering and fertilizing regularly. You also may find that the roots from these large neighbors have made it all but impossible to stick a spade in the ground. If so, you can still have a shady flower garden, but in containers.

Here is a mix of woodland candidates, most with subtle, muted blossoms rather than the knockout effect of a zinnia.

- Wild Canada columbine (*Aquilegia canadensis*)
- Jack-in-the-pulpit (*Arisaema triphyllum*)
- Spring beauty (*Claytonia virginica*)
- Dutchman's breeches (*Dicentra cucullaria*)
- Trout lily (*Erythronium americanum*)
- Hepatica (*Hepatica americana*)
- Cardinal flower (*Lobelia cardinalis*)
- Virginia bluebell (*Mertensia virginica*)
- Jacob's ladder (*Polemonium reptans*)
- Solomon's seals (*Polygonatum* spp.)

- ✤ Bloodroot (*Sanguinaria canadensis*)
- ✤ Meadow rues (*Thalictrum* spp.)
- ✤ Trilliums (*Trillium* spp.)
- ✤ Wild pansies (*Viola* spp.)

ROSES

There really aren't roses that love shady nooks. But if you have a sun-scarce yard and long to have roses, the queen of flowers, there is some hope. Here are a few roses that you might look into.

ROSE	FLOWER COLOR
'Ballerina'	White, pink-rimmed
'Celestial'	Pink
'The Fairy'	Pink
'Greenmantle'	Red
'Gruss an Aachen'	Cream
'Harrison's Yellow'	Yellow
'John Franklin'	Red
'Maiden's Blush'	Pink
'Robin Hood'	Red
'Sea Foam'	Cream

Give roses at least 3 to 4 hours of sunlight per day. You might prune nearby shrubs and trees to allow more sun. It also can help to give the roses themselves a light summer pruning if the shade is causing them to grow too lanky.

ROSES FOR COLOR IN THE FALL

While the bloom may be on some roses in summer, these double-feature roses put on a display in fall as well.

Chances are that you've forgotten all about roses by the end of summer. They've done their thing, and now it's time for asters and mums. There are a few roses, however, that bring colored foliage to the autumn landscape.

ROSE	BLOSSOM COLOR	FALL FOLIAGE COLOR
'Father Hugo'	Pale yellow	Red
'Fru Dagmar Hastrup'	Pink	Yellow
'Fruhlingsgold'	Pale yellow	Yellow, orange
'Pink Grootendorst'	Pink	Yellow, orange, scarlet
'Therese Bugnet'	Pink	Yellow, orange

SEND A ROSE UP A TREE

Climbing varieties add another dimension to the rose garden.

Trees, living or not, make good supports for climbing roses. Once you've identified a good climber, plant it on the south side of the tree to provide as much sunlight as possible. Because the tree (if living) is apt to use up much of the soil's moisture and nutrients, you'll need to water in dry weather and add fertilizers.

CLIMBING ROSE	BLOSSOM COLOR
'Cecile Brunner'	Pink
'Chaplin's Pink Climber'	Pink
'Climbing Iceberg'	White
'La Mortola'	White
'New Dawn'	Pink
'Rambling Rector'	White

MAKE ONE ROSE DO THE WORK OF FOUR

By pegging roses, you can stimulate them to put out more flowers.

Many roses like to ramble randomly, and gardeners tend to manage that by pruning them back to a reasonably tidy form. Instead, you can take advantage of their waywardness by *pegging*. This is a traditional method of directing that lavish growth along horizontal canes held in place with some sort of peg. The plants will respond to this positioning by sending up flowering shoots and producing far more flowers than you'd get otherwise. Good candidates may include Bourbon roses with long canes, Albas, hybrid perpetuals, and mosses.

1. Select young, supple canes; older ones may break and will be less productive.
2. Gently bend the canes horizontally and cut off the tip to direct the plant's energy to forming the new vertical shoots.
3. Hold the canes roughly 8 to 16 inches above the ground by running them through wire hoops made from coat hangers inserted in the soil.
4. Prune these canes after 2 or 3 years and select new canes to peg.

CUTTING UP PELARGONIUMS IN FALL

It seems cruel, but you may be better off bringing pelargonium cuttings inside in fall rather than potting up plants.

If you grow pelargoniums in beds for the warm months, you may feel obliged to pot them up to spend the winter on sunny windowsills. But some gardeners prefer to skip the mess, skip the pruning, and bring only cuttings indoors for rooting. Taking cuttings is also a way to avoid having to repot pelargoniums, which otherwise need this attention every year or two if they are to remain vigorous. For success with cuttings, snip 4-inch-long pieces of new, nonflowering shoots at summer's end. Trim the lower leaves. Tuck the cuttings 1 inch deep into a moist mix of compost and sand.

BLOSSOMS IN THE SNOW

Here are cold-weather flowers for the winter-weary gardener.

Winter doesn't have to mean that your only gardening activity is paging wistfully through seed catalogs and books of pretty landscapes. There are a few oddball plants that blossom after the rest of the yard has gone to sleep and before things start cooking again in spring.

- **Spurge laurel (*Daphne laureola*)** may put out its shy little green flowers as early as January. Mezereon *(D. mezereum)* is another good choice, with small white or purple blossoms. As with other Daphnes, the fragrance of this duo is remarkable. Both will do well in the shade.
- **Witch hazel (*Hamamelis virginiae*)** is a native shrub that puts on a quiet show with its yellow, threadlike blossoms from late autumn into December. As another cold-weather curiosity, capsules on the plant shoot out seed as far as 20 feet.
- **Lenten rose (*Helleborus × hybridus*)** thrives in shady areas and can begin blossoming as early as February, in colors ranging from white to a deep plum that borders on black.
- **Winter honeysuckle (*Lonicera fragrantissima*)** is a shrub from China that will blossom toward the end of winter or in early spring. The creamy flowers aren't dramatic, but their sweet, lemony scent will draw you out into the yard.

DEICERS DECIMATE PLANTS

People who garden organically tend to focus on the drawbacks of using chemical fertilizers, herbicides, and pesticides, but these aren't the only potentially harsh products used in the home landscape.

Chemical deicers prevent wintertime spills, but they don't do any favors for nearby plants. Shrubs may suffer bud death and twig dieback, and evergreens turn yellow or brown where affected. And over time, chemical levels can build up in the soil to cause chronic wilting and declining vigor, no matter how attentive you are with the hose. Common salt (sodium chloride) is the most harmful, and calcium chloride may be a less damaging alternative. Better still, get out the snow shovel and follow up by scattering kitty litter or sand where the walks are slippery.

OLD-TIME BLOSSOMS

Grow a bit of history, planting flowers that have been traditional favorites since Colonial or Victorian times.

Nurseries tend to stock flowers that snare a customer's attention—bright, shouting sorts of blossoms that may not quite fit in with the setting of a traditional home. That's just one reason that gardeners are taking a new interest in old flowers. These time-tested plants tend to be sturdy, somewhat disease resistant, modest in appearance, and fragrant. They lend themselves to informal groupings, more like natural wildflower patches than planned features of the landscape. Contrast that with the bright, regimented look of bedding geraniums in their unwavering display of white and magenta blossoms.

An easy way to get started with old-time flowers is to poke around the gardens of neighbors and friends and make it known you wouldn't mind going home with a cutting or clump of something interesting. So-called "pass-along plants" are the means by which many vintage varieties have survived over the years. They tend to have a very high rate of success because they're from just down the street, rather than suffering a long ride via mail order to your address or on a long-haul truck to a nursery.

But mail order is the way to go for many obscure treasures. A number of firms specialize in older plants, and their catalogs may even delineate the defining period for each flower—the span of years with which it is most closely associated. And then there's the Flower and Herb Exchange, a not-for-profit branch of Seed Savers Exchange, 3094 North Winn Road, Decorah, Iowa 52101. In an annual publication, some 200 members offer nearly 2,000 unusual varieties of flowers and herbs for sale—a greatly expanded version of passing plants along from one yard to the next.

In your search for old-time varieties, don't overlook your own yard. If you bought the property from previous owners, there may be little treasures tucked away under shrubs or in overlooked corners. It's something like rooting around the attic of an older home—you never know just what forgotten gem you might come upon.

A GOOD-TASTE FILTER

When it comes to flowers, white never looks out of place, and white varieties can come to the rescue of beds that are a riot of clashing colors.

Some of us have a hard time resisting flashy effects both in home decorating and in choosing plants for the yard. If you are one of this troubled group, you can help ensure that your selections will work harmoniously by specializing in one color. The most harmonious color of all is white, so you might start there when shopping for seeds, bulbs, and plants. Here are a few plants to get you started.

ANNUALS

Alyssums (*Alyssum* spp.)

Cleomes (*Cleome* spp.)

Malvas (*Malva* spp.)

Moonflower (*Ipomoea alba*)

Nicotianas (*Nicotiana* spp.)

Petunias (*Petunia* spp.)

Zinnias (*Zinnia* spp.)

PERENNIALS

Goatsbeard (*Aruncus dioicus*)

Azaleas (*Azalea* spp.)

Coneflower (*Echinacea purpurea*)

Daffodils (*Narcissus* spp.)

Peony (*Paeonia*) 'Festiva Maxima'

Phlox (*Phlox*) 'David'

Balloonflower (*Platycodon grandiflorus*)

Roses (*Rosa* spp.)

Spireas (*Spirea* spp.)

Tulips (*Tulipa* spp.)

A BLUE HORIZON FOR PINCHED YARDS

Blue flowers have the remarkable property of receding from view, an effect that landscape designers long have been aware of.

Look at a landscape painting with distant mountains, and you're apt to see an optical trick used by artists for generations. The color *blue* seems to recede from us. Painters use that effect to give their two-dimensional canvases the illusion of depth, and you can do the same to make a shallow yard look deeper. Try arranging a border of blue-flowering plants, and even plants with bluish foliage such as hostas down low and spruces above. You probably can come up with a list of your own favorite blue flowers, but here are a few suggestions.

Agapanthus (*Agapanthus* spp.)

Anemones (*Anemone* spp.)

Asters (*Aster* spp.)

Larkspur (*Consolida ambigua*)

Delphiniums (*Delphinium* spp.)

Cranesbill (*Geranium sanguineum*)

Hydrangeas (*Hydrangea* spp.)

Irises (*Iris* spp.)

Virginia bluebells (*Mertensia virginica*)

Nepetas (*Nepeta* spp.)

Russian sage (*Perovskia atriplicifolia*)

Balloonflower (*Platycodon grandiflorum*)

Plumbagos (*Plumbago* spp.)

Scilla (*Scilla sibirica*)

Spiderworts (*Tradescantia* spp.)

THE GRAY GARDEN

Play up your architecture with a bed of gray plants.

Gray-leaved plants are a good match for homes of stone, white clapboard, or silvery cedar. They also bring harmony to beds that seem to be a jarring mix of brilliant hues. Try growing dusty miller, horehound, lamb's ears, a few varieties of lavender, nepeta (catmint), rose campion (this one comes with attractive magenta blossoms), Russian sage, santolina, southernwood, and wormwood. Plants with gray foliage tend to be happy in relatively dry locations, and a house with rain gutters likely will provide just that type of soil around its perimeter. Keep the bed tidier than you might otherwise—because the effect of these plants is subtle, neatness counts for a lot.

ROLL UP SOME LAWN AND PUT IN AN ISLAND

Island beds not only break up a boring lawn, but also allow you a refreshing view of your plants from all sides.

ADVICE OVER THE FENCE

For Another Point of View . . .

It can be difficult to evaluate the shape of a new bed by staring at an outline of rope or hose. Try going up to a second-story window of your house for an aerial perspective.

There is no landscaping law that says beds must adjoin a structure or wall or property line. They can be freestanding islands, taking whatever shape you choose. A relaxed kidney shape is popular, but you may have to take some care to be certain it doesn't look artificial in form, like an amoeboid 1950s end table. Be guided by the shape of surrounding beds. If their outlines undulate gracefully, then try for the same feeling with the island. Or, if your beds are primly rectangular, go with a rectangular island. Another formal shape is a circle, with some sort of visual feature at its center.

Size is as important as shape. A tiny island placed smack in the middle of an expanse of lawn may look as lost as if it were in the middle of the Pacific. Try sketching various outlines on the lawn with garden hose or rope. To make the outline of a circular bed, tap a stake in what will be the center and use a length of twine as a compass with you at the swinging end, laying down the fairly precise circumference with a length of rope.

You may already have the makings of an island if there is a grouping of shrubs or a tree that you scoot around on your mower. Instead of hassling with mulching around them, consider expanding this no-mow area to an interesting island. You already have established shrubs or a tree as a tall centerpiece.

Finally, if the island's plantings will need to be watered, you'll save time and effort by placing it within the range of hoses or an extension of a drip-irrigation system.

1. **Lay it out.** Once you've arrived at a shape you like, use spray paint to draw its outline on the lawn; or, if this is a rectangular bed, you can place stakes at the four corners, 18 inches or so back from the outline, and run twine between them as your guide (in this way, the twine will be less likely to get in the way of your work).

2. **Scalp it.** You can scalp back the grass with a flat-bladed spade. But for larger projects, you may want to rent a sod cutter. It peels off a slice of sod, which then can be planted as needed elsewhere on the property.

3. **Prepare the soil.** This may or may not be a big chore, depending on the quality of the earth that's been lurking below your lawn. Proceed as you would for any bed.

4. **Pick the plants.** Again, this step isn't out of the ordinary, except that you will be considering how the island will look from all sides. And to establish this floating feature of the yard, you may want to include plants with a vertical presence—a tree, shrubs, or tall perennials such as black cohosh, buddleia, flowering tobacco, hollyhocks, joe-pye weed, lilies, larkspur and delphinium, monarda, pale and purple coneflower, Russian sage, swamp milkweed, and yarrow, as well as tall, graceful grasses.

5. **Add a landscape feature.** To help place the island more confidently in the home landscape, you might add an arbor, small statuary, birdbath, urn, or bench. If the island is large enough, you could even arrange plantings to create a sheltered nook for the bench.

AN EDIBLE BORDER

Define flower beds with a prim edging of lettuce.

Any number of neatly growing lettuces are attractive enough to serve as a mini-hedge around beds of ornamentals. A variety with some red coloring will be more obviously an intentional addition than those that are a straight green. And lettuces that form a small, compact head early on will work especially well as a border. Try 'Eruption', 'Ferrari', 'Oscarde', and 'Red Star'.

A MULTICOLOR LAWN

Lawns are a yawn sometimes. Why not sprinkle your bluegrass with blossoms?

Next Year's Garden
Storing Bulbs without Shriveling

If you dig up tender bulbs each fall for replanting the following year, you may have noticed that they sometimes have a way of drying out. You can protect them by dipping them in a 1-to-10 solution of Wilt-Pruf anti-transpirant in water. Allow the treatment to dry, then store the bulbs in peat moss in an unheated basement or a garage that stays above freezing.

There's no more refreshing sight in the home landscape than a lush lawn—expect for a lush lawn dotted with spring-blooming flowers. When set out in relaxed "drifts," the flowers look as though they've sprung up all by themselves. It's best to plant these naturalizing bulbs in low-maintenance lawns or meadows that you won't feel compelled to mow until the foliage has died back, about a month after the blooming period. The flowers need their green tops to generate energy for the following year. Try the edges of the yard, or an area under spreading deciduous trees. The site should have well-drained soil that's of a good quality down to a depth of at least 1 foot; dig a test hole or two in order to make sure that the bulbs won't be dealing with a layer of hardpan just below the surface.

To create a carpet of springtime bloom in an existing lawn, simply make a hole in the grass with a narrow trowel, dandelion digger, or garden knife. For small bulbs, you can rock the tool back and forth to create a small hole and slip the bulb in place. For larger bulbs, you may have to actually lift the sod and soil, insert the bulb, and put the flap of turf back in place.

If you have a lot of large bulbs to place, use a spade or shovel and remove larger areas of turf—about 1 foot square. Loosen the soil, plant the bulbs, replace the turf, and water.

Even if you spread lawn fertilizer over the area, you may want to top-dress the flowers with bulb fertilizer in order to ensure the plants get their requirement for phosphorus and potassium.

BULBS FOR LAWNS AND MEADOWS

Here are a few of the most popular choices for planting in lawns.

Crocus	*Iris danfordiae*
Daffodils	*Iris reticulata*
Grape hyacinth	Scilla

AFFORDABLE DRIFTS

A natural-looking "drift" of spring-blooming flowers requires more than a half-dozen bulbs. But, oh, the expense . . . !

There are a few ways to go about establishing an impressive display of spring bloomers without exhausting your gardening budget.

BUY WHOLESALE

Some mail-order bulb firms specialize in selling at wholesale prices—if you purchase in wholesale quantities. Check with gardening friends to see if they will go in with you on a big order. The incentive? You all stand to save up to 50 percent. And by ordering lots of bulbs, you'll be able to indulge in a broader variety.

STICK TO THE TRIED AND TRUE

While you're paging through catalogs, pay particular attention to bulbs described as being "naturalizers" or "perennializers"—varieties that, given conditions that make them happy, will make you happy by increasing in number or at least reappearing for some years to come. Generally speaking, older varieties stand a better chance of showing up each spring, with some traditional favorites good for a half-century of blooming.

GIVE THEM ROOM TO PROLIFERATE

If you're planting for the long run rather than just a year or two, consider allowing more than the standard spacing between bulbs to allow them to multiply.

AN ENCHANTED EVENING GARDEN

Plan for a garden of vesper bloomers, locating it near the house, by a porch, or along a walk where you're most apt to take pleasure from it each evening.

Next Year's Garden

Build a Bench

Enjoying an evening garden doesn't have to mean stumbling around in the dark. If you arrange comfortable outdoor seating, you may find yourself returning to this spot often. Several mail-order companies sell attractive wooden lawn chairs and benches as kits, giving you a chance to save money by doing some of the assembly yourself. When shopping for a piece of furniture, consider both the durability and the appearance of the wood used (teak holds up best, followed by cedar, mahogany, and pine) and the beefiness of construction (cheaper chairs and benches may look spindly). How much work is involved? Typically you'll have to use a screwdriver and hammer, as well as mix up the two-part epoxy included with the furniture. The directions may be quite involved, depending on how much of the piece has been preassembled.

When the sun goes down, senses other than sight are heightened—for pollinating creatures, as well as for ourselves. Several flowers have a remarkable nighttime presence, with large white or pale pastel blossoms visible in the dimmest light and enchanting fragrances that hang in the cooling air.

❧ *Datura inoxia* subsp. *inoxia* 'Evening Fragrance' (also known as moonflower) is a variety that unfolds its hanky-size blossoms at dusk and closes them before dawn. A single blossom, plucked just after opening, will scent an entire room. The white petals show just the palest violet tinge around the edges. Seeds are dropped generously from spiky pods, and seedlings are likely to appear the following spring.

❧ Another item that goes by the name of moonflower, *Ipomoea alba*, also produces large white blossoms. It grows as a vine, reaching 10 to 15 feet in height.

❧ Flowering tobacco (*Nicotiana alata*) unfolds large blossoms—in white, if you grow the highly fragrant species form rather than later developments that offer a range of colors but less enticement for the nose. It grows to 3 or 4 feet without needing support.

❧ Evening flowering stocks (*Matthiola longipetala* subsp. *bicornis*) look like last week's bouquet when viewed in the garden by daylight, but their weedy appearance is redeemed after sundown when they put off a perfume that has been likened to vanilla, jasmine, and nutmeg. The plants aren't dramatic in themselves, growing to just 12 to 18 inches in height.

❧ The blossoms are smaller and don't unfurl dramatically each night, but dame's rocket or sweet rocket (*Hesperis matronalis*) comes into its own after dusk, when the white to dusty lavender flowers glow and their clovelike scent comes on strong. Once you establish them, they may freely volunteer.

BIENNIALS: PATIENCE PROSPERS

Annuals and perennials have obvious advantages—you put the plant in the ground, and before long you get flowers—but discover how biennials can be all the more precious for delaying gratification.

EASY DOES IT

Try for Triennials

You may be able to coax a second, modest year of flowering. Just cut back the flowering stems to their lowest rosette of leaves, doing so just after the blossoms are spent.

Some of the best-loved flowers of all time fall into the odd category of biennials, those plants that just won't be rushed. A biennial needs 2 years to get its act together—its act, like all other living things, being to propagate itself. In the first year, you are rewarded with foliage, period. The plant overwinters, and in year two, you are rewarded with the blossoms. And what blossoms! Foxglove, hollyhocks, sweet William, Johnny-jump-up, honesty plant, English daisy, and Canterbury bells, to name a few.

As for year three—well, there typically is no year three. The plants die. But many will self-seed, as long as you allow some flowers to form seedheads (and after the plant has labored for 2 years to come to fruition, it seems only fair to allow a few plants to go the whole distance).

DON'T GO TO THE FLORIST FOR CARNATIONS

That staple of flower shops, the carnation, is surprisingly easy to grow. Give it a try!

Gardeners routinely grow the demure little border pinks of cottage beds, but purchase bunches of carnations. The florist type of carnations can be started readily from seed. Your homegrown flowers aren't likely to grow as tall as commercial carnations flown in from Colombia or Kenya, two centers of production, but they will be every bit as attractive and spicily scented. And fresher, too.

Plant seed in moistened potting mix; cover with a ¼-inch layer of the mix; then place the containers in a clear plastic bag and close the top loosely with a twist-tie to maintain an even level of humidity. Keep the bagged containers in a warm place, ideally with bottom heat supplied by a seedling mat or heat tape. Once seedlings are well under way, you can transfer them to large pots and move them outdoors. As they reach a height of 4 inches or so, they're ready for the garden. Carnations tend to be floppy, especially if grown with less than full sunlight, and they likely will need staking. By pinching off the terminal flower bud, you may be able to encourage the growth of smaller flowers along the stem; or, to produce a single large flower, pinch all buds *except* the terminal.

A DEDICATED CUTTING GARDEN

Rather than make unsightly holes in your flower beds when making bouquets, devote part of the yard to flowers intended solely for the vase.

To have plenty of bouquet fodder on hand, it helps to have a bed devoted solely to cutting flowers. If possible, place it close enough to the house that you will be more likely to cut flowers regularly, catching them at their best. These gardens traditionally have been coupled with the vegetable garden; both tend to be primarily about production rather than functioning as landscape features. Include not only annuals and perennials, but also flowering shrubs (flowering quince, lilac, mock-orange, and weigela) and a patch of ferns to add feathery greens.

PLANT AN AUDITION BED

Set aside a trial garden to see how new plants perform.

When growing flowers from seed, it's often the case that you don't know just what you'll get. The seeds may give variable results—different colors and aspects, and both double and single blossoms. Or the plants may not even survive. So before setting the seedlings out in your most visible beds, you might want to "audition" a few dozen in a bed tucked somewhat out of sight but convenient to where you do your seed starting. Watch them as they begin to come into bloom and select the most outstanding for show. And what about the rest? Chances are you can find good uses for them, too.

- They can serve as fillers for gaps that are apt to appear in even the best-tended beds.
- Transplant them to wildflower meadows.
- Clip them for bouquets.
- Give them away as pass-along plants to neighbors and friends.
- Allow them to set seed for sowing next year.

SALVAGING FORCED NARCISSUS

A pot of fragrant narcissus will add cheer to your home in winter, but it's a real anticlimax to toss the faded flowers once the show is over.

Pity the forced narcissus. It's tricked into flowering, then chucked. That's because forcing these flowers and offering them only water will drastically deplete their store of nutrients. Instead, as soon as the flowering is over, place the plants in soil and fertilize them. Given nutrients, a sunny windowsill, and careful watering, the bulbs may build up the energy required to bloom the following year. When the ground becomes workable and only light frosts are forecast, plant the bulbs outside. It's best to allow them to remain in the soil, rather than trying to dig them up in hopes that they can be forced again.

A DETACHABLE WINDOW BOX

Window boxes look downright depressing in winter months; here's one that goes away when the weather turns cold.

Winter weather is tough on wooden window boxes, shortening their serviceable lives. In particular, the planting medium will expand as it freezes, possibly causing the joints to fail. The design shown here is easy to build, is light enough to manage easily, and can be lifted off of its support come cold weather. There's no need to paint (and scrape and repaint) the box because it's made of cedar and assembled with stainless-steel screws.

1. From 1 × 6-inch cedar boards, cut the sides, ends, and bottom to length. You'll also need to cut two mounting pieces, one that will be attached permanently to the windowsill and the other for the box itself. Note that one long edge of each piece has a 45-degree angle; you can make both pieces with a single angled cut down the middle of a 1 × 6.

2. Assemble the box by drilling pilot holes, then driving the screws. Drill the drainage holes in the bottom. Attach the other mounting piece to the windowsill, bevel side up as shown.

3. Line the box with a piece of plastic sheet, tucking in the corners. Punch drainage holes through the plastic over the holes in the bottom.

4. Mount the window box and either add a potting mixture or use individual potted plants.

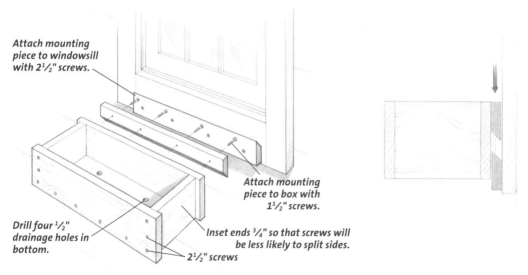

Attach mounting piece to windowsill with 2¹⁄₂" screws.

Attach mounting piece to box with 1¹⁄₂" screws.

Drill four ¹⁄₂" drainage holes in bottom.

Inset ends ³⁄₄" so that screws will be less likely to split sides.

2¹⁄₂" screws

You can construct a detachable window box that disappears from its highly visible location as soon as the plants within are battered by the first frosts of autumn.

A WINDOW BOX FOR ALL SEASONS

Unless you'll be taking down window boxes in the off-season, give some thought to keeping them looking productive throughout the year.

ADVICE OVER THE FENCE

For Window Boxes, Don't Go with Dirt

Garden soil works well in the garden, but it isn't your best choice for the highly artificial conditions of a window box. Instead, use a blend of soil, compost, and soil-less potting mix for a lightweight, moisture-retaining medium.

Most of us plant a window box once, early in the gardening year, and then forget about it. And for the usual ever-blooming, ever-cheerful sorts of flowers, that's fine. But to change the display with the season, use potted plants in the window box and swap them out as they begin to look tired. You might begin with daffodils and other bulbs, switch to geraniums and other low-maintenance flowers for summer, and then close out the growing season with mums and dwarf asters. Plants should be in plastic pots to reduce weight. If you surround the pots with vermiculite and top them off with a fine, attractive mulch, they will be concealed.

A WINDOW BOX IN WINTER

Nothing looks gloomier than abandoned window boxes, with dead plants fluttering in the wind. When fall frosts have laid waste to the plants in a box, empty it, planting medium and all. Wooden boxes will last longer if you do. This is a good time to renew a paint job. And if the empty boxes aren't to your liking, you can use them to hold displays of evergreen branches and bittersweet.

AN INDOOR WINDOW BOX

Windowsills are nearly the perfect spot for indoor plants—nearly, because pots tend to leave unsightly rings, and a row of circular pots necessarily isn't the most efficient use of valuable sunny space. Instead, build or buy an attractive window box and install it adjacent to the ledge. You can rest it on a plant stand, perhaps one with wheels so that you can roll light-hungry plants to take advantage of both morning and afternoon sun. Or mount it on sturdy L brackets that are attached with screws to studs within the wall. (In most houses, studs are located every 16 inches on center, and usually there will be studs on either side of the window opening.) To contain water within the box, use a plastic liner or baking pans of aluminum foil, and top with a layer of gravel.

GIVE EACH HOUSEPLANT THE LIGHT IT NEEDS

Think of light as a vital nutrient, one that a plant needs in a particular dosage each day.

Plants rely on light energy to drive the metabolic machinery of photosynthesis. With too little light, the machine slows and a houseplant performs poorly and may die. If the light is too intense, foliage may be burned. And one variety's sunlight requirement can cause another variety to drop all of its leaves. Plants are sensitive not only to the brightness of the light they receive, but to its duration and even the colors from which it is composed. For healthy windowsill greenery, you need to pay as much attention to light levels as to fertilizer and water.

A GROW-LIGHT LIKE THE SUN ITSELF

For years, greenhouse growers have relied on high-intensity discharge (HID) lamps for a blaze of light to supplement sunshine. For commercial operations, that supplemental light is especially important in northern states and in the winter. Most of us homeowners make do with too little light for many of the plants we'd like to grow indoors, but now HIDs are available in lower wattages. The smallest of them aren't terribly expensive, although powerful ones rated at 300 watts or so require a ballast (transformer) and are something of an investment. On the positive side, the bulbs last for 10,000 hours or more. And the quality of light resembles the sun's own, covering much of the spectrum. If you're serious about having a grouping of houseplants perform at their best, consider the purchase of an HID.

A LIGHT MOVER

Unless you can afford a bank of HIDs, you'll be limited to focusing a single fixture on one or a few plants that need a lot of light. Or, you can install a nifty automatic *light mover* that slowly propels the high-powered fixture along a ceiling track, increasing your growing area by 30 to 60 percent. There's no need to go up onto a stepladder to adjust a light this way and that—a 5-watt-motor does the work. Check the Internet for a supplier.

USE A MIRROR FOR NICELY GROOMED PLANTS

If you have a spare dressing mirror, you can use it to reflect the sun's energy and bathe the dark side of seedling flats placed by windows or large potted plants (especially ones in heavy clay pots). You not only make better use of the solar energy trickling in through the panes, but also distribute it more evenly so that plants will grow symmetrically rather than leaning into the light. Painting adjacent walls and trim a semigloss white will also help bump up light levels. And you can cover the windowsill or window-side table with shiny Mylar, serving both to protect the surface below and to bounce light back up at the plants.

Make the sun do double duty by placing a spare mirror behind large houseplants that aren't easily turned or moved. The plants will be more likely to grow to a well-rounded form because there is more than one light source.

A WINDOW GREENHOUSE

Go ahead and splurge. Attach a miniature greenhouse to a sunny window to put plants at your fingertips—and eye level.

Within a few hours, you and a helper can graft a window greenhouse onto the side of your home, for a greatly expanded version of your favorite sunny window ledge. A greenhouse with two or three shelves gives you room for flowers and kitchen herbs. For heat in cooler months, there's the sun shining through all that glazing, as well as warmth that comes from the house when you open the window.

In order for you to have full access to the height of the greenhouse, you can attach it outside an opening from which the window has been removed. Or, to be able to control the flow of heat into and from a greenhouse, mount it outside a *double-hung* window—one with two sashes that slide up and down in tracks. (A *single-hung* window, in which only the lower sash is moveable, will allow you to reach only the bottom half of the space within.) You may have to gently free the upper sash with a putty knife if it has been painted shut over the years.

1. Choose a window with a good location. You'll want to go with a window that gets a lot of sunlight throughout the day—at least in cool months. Shade from deciduous trees might be welcome in late spring through early fall. Measure the dimensions of the window from the outside, deciding if the frame of the greenhouse will mount on the window trim or on the home's wall just outside the trim. Order a greenhouse to suit your situation.

2. Assemble the greenhouse frame, omitting the glazing for now. With a helper holding the frame in place over the window, attach it by driving screws into the wall. If yours is a wood-framed house, it's best to sink screws into framing members around the window. For a brick house, drill holes for plastic anchors, then drive screws into the anchors. There may be support brackets with the kit as well; install them as directed in the manufacturer's directions.

3. Using a good grade of exterior caulk in a caulking gun, seal around the perimeter of the greenhouse.

4. Install the glazing as directed by the manufacturer.

PLANTS TELL YOU WHEN THEY'RE IN THE DARK

Keep an eye on your houseplants, and outdoor plants brought in for the winter, and there may be telltale signs that they're getting too little—or too much—light from nearby windows. If you see leaf burn, it may be time to move the plant away from the window. And if foliage is an unnaturally dark green or the plant just isn't growing, suspect insufficient light.

You can have a greenhouse at your fingertips, while making it possible to enjoy the plants from inside your home.

THE FIRST VISITORS OF SPRING

Plant these harbingers of the growing season and it's likely you'll find yourself pleasantly surprised by them each year.

ADVICE OVER ⌂T⌂H⌂E⌂ FENCE
Leave the Leaves?

After enjoying the display of spring-flowering bulbs, gardeners are apt to find themselves wondering about what to do about the aftermath—leaves, either healthy or on their way out. You should remove spent flower heads from tulips and daffodils so that the plants will invest energy in the bulbs rather than in seed pods. But generally the foliage of spring-flowering bulbs isn't trimmed until it has yellowed and is dying back. That might not be until summer in the case of tulips and daffodils, or earlier for the smaller bulbs that appear before spring is well underway. If you remove the foliage while it is still at work generating energy for the plant, the next year's performance will be compromised.

The early flowering bulbs of spring can be an encouraging sight, as they thumb their noses at freezing temperatures and the last snowfalls of winter. They often are described as "minor bulbs," playing second fiddle to the showier tulips and daffodils. But they deserve credit (and planting) as the vegetative world's accompaniment to the first migrating birds.

Glory-of-the-snow (*Chionodoxa luciliae*). This sun-loving bulb is most often seen with star-shaped blue blossoms, and there are also white- and pink-flowered varieties. It prefers sunny sites.

Crocuses (*Crocus* spp. and hybrids). These modest-size flowers can handle some shade, and they work best when planted in groupings of just one color or a similar shade. They don't do well in the lawn, unless you can put off the year's first mowing until the tops die back.

Snowdrops (*Galanthus nivalis*). These stalwart little plants seem unfazed by the worst that early spring weather can bring. The drooping blossoms make a quiet display, so you may overlook them unless you plant a fair number.

Spanish bluebell (*Hyacinthoides hispanica*). Plant this one wherever shade has meant a sparse visual show. Allow the foliage to remain after blooming so that the plants can generate food for the following season.

Spring snowflake (*Leucojum vernum*). Like snowdrops, the blossoms are white and drooping, but distinguished by green ends on the petals. They can be grown in partial shade or full sun.

Grape hyacinth (*Muscari armeniacum*). Whether or not you think the blossoms look like clusters of grapes, these cheerful plants return dependably each spring. By shopping in mail-order catalogs, you can find a range of colors including yellow and a chilly white with the slightest blue cast. *Muscari* do well with plentiful sun.

Siberian squill (*Scilla sibirica*). The bright blue flowers are eye catching in early spring, when the rest of the yard has yet to shake off its wintertime slumber.

BOUQUET BOOSTERS

You may know some of these tricks already, but read on! There are all sorts of pet ways of keeping cut flowers from collapse.

The delicate glory of a bouquet from the garden is all too fleeting. Not that gardeners have spared any effort in coming up with ways of forestalling the day when the faded flowers become compost fodder. Here are a few tricks that have worked for others.

- Add lemon-lime soda (not the diet variety) to the vase water.
- Drop in a penny (the theory being that copper is a fungicide).
- Stir in an aspirin (these fast-dissolving pills are acidic, which is said to promote the flow of water up stems).
- Pour in a bit of mouthwash (look for a brand that has both sucrose, to feed the flowers, and antibacterial properties).
- Plug the stems, if they're hollow. Use an eyedropper to fill the stem with water while holding individual flowers upside down, then make a tiny plug from a dampened cotton ball.
- Singe the stems of plants that have a milky exudate when snipped, by holding a match or lighter under the newly made cut.
- Mash the stems of woody plants to encourage them to draw in more water, using a light tap with a hammer.

Probably the soundest advice is the most ordinary (and the most troublesome): Change the water daily. You already know that old vase water ranks among the vilest liquids on the planet.

GET THE LIGHT RIGHT

Plants vary greatly in the amount of sunlight they need—and can tolerate. If you have a perennial or shrub that languishes each year, try moving it to another site—either shadier or sunnier.

Here is a rundown of how you can meet the light needs of houseplants throughout the year, compiled by Paula Szilard, master gardener at the Colorado State University Cooperative Extension in Arapahoe County. Note that the distance from a window makes a dramatic difference in how much light a plant receives. The seasons matter as well, because the sun becomes less intense and travels a lower arc as the days approach December's vernal equinox.

FOR PLANTS NEEDING HIGH LIGHT LEVELS

- Give 4 to 6 hours of sun or the equivalent
- Place 2 to 6 feet from a south-facing window, October to March
- Place within 2 feet of an east- or west-facing window, year-round

FOR PLANTS NEEDING MODERATE LIGHT LEVELS (BRIGHT LIGHT BUT NOT DIRECT SUN)

- Place within 2 feet of a north-facing window, April to September
- Place 2 to 6 feet from a south-, east-, or west-facing window, year-round

FOR PLANTS NEEDING LOW LIGHT LEVELS

- Place within 2 feet of a north-facing window, October to March
- Place 6 to 10 feet from a south-facing window, April to September

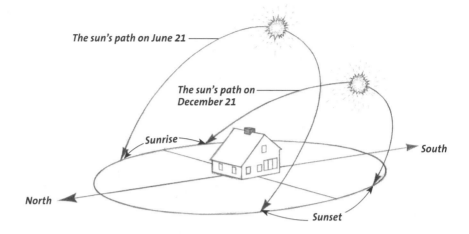

The sun's path on June 21

The sun's path on December 21

Sunrise

South

North

Sunset

When positioning houseplants, it's good to keep in mind that in winter, the sun's rays are weaker and enter the home at a lower angle.

NATURAL AIR FRESHENERS

Rather than spray household air with aerosols that claim to smell like the country-side, use houseplants to relieve indoor air pollution.

Houseplants are more than just a pretty face. They can improve the home's environment quality—and indoor air quality is apt to be compromised by solvents, cleaners, outgassing building products, and scented products. The best all-around houseplants for clearing the air are reported to be three palms: areca, lady, and bamboo. This trio may not only remove pollutants but may also contribute humidity to dry household air. They're easy to take care of, too. In addition, Boston fern is said to do a good job of removing formaldehyde (used in some construction materials and carpeting), and peace lily may be effective in lowering levels of acetone (found in nail polish remover).

TREATING GERANIUMS AS PERENNIALS

Don't give up on geraniums (Pelargonium × hortorum) as the frosts of fall approach.

With a little trouble, you can bring your beloved geraniums through the winter in good shape so that they are raring to go come the return of warm weather. Before the killing temperatures arrive, dig them up and cut back their growth by half. Then follow either of these two procedures.

POT THEM UP

Shake off the soil from around the roots, and pot up the geraniums with potting mix. Place them in a cool spot with generous sunlight. Pinch back weak growth so that the plant maintains a full appearance. Before returning the plants to the outdoors, give them a dose of fertilizer.

LET THEM GO DORMANT

It may seem strange, but this involves carefully removing all the soil from around the roots and then leaving the plants alone. Place them in individual paper bags, fold over the end, and store for the winter in a cool, dark place, ideally around 40°F. Inspect them a couple of times during the cold-weather months. The leaves will yellow, but the stems should remain rigid. You can help ensure that the stems won't shrivel by soaking the roots in water for an hour or two, twice during the winter. If some plants do shrivel nonetheless, throw them out. Around April 1st, pot up the dormant plants with potting soil. Prune back any dead stems. Place the plants along a cool, sunny windowsill. Return them to the garden when all danger of frost is past.

TAKE CUTTINGS

If you customarily move your scented geraniums outside for the summer, then back indoors at summer's end, you also may be bringing diseases and pests along with them. And you might not have enough sunny windowsills to keep an ambitious collection of full-grown plants alive inside. Many gardeners prefer to start fresh by taking cuttings in the fall, placing them in water until they send out roots, and then potting them up with a soil-less medium. Leaves from the unused parts of the plant can be used in potpourris.

CARE FOR CUTTINGS

Allow breathing space around cuttings to promote air circulation and prevent diseases, and keep humidity high by putting the container in a plastic bag, open side up. Place the cuttings in a bright area that receives only indirect sun. If the temperature in the bag climbs too high for the young plants, open the top of the bag. Cuttings are ready for planting out when you give them a gentle tug and they seem anchored in the planting medium. Set the cuttings at the same depth, and gradually expose them to more sun.

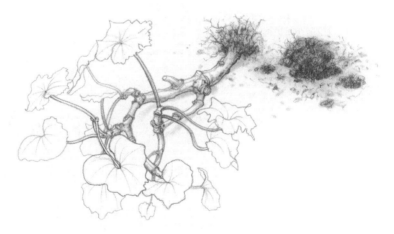

To keep geraniums over winter, encourage them to go dormant by gently removing the soil from around their roots and storing them in paper bags in a cool place.

NATURAL POTPOURRI

Don't let your hard work fade with time. Use essential oils and a natural fixative to make your potpourris more permanent.

EASY DOES IT

Err on the Side of Subtlety

When making a potpourri, whether from a recipe or according to your own notions, keep in mind that it's easy to overdo the highly scented oils and such olfactory powerhouses as cinnamon and cloves. Begin by focusing on leaves and blossoms from your own gardens, then judiciously add other ingredients as needed for a well-balanced scent that complements, rather than dominates, your homey atmosphere.

The scent of most flowers is fleeting, but there are steps you can take to make a potpourri that lasts longer—without resorting to harsh-smelling additives. Orris root is a commonly used fixative, taken from a variety of iris. It may be available at drugstores and herb shops, as well as through on-line firms selling perfume supplies. You also can stir in brandy—not a frilly, flavored brand but the straight stuff—to help bring out the flavor of shy-smelling flowers and herbs. And many formulas call for scented oils, including rose, lavender, bergamot, lemon, bayberry, vetiver, cedar, and sandalwood.

If you want the potpourri to be pretty as well as perfumed, add visual bits and pieces; delphinium blossoms, rosebuds, citrus rinds, curlicues of cedar wood, and little pinecones. If you have balsam firs, or will be visiting a forest where the trees grow, the needles have a long-lasting scent that blends well with other ingredients.

1. Harvest the ingredients. For best fragrance, pick flowers early in the day but after the dew has evaporated. The best roses for potpourri are highly scented (of course) and also have some fleshy thickness to the petals; catch them before they've fully opened.

2. Dry blossoms and leaves on several thicknesses of paper towel, out of direct sunlight. You also can use a food dehydrator, or an oven set to 100°F and with the door ajar. (The exception is for making a *moist* potpourri; see the opposite page.)

3. Combine your harvested flowers and leaves with any purchased ingredients—herbs and spices, and fragrant oils if you choose to include them.

4. Stir in about 1 tablespoon of orris root powder for every 2 cups of ingredients.

5. Place the potpourri in a sealable container and age out of the light for a couple of months, stirring every couple of days. Then place the potpourri in a decorative bowl or fill sachets with it.

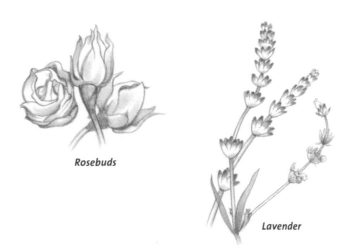

Rosebuds

Lavender

For the finest possible potpourri, grow your own flowers and herbs rather than relying on commercial ingredients that may irritate your nose instead of pleasing it.

A MOIST POTPOURRI

This recipe may come closer to the original potpourris of centuries past, when the ingredients were fresh and pulpy rather than dry. After all, *potpourri* comes from the French for "rotten pot."

What You'll Need

4 cups rose petals, partially dried

2 cups lilac flowers

2 cups lavender buds

1 cup rose geranium leaves

1 cup lemon verbena leaves

4 tablespoons unflavored brandy

Dry Mixture

¼ cup powdered orris root

¾ cup noniodized salt

¼ cup ground allspice

¼ cup whole cloves

½ cup brown sugar

(continued)

1. In a bowl, mix the petal and leaf ingredients.
2. In another bowl, mix the dry ingredients.
3. Make alternate layers of the two mixes in a crock with a lid. Cover for 1 month, stirring daily.
4. Uncover the crock. As needed, you can pour in more brandy to revive the scent, stirring it into the other ingredients.

POTPOURRI LITE

If you find that most potpourris are simply too much of a good thing, with a cloying and heavy effect, try making this clean-scented variation from easily grown ingredients.

1 cup marigold leaves and flowers

1 cup thyme

1 cup spearmint leaves

1 cup lemon balm leaves

1 cup noniodized salt

Prepare as for "Natural Potpourri," on page 236.

POISONOUS POTPOURRIS?

Potpourris are intended to make the home seem cozy and welcoming, but in fact certain mixtures may function better as people repellents. Commercial blends may have synthesized chemicals that cause allergic reactions, as do some scented candles. So, make your own and be assured that you aren't polluting the indoor environment.

CHAPTER 8

Growing and Enjoying Herbs

Herbs are multipurpose plants that gardeners grow for any number of reasons. There's the fascinating folklore attached to them, going back to a time when all sorts of magical properties were associated with these plants. There's the astounding range of bewitching scents (and some of their perfumes continue to be credited with special powers over the mind and body). Many of them produce lovely (if small) blossoms. They can be used in cooking—and should be, because the flavor of homegrown herbs is so much more complex than that of the dried stuff that comes in little bottles. By interplanting certain herbs with vegetables, you can ward off pests. Add to this list the fact that most herbs are very undemanding, and it's no wonder that they have such an enduring appeal.

A CHAMOMILE LAWN

Roman chamomile is a low-growing herb that can serve as a sturdy ground cover, with tiny daisylike flowers and an intriguing scent reminiscent of apple.

If Roman chamomile (*Chamaemelum nobile*) is to thrive as a ground cover, you'll need relatively moist conditions and a low-traffic area. You can start plants indoors 8 to 10 weeks before the last frost date, or sow seed outside 2 weeks before that date. Plan on a 6-inch spacing. Water as needed to help the plants become established. To minimize the impact of people crossing the area, run a path of stones or brick across it. To keep the plants looking like a lawn, mow regularly at between 3 to 4 inches. This prevents flowering and encourages the chamomile to grow vegetatively. And, with luck, there you have it—a fragrant lawn that demands little in the way of maintenance.

THYME FOR A NEW CARPET

Try planting low-growing thymes for those in-between places that weeds love to colonize—around steps and between pavers, in particular.

Thyme can be tucked into all sorts of nooks and crannies in the garden, and once established, they'll help keep weeds from colonizing in these spots. You can grow varieties that will lend a hint of lemon, nutmeg, and caraway (not to mention thyme flavor) to salads, savory dishes, and even butter. The flowers are tiny but attractive and often profuse. And you can walk barefoot on these plants, as long as you don't indulge yourself too often.

Most choices will be either of two species. Creeping thyme (*Thymus serphyllum* or *T. praecox arcticus*) forms mats growing to about 4 inches in height. A single plant may eventually cover an area 3 feet in diameter. The wooly thymes (*T. pseudolanuginosis*) grow to no more than 1 inch high and tend to bear fewer flowers. Plant them in a sunny spot with well-drained soil that's on either the sandy or the loamy side. Brush off fallen leaves as necessary, and keep an eye on weeds.

AN HERB TO GAZE UPON

Bronze fennel is bold and beautiful. Make an effort to find it.

For a dramatic addition to an herb or flower garden, plant bronze fennel (*Foeniculum vulgare*), with its unusual color, feathery tops, and graceful aspect. Unlike the bulb-forming fennel, this one is grown for the leaves and, if allowed to overwinter, for the flavorful seeds that find use in baking. Start bronze fennel by sowing directly in the garden, about 2 weeks before the last frost date. If these semi-hardy perennials like their site, you can look forward to having them reappear each year.

KEEP LAVENDER FROM LANGUISHING

Plant catalogs illustrate lavender listings with photos of great purple swaths of the herb. How do they do it?

Suspect digital enhancement. It can be a challenge to grow a flourishing bed of lavender. The basic requirements are 6 to 8 hours of sun a day and well-drained soil with a pH between 6.5 and 7.5. Where summers are hot and humid, lavender may do best in a raised or mounded bed. In cooler zones, the plants often don't survive the winter in good shape, so that you may be better off thinking of this herb as an annual and beginning with fresh stock each spring.

TEA TIME IS A GARDENER'S REWARD

Go beyond plain mint in your tea. Come up with a custom blend of teas from your own herbs.

Next Year's Garden
Refresh with Mint

Even if you experiment with flavored teas, you'll still be amazed with the cool, refreshing taste of homegrown mint. Most mints are tough perennials, so they're easy herbs to grow. Be careful where you plant them though because they spread aggressively. Mints do best in Zones 5 to 9 and usually reach 2 feet high. Plant mints in full sun or partial shade in rich, moist, well-drained soil. Or try planting mint in a 5-gallon container with holes punched in the bottom for drainage. Most mints don't come true from seed, so be sure to buy a seedling or take a cutting from another plant.

By brewing tea from fresh garden-grown ingredients, you'll enjoy the full-bore complexity of scents and flavors that dried store-bought teas only approach. You also can come up with a nearly inexhaustible variety of blends.

Experiment freely, recording your hits and misses. But when you find a blend you like, work methodically, measuring out herbs by the teaspoon or tablespoon if you've dried them, or possibly by weight if they are fresh. Try the blends with and without various sweeteners—sugar, honey, or even a light grade of maple syrup. And don't overlook using *true* tea, black or green, in your blends. Chances are you won't be growing and processing it, although the plants can be had through mail-order sources. But other easily grown plants have traditionally been used along with tea (*Camellia sinensis*), including spearmint (and occasionally valerian) in Moroccan green tea, rose petals, and jasmine blossoms. Bergamot can be added to either black or green tea to approximate the flavor of Earl Grey tea, although this famous blend draws its distinctive character from the bergamot orange, a citrus fruit seldom seen in the garden.

Brew your homemade tea with boiling water from the stove. Take care not to allow the leaves or flowers to sit in hot water so long that the tea takes on a "stewy" flavor. A gentler way to steep herbs is to put them in a glass bottle full of room-temperature water and set it in a sunny place.

Here a few suggestions to get you started.

- In the mint family alone, there are dozens of experiences to be savored. The standards are peppermint and spearmint. Also try orange mint or pineapple mint.

- Chamomile is easy to grow, and it is credited with having a calming effect that can help *you* to take it easy, too. The taste is likened to both pineapple and green apple.

- For a lemony taste, try lemon balm and lemon verbena.

Keep Mints from Mingling

Mints have a beguiling scent but a bullying manner in the garden, so you may want to take steps to prevent them from wearing out their welcome.

Pot-bound plants are something to avoid, correct? Not necessarily.

Plant catalogs and nurseries offer a tempting array of exotically scented mints, which might have you thinking about setting out a half-dozen or so varieties for teas or just plain sniffing. Trouble is, most mints grow with unrestrained enthusiasm, and what was a tidy herb patch in your imagination can turn into an herb jungle in reality. To maintain order, use sturdy scissors to cut the bottoms out of large black plastic nursery pots and set them near one another in the mint patch with the rims just above soil level. Plant the various mints in the pots. Before long, the pots will be invisible beneath the fragrant greenery.

❖ Kids may like the noncaffeinated root beer taste of iced tea made from anise hyssop (*Agastache rupestris*).

❖ Rose hips add color, vitamin C, and a bracing tartness to tea blends.

❖ You also may be lucky in having potential tea ingredients growing wild nearby, such as spicebush (*Lindera benzoin*), the anise-scented sweet goldenrod (*Solidago odora*), and wintergreen (*Gaultheria procumbens*).

❖ For a little added zip, combine herbs with either green or black tea. Traditionally, Moroccan mint tea is made from both fresh spearmint and green gunpowder tea.

For a refreshing summertime tea while gardening, combine spearmint out of the garden with green gunpowder tea. It's the national drink of Morocco, and typically is served very sweet, but be guided by your own taste.

SAGE ADVICE ON SMUDGING

Native Americans in the Southwest used smoldering wands of wild sage as incense for purification rituals known as *smudging*, and these wands still are widely used to foster a positive atmosphere in homes. A popular variety is white sage (*Salvia apiana*), easily grown in a sunny spot and ornamental in its own right. To make a wand, form a cigarlike bundle of the leaves and bind them together by wrapping with string. Allow the leaves to dry so that they will smolder. Then light the end and blow out the flame to produce fragrant smoke.

SHADY HERBS

Some herbs will do just fine without a day-long sunbath.

EASY DOES IT

Learn about Lovage

Bet you didn't know that lovage makes a great trivia subject! It's a fascinating herb with a long history. Lovage was very popular in the Middle Ages, when people grew it in kitchen gardens. Early herbalists recommended lovage as a diuretic, and occasionaly as a cure for rheumatism, jaundice, and kidney stones.

Modern gardeners can use the leaves fresh in salads and fresh and dried in soup, stews, and sauces. You can chop and add the stems to salads. The seeds, whole or ground, work well in pickling brines, cheese spreads, salads, salad dressings, and sauces. Lovage also enhances tomatoes, steamed vegetables, rice, chicken, and poultry stuffings.

When we think of herbs, we're apt to think of the sunny Mediterranean, with nearly treeless landscapes blanketed with rosemary and lavender and thyme. If that doesn't sound like a description of your yard, don't despair. There are a number of herbs that will do well for you in partial shade.

* Lemon balm (*Melissa officinalis*) is an enthusiastic grower with soft lemon-scented leaves that carry a suggestion of mint. Try it as a tea, in punch, and chopped finely in salads and marinades for fish.

* Lovage (*Levisticum officinale*) is a good candidate for the back of a shaded bed, reaching a height of 5 feet. With a flavor resembling celery, it's a good addition to soups and potato salad.

* Mints (*Mentha* spp.) offer you an enchanting variety of scents and flavors. They tend to roam, so plant them in buried nursery pots with the bottoms cut out. Mints can be brewed in tea, either alone or in addition to green or black tea for an interesting blend. Try them also in Greek dishes, in jellies, diced small for a frosting flavoring, and as a garnish in tall drinks.

Sweet woodruff appreciates well-drained, humus-rich soil, and it can handle shady locations.

- Sweet woodruff (*Galium odoratum*) makes a pretty picture unto itself, with dainty white flowers and radiating leaves. It often is used as a ground cover in the grass-free circle around trees and shrubs. When dried, sweet woodruff takes on the scent of vanilla, and it can be used in potpourris or tucked between sheets before they're folded and put in the linen closet.

- The French variety of tarragon (*Artemisia danunculus* var. *sativa*) has a character all its own, coming closest to anise. Its most familiar use is as a flavoring for vinegar; just add a leafy stem or two to a jar of malt vinegar. It also finds its way into recipes for mayonnaise, soups, and sauces.

- Other herbal plants to consider for partially shaded areas include bay, bee balm, chamomile, chervil, coriander, gentian, ginseng, rosemary, saffron, sorrel, sweet cicely, thyme, wintergreen, and wormwood.

A MEADOW OF HERBS

Sow tall, free-growing herbs for a pleasantly scented meadow that will need little attention.

There are low-growing, delicate herbs, and also herbs that would like to take over your entire property. If you have a good-size yard, try devoting a corner of it to a few of the latter type. Their robust vigor won't be lost on butterflies and beneficial insects, which will flock to the area of massed blossoms. Try spearmint, horehound, agastache in any number of colors, lemon balm, bee balm, tansy, and yarrow for a tough little patch that you won't have to pamper.

After the growing season, when the plants have set seed, cut down the tall herbs with a string trimmer or a lawnmower on a high setting. This clears away dead stalks and also nips in the bud any invasive brush or tree seedlings. Allow the clippings to remain in place to encourage self-seeding, but remove any weeds that have set seed.

A BACKDOOR HERB GARDEN

Dedicate a piece of real estate right outside the back door to culinary herbs.

Next Year's Garden
An Italian Herb Garden

There's no need to compromise the flavor of your homegrown peppers and tomatoes with dehydrated garlic and dried spices. Plant a dedicated garden or a garden row with basil, marjoram, oregano, rosemary, parsley, and thyme, and tuck garlic in the ground in November for harvest the next summer.

If you like to cook with herbs, you'll be more apt to actually pick them if the plants aren't growing very far from the kitchen door (within 15 feet is a good guideline). An ideal site would be well drained and sunny for at least 6 hours a day. For a practical plot of culinary herbs you might favor a relaxed design, with mounded beds setting off a section near the kitchen door. Simple stepping-stones will add a bit of ornament, while allowing you easier access to the plants so that you don't end up admiring them from a distance. A stepping-stone path also can help segregate aggressive growers, such as mints. You might place ornamental potted herbs in each corner of the herb garden to lend definition to the bed; try large specimens of scented geranium, bay, kaffir lime, sage, or rosemary.

A SIMPLE BRICK WALK

Brick seems like such a natural material with which to make a walk. The components are inexpensive, durable, easy to lift and move about, and attractive. Their one big weakness is that all those cracks between the bricks are apt to be weed nurseries. And weeds that get their feet into a brick walk can be tough to eradicate.

The best solution is the most involved: set the brick in a bed of cement. If you aren't up to that bother and expense, an easier alternative is to lay the brick in a bed of sand.

1. Dig a shallow bed for the walks, just deep enough for a 2-inch layer of sand and the brick. A straight-bladed shovel will help you keep the bed level and its edges sharp.
2. Spread sand evenly over the beds. You can use a 2 × 4 to help grade the sand to a level surface.
3. Lay permeable landscaping cloth over the sand.
4. Put the brick in place, staggering the courses. This will mean

What to Plant?

Until perennial herbs get under way later in the season, the herb patch may look pretty patchy indeed. Annual flowers can come to the rescue for the first couple of years, particularly those with culinary uses: lemon gem marigold, nasturtium, and borage are good choices. As for the herbs themselves, the selection is up to you, but the baker's dozen listed here will get you started.

Basil, Italian	Peppermint
Basil, Thai	Rosemary
Chives	Sage
Cilantro	Spearmint
Dill	Tarragon
Oregano	Thyme
Parsley	

starting off every other course with a half brick. Use a hammer, a *brick set* (a chisel with a broad, heavy-duty blade), and safety glasses to tap bricks across the middle and snap them in two. To define the sides of the walks, you can run a row of bricks set on edge or on end.

5. Scatter sand over the brick surface, and use a broom to brush the sand into the spaces between bricks. By doing this regularly from time to time, you'll have more sand between the bricks than dirt, and weeds will be less likely to invade.

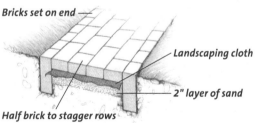

Bricks set on end

Landscaping cloth

2" layer of sand

Half brick to stagger rows

By having a couple of short brick paths meet at right angles, you can establish a simple herb garden within an expanse of lawn.

A BALL-SHAPED BASIL

It tastes as great as it looks!

Spicy globe basil is a compact form of the herb that tends to take the shape of a small globe. By spacing the plants at regular intervals, you can make an attractive mini-hedge or border to run along beds. Or pot up a row of three or five in a rectangular planter to show off their tidy shape. To harvest leaves when cooking, take modest pinches in order to maintain the form.

Here is a basil that grows naturally into a tidy form that looks as though it had been carefully sheared into shape.

WHERE DEER ROAM, GROW HERBS

Grow a garden of herbs, and dispense with a fence.

If you are plagued by the ravages of deer, one strategy is to turn your attention to growing herbs. Most of the better-known herbs are relatively untroubled by deer, an animal with a famously broad appetite. That could be because herbs are strong flavored and their leaves tend to be less than lush. For whatever reason, you may be safe with anise, horehound, hyssop, lavender, lemon balm, marjoram, mints, oregano, rosemary, tarragon, and thyme.

A KNOT GARDEN FOR THE AMBITIOUS GROWER

If you prefer a formally laid out yard, try sketching patterns for a traditional knot garden. It's a way to keep your garden looking fresh and vibrant.

In centuries past, knot gardens were formed from interlocking mini-hedges of herbs and edging plants. Good candidates include Munstead lavender, germander, green santolina (*Santolina virens*), lavender cotton, mother-of-thyme and golden lemon thyme, rosemary, and hyssop. For variety and an attractive appearance in every season, consider adding dwarf plantings of box, as well as blueberry or barberry for their brilliant fall foliage. And then you have to fill in the blanks—the spaces within the edging. Choose from gravel, stone paving, bricks, or mulch, depending on your vision for the garden. Or grow grass or a low, tidy ground cover.

A traditional knot garden gives the lawn a formal touch that remains attractive throughout the seasons.

INDOOR HERBS APLENTY

Grow a living spice shelf of your favorite culinary herbs.

ADVICE OVER THE FENCE

A Turn for the Better

Sunny windowsills are a fine place for herbs, with one reservation. That light source is beaming in from one direction, and over time a plant's growth will tend to look lopsided. Try to get in the habit of rotating pots a quarter turn or so each time you water them.

A pot of carefully pruned rosemary or spicy bush basil makes an attractive windowsill plant, but you'll probably be reluctant to snip off much for cooking. And chances are that if you love plants, your south-facing windows are already filled to capacity. So, if you really like to cook with fresh herbs year-round, consider arranging a light table for them. This involves setting up fluorescent shop lights over a sturdy table or shelf that won't be marred by water. It's almost like having an attached greenhouse—on a far more modest scale, of course.

For most plants, provide at least 12 hours of light a day from a two-tube fixture suspended about 6 inches above the plants. You can hang the lights from two or three sturdy brackets. Place the brackets over studs in the wall above the windows and drive screws to anchor them securely. To locate the studs, you can use a magnetic or electronic stud finder. Or, look at the baseboard or chair rail trim and note where it has been nailed; if these locations are 16 inches on center, they indicate the studs' positions within the wall.

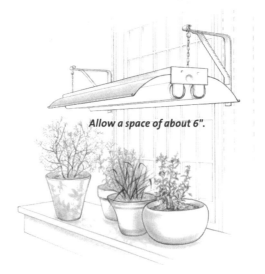

Allow a space of about 6".

To make sure that windowsill plants get sufficient light, you can supplement the sun's energy with a fluorescent fixture mounted on wall brackets.

GIVE INDOOR HERBS A BOOST

If you bring your favorite herbs indoors for the winter rather than sacrificing them to the frosts of fall, they may not reward your kindness with lush growth. They are apt to go dormant, performing sluggishly. Here's a way to goose them into growing with youthful energy.

1. Pot up the plant and boldly cut back the top growth to just 2 or 3 inches.
2. Place the plant in a clear plastic bag with the opening on top and seal it.
3. Create a false winter by placing the potted plant in the refrigerator for 2 weeks, subjecting it to another 2 weeks in the freezer, and then moving it back to the refrigerator for a final 2 weeks.
4. Place the plant on a sunny windowsill with the bag open and look for new growth.

OVERHEAD HERBS

Traditionally, herb plants were plucked by the handful and hung up to dry a couple of steps from where they'd be used.

It may be ornamental rather than strictly practical, but a kitchen seems to look more like a no-nonsense workplace if there are bundles of herbs hanging to dry from joists. Or, if you don't have an old farmhouse with authentic exposed joists, simple hooks on a wall will do. Cut the stems just above ground level to facilitate tying bundles with twine. The less-humid air of fall may help the herbs to dry. But unless your house is unusual, kitchen oils and dust will conspire to coat these herbs with an unappetizing fur. So either use them fairly promptly or treat them as nonfunctional decoration, something like wax fruit in a glass bowl.

SCULPT A ROSEMARY

Rosemary lends itself to being trained in any number of geometrical or fanciful shapes.

Come winter, give rosemary plants a prominent, sunny spot in your home. And avoid the fate that befalls so many of these plants when brought inside by well-meaning gardeners. As sturdy as they seem, rosemary plants are highly vulnerable to drying out. Skip a single watering, and you may lose them. (If so, harvest the leaves before discarding the plant, give them a good rinse to remove household dust, allow the water to evaporate, then put them in a plastic bag and pop in the freezer.) Left to its own devices, rosemary takes on a relaxed form. But with its fine needlelike foliage and the promise of delicate flowers, this herb is an excellent candidate for shaping into any number of forms. You can coax the potted plants into *standards,* with a trunk below and ball of leaves above in the manner of a manicured park tree. They also can be trained around a wire hoop, homemade or bought at a nursery. Or trim them into the form of a miniature Christmas tree.

Shape rosemary according to your whim, clipping or training it with wire for an ornament that produces edible trimmings.

A SCENTED CURE FOR SLEEPLESS NIGHTS

Rest sweetly and soundly on an herbal pillow.

ADVICE OVER THE FENCE

Snip Hops Shoots

In spring, the fast-growing young shoots can be snipped off and added to salads, steamed like tiny asparagus, or dropped into the brine of an empty pickle jar for later nibbling.

Herbs have long been used to influence people's moods and emotions. For example, lavender was once strewn between sheets back in a day when bed linens were routinely ironed, so that sleepers would be calmed by the clean scent. And pillows were stuffed with hops blossoms for the supposed sleep-inducing effect of this plant. Abraham Lincoln, troubled by mood swings and sleeplessness, used a hops pillow. Unless you like the sound and sensation of resting your head on dried leaves, it's best to make a small herbal pillow, sew or zip it shut, and place it *near* your head rather than under it. The scent of hops isn't to everyone's liking, so you may want to also include rose or rose geranium petals, lavender, and lemon balm.

Chances are you're familiar with the last three ingredients. To grow hops (and homegrown flowers will be especially fragrant), you'll need something for these vines to climb on—an ornamental arch, or tall poles lashed together in the fashion of a teepee. To shade a patio or porch that takes a beating from the late-day sun, train hops up a trellis.

INTERNATIONAL HERBS

Expand your herb garden to embrace the world.

Do you find yourself frustrated by fascinating ethnic recipes for which you can't find the ingredients? Mexican, Italian, Thai, Indian, Chinese—these are just a few cuisines that rely on exotic herbs and spices. And while the Internet is a boon for tracking down unusual dried ingredients, you can grow a row of hard-to-locate herbs.

❖ **Basil.** Broadly speaking, there are two types of this famously fragrant plant—Italian basil, the main ingredient of pesto; and East Asian basil, which can be redolent of anise, lemon, or lime. All will grow easily in the garden. Just be aware that the first frost will do them in. Pot up a few plants for use indoors.

❖ **Coriander.** Here is another well-traveled herb, figuring importantly in the cooking of both Latin America and East Asia. The pungent leaves are used fresh, either whole or ground into a condiment. Allow the plants to flower and go to seed, and you'll have a supply of another popular form of the plant. Even the roots are put in a stone mortar along with other ingredients to make Thai curries.

To take your garden a bit beyond the ordinary, try the curry plant, native to India and Sri Lanka. The flavor is exotic, and its growth habit is eye-catching as well.

- **Curry.** There's curry powder, commonly available at supermarkets. The curry *plant* is a different item altogether. The rather leathery leaves aren't eaten but added to Indian dishes in the manner of bay leaves for their unusual flavor.

- **Epazote.** Mexican bean dishes often are flavored with this sharp-scented, easily grown herb. Epazote is said to aid in the digestion of beans. There's a medicinal value, too: A substance in the plant, ascaridole, has been found to be poisonous to intestinal worms, should you be so indisposed.

- **Lemongrass.** The thickened base of this tall, attractive grass is used to lend a lemony fragrance to Thai soups and curries. With a bit of luck, you can root clumps from a supermarket or East Asian grocer. Make sure you give lemongrass plenty of light and water, and you'll be rewarded with a good-size stand of plants.

- **Kaffir lime.** Mail-order nurseries sell this small citrus tree, central to the essential flavor of several East Asian cuisines. The leaves are the most commonly used part of the plant, but you also can grate the zest from the hard, nearly juiceless fruits. Kaffir lime will do well in large pots.

- **Zatar.** This Middle Eastern relative of oregano has its own assertive scent. It is mixed with sesame seeds, sumac powder, salt, lemon juice, and olive oil for spreading on pita bread.

For Thai cooking, a vital ingredient is kaffir lime. Recipes most frequently call for the leaf, minced into tiny shreds, but you also can use the zest of the nearly juiceless limes.

MAKE YOUR OWN HERBAL BLENDS

Whether you preserve herbs by drying, freezing, or embalming in bottles of vinegar, try putting up blends of several herbs.

EASY DOES IT

Herbs in a Bunch or a Bag

A traditional way to have the flavor of herbs without the plant parts themselves is to make bouquet garni. Gather sprigs of parsley, thyme, and rosemary, leaving a good length of the stem intact. Pick a bay leaf, again with its stem. Gather these plants in a bunch and bind their stems tightly with enough twine that you can dunk and remove the bundle from soups and stews as they simmer.

You can add the flavor of herbs to soups and stews without having them floating in the final preparation by making a mix of herbs and placing them in a reusable cotton bag with a drawstring. The bags are sold by some mail-order herb nurseries. (By the way, the bags can be used to make sachets for dresser drawers and clothes closets, with no need for sewing.) Toss in anything that appeals to you, fresh or dried. Possibilities include parsley, thyme, bay, rosemary, marjoram, celery and fennel leaves, cloves, and orange or lemon zest.

There is an old tradition of devising well-rounded herbal blends. You can develop your own favorites, or use time-tested recipes that embrace the characteristic flavors of a region. (Consider what our own North American pumpkin pie would taste like without the spices!)

- **Bouquet garni** (France): Bay, parsley, and thyme
- **Fines herbes** (France): Chervil, chive, and tarragon
- **Herbes de Provence** (France): Basil, fennel, lavender, marjoram, rosemary, and thyme
- **Recado rojo** (Mexico): Allspice, annatto, black pepper, cinnamon, clove, cumin, garlic, Mexican oregano (*Lippia graveolens*), salt
- **Chermoula** (Northern Africa): Chili peppers, coriander leaves, cumin, garlic, lemon, olive oil, paprika, saffron
- **Harissa** (Northern Africa): Caraway, chili peppers, coriander, cumin, garlic
- **Zatar** (Middle East): Sesame, sumac, zatar (*Origanum syriacum*)
- **Garam masala** (India): Black pepper, cardamom, cinnamon, clove, coriander, cumin, mace
- **Curry** (India): Black pepper, coriander, cumin, curry leaves, fenugreek, ginger powder, mustard seed, red chilies, turmeric
- **Five-spice** (China): Cinnamon, clove, fennel seeds, star anise, Szechuan peppercorns

You can use branches of herbs as you do a tea bag, dunking them in broths and other dishes long enough to impart flavor, then pulling them back out. To make things tidier, you can wrap a leek stem around the bunch.

AN HERBAL EDUCATION

It's one thing to grow an impressive selection of herbs, and another to know how to use them in the kitchen. A good way to start is to sit down with your favorite cookbooks and a pad of self-adhesive notes. Look up herbs in the index of each book, and turn to recipes incorporating them. Stick a note to mark the place of recipes that sound good to you. Then work your way through these dishes, leaving the note for those that meet with your household's approval. You're apt to find your herbal knowledge expanding considerably. And if your imagination is sparked by recipes for which you don't have herbs on hand, next year's herb garden may expand as well.

A SPICE SHELF IN THE FREEZER

Keep your herbs cold and close at hand.

It's not as convenient as having a spice rack next to the stove, but a well-labeled row of herbs in the freezer will do a superior job of maintaining flavor and aroma. Clip the leaves, including a few flowers if you like. Use scissors or a knife to cut up the herb to the best size for use in the kitchen. Place the herb in resealable plastic bags or small jars. Use an indelible marker to clearly note the name of the herb and the year of the harvest. Devote at least a part of one freezer shelf to these containers, arranging them with their labels facing out.

Assuming the freezer compartment of your refrigerator isn't already crammed, try reserving a shelf in the door for herbs out of the garden that are stored in resealable plastic bags.

NOT THE SAME OLD GRIND

To bring out the full flavor of both fresh and dried herbs, grind them with a traditional mortar and pestle.

Pinching a bit of herb between your fingers will help to bring out its character. You can do this on a larger scale with a mortar and pestle—a sturdy vessel in which a stout, rounded rod is used for grinding. These are available in different types of stone, wood, and pottery, and each material has its advantages. Try grinding Thai curry pastes, Indian spices, and Italian pesto from your own garden-grown ingredients.

CHAPTER 9

Tools, Supports, and Storage

Every gardener starts out with a plot of ground, a shovel, and a few packets of seeds. And that's all you need, at the absolute minimum, to coax edibles and ornamentals from the yard. For most of us, however, the equipment tends to proliferate. Tools, sprayers, fencing, gadgets to scare away pests—all have the potential to make gardening easier and more productive. Some, like a good trowel or clever one-wheel cultivator, can be a pleasure to use as well.

Eventually, the well-equipped gardener may feel a bit overwhelmed by the need to clean and maintain and store this hardware. There can be a move toward simplicity, scaling back just a bit in order to get closer to the simple pleasures of collaborating with nature on a lovely day. It's a matter of balance between convenience and complexity—between time-saving equipment and finding the time to manage a garage full of stuff.

HOE HONING

Wield a sharp hoe and make short work of guillotining the weeds.

In the kitchen, you wouldn't waste your energy chopping up vegetables with a dull knife, but chances are the blade of your garden hoe hasn't gotten much attention lately. And yet if you want to efficiently deal with weeds, a sharp blade is important.

To put a keen edge on a hoe, use a *mill file,* a flat file with fine teeth that's available at hardware stores. Since you'll be turning your homely hoe into a weed weapon, you should wear work gloves and sharpen with care. Support the hoe, blade up, and go over the beveled edge of its blade, typically along the outer side. Hold the file at about a 45-degree angle, drawing it away from the handle as you slide it along the entire width of the blade. Repeat the stroke as needed.

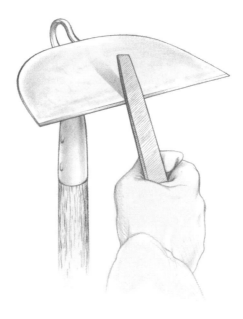

A hoe does have a blade, so it shouldn't be surprising to learn that it will be a better weapon against weeds if it's kept sharp.

TOOLS, SUPPORTS, AND STORAGE

REPLACE A HANDLE, SPARE A SHOVEL

You may know the humorous story of the 300-year-old axe that still cuts beautifully: The only maintenance it needed was the occasional replacement of the head or the handle. You're better off replacing just the handle of your tools.

EASY DOES IT

Handles with Care

To get more years of use out of garden tools, take extra care with wooden handles. First and foremost, bring tools undercover when they aren't in use, rather than subject them to the elements. And treat them to an occasional restoring treatment with sandpaper and penetrating oil. Sand the handles smooth, then rub linseed, Danish, or tung oil on them with a piece of cloth.

If a shovel or hoe has served you well, you may be reluctant to chuck it when the handle breaks. Chances are you'll be able to replace it.

To remove an old handle, either grind the rivet down with a mill file or saw it off with a hacksaw. Drive out the rivet by tapping with a punch or a large nail. Take the shovel or hoe head to a hardware store to find a handle that will fit. A bit of filing may be necessary; use a wood rasp with coarse teeth for this part of the job. Drive the handle into place by tapping its end with a hammer cushioned with a piece of scrap wood. Secure the handle by drilling a ⅛-inch-diameter pilot hole for a wood screw.

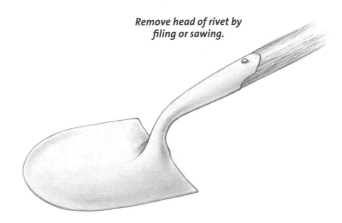

Remove head of rivet by filing or sawing.

To remove the broken handle of a shovel, file away or saw off the rivet holding it in place.

THE LONG AND SHORT OF SHOVELS

Choosing a shovel is a matter of personal preference and personal stature.

Check Out Your Tools

You may be the exceptional gardener who rarely leaves implements outside and returns them to their proper place. If not, try a simple check-out system to keep track. Hang a clipboard where you store tools, attach a pencil on a string, and get in the habit of noting what you'll be taking out in the yard and where. This is also a handy place to keep a shopping list for the hardware store and garden center, so that you don't end up standing in the aisles on a Saturday morning wondering just what it was you needed.

Shovels come with short D-handles and long straight handles. Which is best? That depends on you, and what you intend to accomplish in the garden. You're apt to experience less back strain with a long handle. Yet while a short handle requires you to bend a good deal more, it will make more efficient use of your energy. You might want to buy one of each, reserving the short shovel for short bursts of relatively intense digging. Chances are you'll find yourself reaching for the longer one most of the time.

GARDEN TOOLS FOR WOMEN

There are female gardeners stronger and taller than some male gardeners, of course. But very generally speaking, women may find that they prefer lighter, smaller-scaled tools, as well as those that have advanced ergonomic designs to make the most of the user's strength. The advantages go beyond comfort. A properly sized tool is more efficient, will be less likely to trigger an injury, and even can give your body a superior workout.

The most obvious requirement is a pair of gloves for smaller hands, rather than settling for the usual one-size-fits-all jumbos. Several companies now market lines of tools especially for women, including trowels, pruning shears, a lightweight cordless drill for outdoor build-it projects, and a lightweight string trimmer. Women may want to look for a border spade rather than a standard shovel, because the blade is lighter and considerably smaller in area. There also are garden clogs and kneepads sized for smaller gardeners. Whatever the tool, it's a good idea to get a sense of how it feels in the hand when shopping, evaluating both weight and size.

GARDEN TOOLS FOR KIDS

There's no better way to introduce children to chores than getting them involved in gardening. The work isn't exactly child's play, but it can be enjoyable on a lovely day and with reasonably defined tasks. And the kids can look forward to the payoff of a flavorful harvest in several weeks' time. To make sure they will really contribute and not just playact at gardening, it helps to equip them with specially made, specially sized equipment—watering can, brightly colored hand tools, shovel, rake, and hoe. There are kid-size wheelbarrows, and Troy-Bilt, the well-known garden equipment supplier, sells a serious-looking metal wagon with beefy tires and wooden sides. Don't forget little work gloves, as well as a sun hat of some kind.

Small but sturdy garden tools, like this stake-sided wagon, can help introduce kids to gardening and yard work.

GARDEN SAFE

A huge percentage of accidents happen within a short distance of home, and that includes the garden.

ADVICE OVER THE FENCE

Treat Cuts and Scrapes with Herbs

For superficial cuts and scrapes that don't require medical attention, consider your garden as a remedy source.

Aloe (*Aloe vera*). It's not just for burns anymore. Aloe reduces inflammation and feels soothing, plus it's antibacterial.

Calendula (*Calendula officinalis*). Anti-inflammatory, astringent, and antiseptic, calendula promotes new skin growth. You can use the fresh or dried flowers in a compress.

Comfrey (*Symphytum officinale*). Comfrey speeds healing. To make a comfrey-leaf poultice, wrap fresh or dried leaves in a clean, wet cloth and apply.

Plantain (*Plantago* spp.). This weed contains antimicrobial and anti-inflammatory substances and the tissue-knitting substance allantoin. Mash a few leaves into a poultice and apply to a wound.

According to the Consumer Product Safety Commission, in a recent year nearly 39,000 people were admitted to emergency rooms with injuries related to gardening tools and supplies. Toiling in the soil needn't be that hazardous to health. Here are a few precautions you might want to take.

- Make like an athlete, and go through a slow, careful set of stretching exercises before and after each session in the garden.

- Be mindful of repetitive motions, which tend to be particularly tough on wrists, elbows, knees, and the back. Get in the habit of taking frequent breaks.

- Use fertilizers, pesticides, and herbicides with care. That should go without saying, but it's good to keep in mind that even natural products may carry potential risks.

- Be sure that electric tools are plugged into ground-fault-interrupter circuits.

- In hot weather, dress right—loose-fitting, light-colored clothes and a hat that does a serious job of shielding you from the sun.

- Stay hydrated, no matter what the temperature is. Don't wait until you're parched to take a sip. And lay off the alcoholic and sugary drinks, no matter how good you think they might taste—they are apt to deplete the body's store of water.

- Make sure your tetanus/diphtheria vaccination is up to date.

HEAVY LIFTING WITH A WHEELED FRIEND

Garden carts and wheelbarrows can be enlisted to help lift rocks, peat moss bales, and balled trees.

Don't test your back by lifting big rocks and bales of peat moss. Let a garden cart do it for you, with another person on hand. Approach the all-but-immovable object with a cart that has a removable front panel. Slide off the panel, and lift the handle of the cart to bring its front edge to the ground. Then roll or slide the payload into the cart while your helper leans on the cart handle to bring it upright.

A version of this no-lift technique works with a wheelbarrow. Tilt the wheelbarrow on its side next to the object. Then push or roll the object into the tray while also pressing on the top edge of the tray, and have a helper assist you in righting the wheelbarrow.

To move a heavy stone, roll it into a garden cart or wheelbarrow that's sturdily constructed and able to safely handle the weight.

HARD-PACKED SOIL A HEADACHE?

Seriously compacted soil calls for a specialty tool. Try a mattock!

◤ Next Year's Garden

Stone Harvest

Stones are an impediment to good gardening, of course. But as you unearth them, consider their merits for various uses around the yard. You might classify them in three piles—big stones for walls, medium ones for edging, and little ones for filling in low places around the property. If you can't get to these projects right away, use a wheelbarrow or sturdy garden cart to move the stones to an inconspicuous spot for storage. Keep weeds from working up through the stones by placing them on a plastic tarp.

There are times when a shovel just won't cut it—won't cut into dense, clay-rich soil littered with stones, that is. For tough jobs, it's good to have a mattock on hand. There are a number of different versions, but a particularly useful one has a narrow blade on one end of the head and a pick on the other. Between the two, you can effectively loosen up any kind of soil to the point that it will be receptive to a shovel. As with swinging an axe (or a golf club, for that matter), you have to make certain that no one is anywhere near the arc of the tool as you swing it.

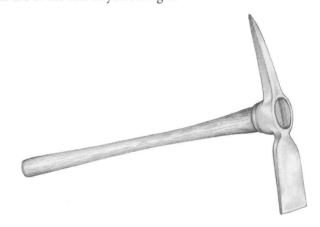

A mattock isn't a tool you'll use every day, but it comes in mighty handy if you need to break up uncooperative soils.

KNIVES FOR GARDENERS

You can get by in the yard with a standard pocket or utility knife, but specialized blades can make work go more quickly and pleasurably.

In the same way that you find yourself reaching for a certain knife in the kitchen, you may prefer a favorite tool when working in the garden and around the yard. Serious gardeners swear by their special-purpose knives, and there are beautifully crafted models that (for a price) have the look of family heirlooms in the making.

❖ It's fascinating (and free) to make new plants by taking cuttings and severing layered stems, and the right knife can be a big help. A *propagation* or *grafting knife* has a short, ultra-sharp blade for making clean cuts. You can buy a model with a fixed blade, or a folding blade that makes it unnecessary to have a sheath.

❖ A *pruning knife* is sturdily built to handle the task of cutting smaller branches, and some models have a distinctively curved blade.

❖ For lopping vegetables in larger plots, it helps to have a *lettuce* or *vegetable harvesting knife*. The shorter edge of the blade is used to sever plants at the stem, while the longer edge is handy for trimming leaves on cabbage as well as harvesting. A plastic-handled version will cost less than one with wood.

❖ To keep blades at their optimal sharpest, you can carry a lightweight set of *mini-hones* with you in the yard. Use them for knives and pruners as you go about your work.

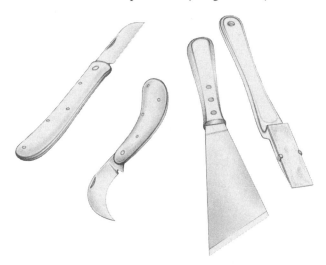

Special-purpose knives will make certain garden and orchard tasks go just a little more smoothly, especially if you regularly sharpen the knives with hones.

A HUMAN-POWERED WEED WHACKER

The scythe is a silent, smokeless way of controlling long grasses and weeds.

EASY DOES IT

Far-Reaching Tools

Not all gardening and landscaping tasks are comfortably close at hand. Trees grow to an inconvenient height, and thorny brambles may be unapproachable. Look into buying "stretch" tools with extensions that allow you to stay on the ground or at a safe distance when cutting and snipping. You'll spend less time wobbling on a ladder and nursing scratches. For versatility, consider loppers with telescopic handles that extend to 36 inches or more. Tree trimming is a lot easier with a pole pruner and lopper; the work is done by both a fine-toothed saw and a rope-activated lopper at the far end of a lightweight pole. If your home center doesn't stock these tools, consult the phone book or go online for orchardists' supplies.

For centuries, the scythe has been used to keep down brushy areas and also harvest crops. You operate it with a gently pivoting motion, feet planted securely and the upper body torqueing to and fro. It's a restful activity, and an ideal way to manage rank growth around the property, without the prep time and maintenance involved with operating a gas-powered string trimmer. They're available in beautifully curved wood, as well as in lightweight aluminum. You also can choose between blades suited for grasses and stouter steel for dealing with brush.

This isn't to say that a scythe is maintenance free. You should pause every 10 minutes or so to run a sharpening stone over the blade (and to lower your pulse rate). Over time, the blade will need to have its edge re-formed by peening with a special-purpose hammer and anvil, sold by the mail-order companies that deal in scythes.

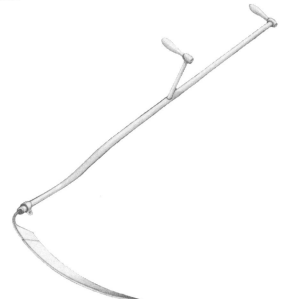

The long, curving blade of a scythe makes short work of felling tall grasses and weeds. You'll get a workout in the bargain.

ONE-WHEEL WONDER

Try this traditional pint-size plow to speed garden work.

Imagine a cultivating tool that's somewhere between a plain old shovel and a fume-belching tiller, one that does its work efficiently but without a noisy engine. That's a fair description of a wheel hoe, a traditional device that you push like a little plow. They've been used for more than a century, and you sometimes can find them inexpensively at yard sales and auctions. If you're willing to spend a bit more, consider buying an updated version, with a pneumatic tire to make the rolling a bit easier and attachments including a variety of hoes, hillers, and cultivators.

A wheel hoe makes efficient use of your energy, while sparing you the jarring, repetitive motions that can be involved with hoeing.

HOSE-TAMING TRICKS

Don't let garden hoses trip you up. Show them who's boss.

A Self-Propelled Sprinkler

Even if you use an oscillating sprinkler to water the lawn, you still face the task of moving the sprinkler to cover the area. Unless, that is, you purchase a traveling sprinkler that uses water pressure to drive itself slowly across the yard. The unit follows the course you've established by laying down a garden hose. Some models have automatic shutoffs, sparing you that bit of bother as well.

Garden hoses have a way of making trouble, sideswiping delicate plantings and getting underfoot. Here are a few ways of managing them.

❖ Put hose bumpers at the corners of beds, using either the commercial type that spins, the screw-in soil anchors sold for trellis wires, or large potted plants set a couple of inches into the ground.

❖ Get reel. Buy a hose reel, either freestanding or one intended to be mounted on a wall. There's even a model that uses the flow of the water to do the reeling for you.

❖ Bury hoses from the faucet at the house to individual gardens or beds.

❖ To avoid tripping on a hose across a walk, dig a tunnel under the walk (in an inconspicuous spot, if possible) and line it with a section of PVC pipe from the plumbing section of a home center or hardware store. It's easy to slip a hose through the plastic pipe.

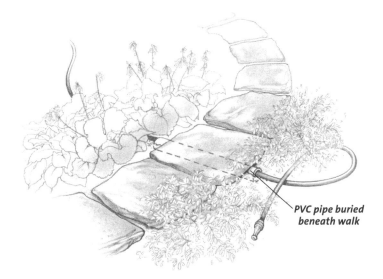

PVC pipe buried beneath walk

By running a garden hose under a frequently used walk, you just might prevent a tripping accident. The hose can be pulled freely through a length of PVC pipe.

A MINDFUL MOWER

Here is the best automatic mower since sheep were invented.

The future is here—or at least it could be out on your lawn. The RoboMower, by Friendly Robotics, is a cute-looking automatic mower that quietly goes about taking care of that most tedious of outdoor tasks. It can operate for 3 hours on a battery charge, and it's kept from wandering off to neighboring lawns by a boundary wire that can be buried in the yard. A basic model sells for about $1,200. For a bit more, you can have a programmable RoboMower that will start mowing at a preset time and even chug on back to its docking station for recharging. And how do you keep a jealous homeowner from pirating your unattended mower? You can't, but the more-expensive model can be made to operate only when the correct four-digit code is input.

This sleek battery-operated robot mower will take over the job of trimming the lawn, freeing you up for other gardening and landscaping tasks.

EVERY GARDENER NEEDS A COAT HOOK

Simple amenities can make the garden a more pleasant place to work.

EASY DOES IT

Postal Tool Garage

To keep your gardening hand tools, twine, and stakes where you need them—in the garden—set up a mailbox on a fence post, either using an old box found at a yard sale or buying an inexpensive one from a discount store. You can spare yourself trips back to the house by also using the box to store spare gloves and suntan lotion.

Each year, on average, gardeners in the United States leave 65,000 jackets, 24,000 hats, 300 pairs of binoculars, 250 cameras, and 200 wristwatches out in the garden to be rained on.

Well, those are fictional numbers. But they help make the case for putting a coat hook or two out in the garden. Mount it on a gate or fence post that you'll pass by on your way back into the house. Rare is the gardener who hasn't left *something* outside to be subjected to the elements. And if you have one spot dedicated to hanging stuff, there's less chance of being forgetful than if you just toss that jacket over the nearest stationary object. While you're at it, you might also put a ring minder on the post, if you're one of those gardeners who doffs a ring or two whenever digging in the dirt.

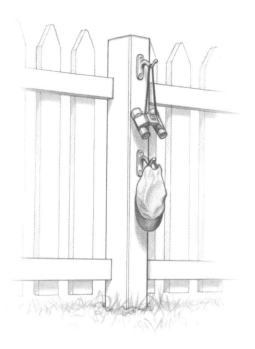

A couple of hooks on a post is all it takes to prevent you from tossing personal items on the ground and forgetting about them. It's best to mount the hooks on a post near the gate so that you'll see these items on your way back into the house.

A PLATFORM BED FOR SQUASH

Build a low platform to keep squash and pumpkins from groveling in the dirt.

Squash plants love to sprawl, casually plopping their fruits right down on the bare ground where nibbling pests and soil-borne diseases are apt to cause damage. An easy remedy is to elevate the vines on a low platform over which you stretch chicken wire.

Build the frame so that the platform is from 6 to 12 inches above the ground, and no larger than you can move easily. Because these plants tend to spread over a wide area, you may want to use several frames, arranged side by side and end to end. Use 1-by-3 lumber for smaller frames, or 2-by-4s for larger ones, with the wider face of the boards vertical. Drive screws at the corners to assemble the frame. Then add the legs, attaching them with screws to the outside of the frame as shown. Cut a rectangle of chicken wire to size and attach it to the top of the frame with a staple gun.

Plant the squash as usual, and be sure to mulch well around the emerging plants—once the frames are in place, it will be difficult to add to this layer. As the vines begin to grow, gently guide them up through the holes in the chicken wire. Not only will the squash survive the season in good shape, but you won't have to bend down quite so low to hunt for them under those broad leaves.

At season's end, clear out the spent vines. Store the frames for the winter in a dry place if possible.

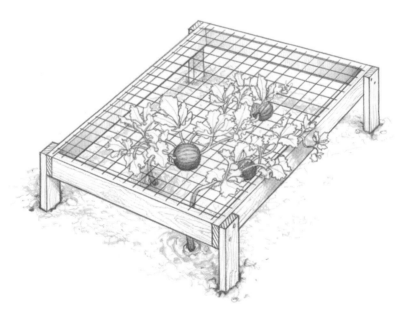

Only the roots of squash plants need to be in contact with the ground. A platform keeps their fruits clean and can help to prevent trouble from diseases.

A STURDIER TOMATO CAGE

These rugged plants need serious support; flimsy alternatives just won't hold up.

Tomato plants can quickly become unruly as they grow lavishly in every direction, and indeterminate varieties are especially vigorous. The best way to contain that green zeal is to construct a cage—a sturdy cage. The standard commercial versions tend to be expensive if you grow more than a few plants, and they're often flimsy as well. As for homemade cages, they are prone to flopping over and often don't last more than a few seasons. Instead, make cages out of wide-spaced cement reinforcing mesh. Chances are you won't find it at a home and garden center. Locate a concrete supply firm in the phone book, and buy a roll of mesh with holes at least 6 inches square—large enough so that you can reach in and extract a nice, big tomato.

Form each piece into a cylinder about 24 inches in diameter, then use pliers to hook the clipped ends of one cut edge around the wires of the other edge. If the cages are too narrow to stand upright by themselves, drive in a pair of wood or metal stakes inside each cage, placing them opposite one another.

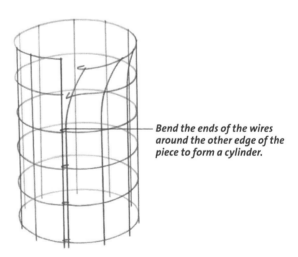

Bend the ends of the wires around the other edge of the piece to form a cylinder.

Reinforcing wire is used to make concrete stronger; a cage of the beefy stuff will do the same for your tomato plants.

TRASH-TO-TRELLIS TOMATOES

Bits of timber, branches, or what-have-you can make for an interesting tomato trellis in a pot.

If your yard is tiny and even your patio seems overfurnished, you still might be able to find room for a tomato plant by training it up a trellis. First, choose an indeterminate tomato variety—one that will keep growing indefinitely rather than remain in a bush shape. (Most older, traditional varieties are indeterminate.) Second, select a pot that will hold at least 10 gallons of planting medium. Third, get creative with your support trellis. You can use a panel of lattice, a section of wrought-iron fence stood on end, an old (and no longer trustworthy) wooden ladder sawed down to size, the stiles from a ladderback chair, or even a tree branch. To make sure the support won't topple in a wind, attach it to screw eyes driven into door or window trim, to shutter hardware, or to metal stakes driven into the ground on either side. Guide the stems up through the support, and tie them as necessary with strips of cloth. Keep in mind that potted plants may get little water if placed along a wall with rain gutters above. You'll have to make up the deficit.

To give a potted tomato plant plenty of sunlight, train it up a trellis you fashion yourself.

A GARDEN GATEWAY

This is an abbreviated arbor, suitable for an entrance to a yard or the garden. It also can be a freestanding object on which climbing plants will have a field day.

What You'll Need

125 feet 1 × 4 pine

#6 × 1⅝-inch galvanized screws

#6 × 2-inch galvanized screws

1½-inch galvanized finishing nails

1½-inch galvanized spiral nails

2-inch galvanized spiral nails

2½-inch galvanized spiral nails

Use this gateway to formalize the transition between spaces on your property. Or simply put it in a highly visible spot—at the edge of a patio, perhaps—and train plants up its sides. The decorative side panels shown in the drawing are just a suggestion. You can substitute store-bought lattice, or a pattern of your own choice. The rafters are decorative, and they also help plants to grow right over the top for a living arch. If the gateway is to serve as an entrance to the garden, you can build a gate for it, repeating the design theme of the sides. The overall dimensions of the project are 84 inches high, 42 inches wide, and 28 inches deep. It is assembled with screws and water-resistant polyvinyl acetate glue (such as Titebond II), as well as with finishing nails and varying lengths of spiral nails. The parts are put together with glue on their mating surfaces, then clamped before driving screws or nailing.

Although this project is fairly straightforward, with no complicated joinery, you may want to turn the job over to a carpenter if you don't have the necessary skills or tools. The structure is made out of 1 × 4 boards. You can rip the narrower pieces from a 1 × 4 with a table saw. Or, if you don't have that tool, you can substitute 1 × 1s and 1 × 2s from off the home center or lumberyard shelf.

1. Make the posts. Each post is a two-piece assembly, with a broad face and a post center. The two are joined with glue and spiral nails.

2. There are little capitals, a design detail that makes a visual transition between the horizontal lintels and the vertical posts. Glue and nail two capitals to the edge of each lintel, setting them in from the ends of the lintel.

3. Each lintel spans a pair of posts, with its capitals resting on the post center pieces. Assembling them goes more easily on a level work surface. Place the posts on the surface and clamp them to it. Next, place the lintel-and-capital assembly across the posts,

with the outside edge of the posts set in from the ends of the capitals. Clamp the assembly together. Use glue, then drive screws through the face of the lintel and into the posts.

4. Add the cornice, which is a horizontal piece that is attached with glue and nails to the lintel and rests atop the posts.

5. Assemble the grille panels on either side of the gateway, gluing and nailing spacer blocks between the strips in the grille.

6. Attach the three grille rails to each grille panel, using glue and screws.

7. Assemble the gateway, clamp the grille rails to the posts, and join them with screws.

8. You may want to add the rafters outdoors, if you've been working inside, because they could make it impossible to get the thing out of the door.

9. To make the job a little more finished in appearance, you can cover the row of screw heads where the grilles are attached to the grille rails. The strips are just ½ inch thick, 1 inch wide, and 12 inches long. Attach them with glue and by drilling pilot holes and driving finishing nails.

10. To install the gateway, place the posts on bricks or flat stones. Anchor the posts by driving wooden stakes into the ground alongside them, and attach the two with screws or by tying.

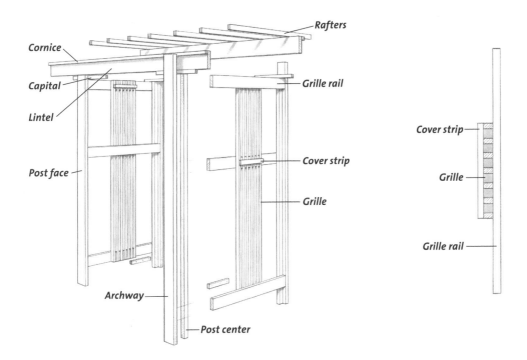

A gracious gateway is lovely to look at, while welcoming us to whatever lies beyond. It also gives you an opportunity to try growing climbing plants—including those you would rather not allow to crawl all over your house.

A SIMPLE SOLUTION TO KEEP POTS FROM TIPPING

To keep potted plants from being knocked over by the first good wind, stake them to the ground.

EASY DOES IT

An ID Card for Tomatoes and Peppers

Standard garden labels tend to disappear as tomato and pepper plants grow. To make sure you can tell what's what throughout the season, make durable plastic tags and place them close to eye level, at the top of cages or stakes. Cut rectangles out of square-sided cider or milk jugs; write the variety name on each tag with an indelible marker; use a hole punch or a nail to make a hole at one corner; and tie the tags to the supports.

If you grow large pepper or indeterminate tomatoes in pots, first of all you'll need a big pot—10 to 15 gallons. Second, to both support the plant and keep it from acting like a sail and blowing over, place the pot where you want it and drive a long metal or wood stake down through the drainage hole and well into the ground below. You may need to make additional holes in the bottom of the pot to ensure good drainage. Add potting medium and plant the tomato or pepper.

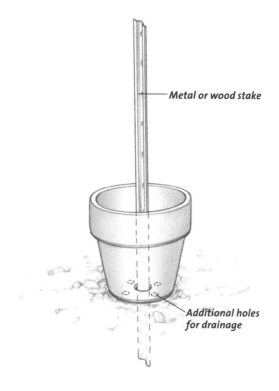

Metal or wood stake

Additional holes for drainage

By driving a stake through the bottom of a large pot, you can anchor it securely to the ground. Add soil after the staking operation.

BUILD A BEAN HOUSE

You can give beans a lot of sunlight and room for climbing with this PVC structure.

Think of this simple structure as a double trellis on which you can grow a whopping harvest of climbing beans. The house is made of 1-inch-diameter PVC pipe, available at home centers and plumbing supply companies. The pipe is a snap to cut with a hacksaw, and the pieces for this project come together easily with 45-degree and 90-degree elbows and 3-way connectors.

1. Assemble the structure to approximately the illustrated shape. For a permanent structure, you can join the pieces with PVC solvent. Or just go with a friction fit if you'd prefer to disassemble and store the house each fall. Use nylon cord to lash the two horizontal pieces at the top of both sides, as shown.

2. To attach the twine for the beans, drill pilot holes at evenly spaced intervals and install cup hooks, at the top, the horizontal side pieces, and the bottom.

3. Run twine between the hooks, then plant the beans.

4. Once the beans have been harvested, snip the twine and clear away the vines. By draping clear plastic sheeting over the house, you can have a temporary greenhouse in which to protect plants from the cold weather that's ahead. Seal the seams between sheets with clear packing tape. Use the greenhouse again in spring to start seedlings, before the soil warms up enough for beans.

For beans that love to climb, this PVC-built frame gives plenty of room to romp.

A TOOL HOUSE

Tired of toting tools? Build a simple shelter for them right in the garden.

What You'll Need

32 feet 1 × 2 pine

16 feet 1 × 4 pine

16 feet 1 × 5 pine

96 feet 1 × 6 pine

⅙ sheet ½-inch CDX plywood

#6 × 1¼-inch galvanized screws

#6 × 1⅝-inch galvanized screws

#6 × 2-inch galvanized screws

Six 4-inch galvanized tee hinges

One 3-inch barrel bolt

Gardening requires enough labor without making repeated trips between wherever you stash implements and the garden itself. An attractive tool house, just deep enough to hold a row of commonly used hand tools, can be a great convenience. The structure is just a box, basically, with a little shed roof. It can be attached to the wall of your house or garage, or anchored to a sturdy garden post. To keep the wood from rotting at the lower edge of the tool house, the sides rest on either bricks or concrete blocks. The inside of the structure measures 9 inches deep, 34 inches wide, and 6 feet high. Although you can make all the cuts needed for the project with a handsaw, the work goes much more quickly with a circular saw. The construction is of solid wood, capped by a plywood roof, and assembled with both screws and water-resistant polyvinyl acetate glue. Parts are put together with glue on their mating surfaces, then clamped before driving the screws. Each door is hung with three tee hinges, and they are secured with a barrel bolt.

The instructions and drawing given here offer general ideas on how to go about building a tool house. If you don't have basic carpentry skills and tools, you can ask a carpenter to do the work.

1. To limit waste, buy 6-foot or 12-foot boards for the 1 × 6s used to make the sides, back, and doors—not 8-footers.

2. Begin by constructing each side, attaching the three rails to its inside surface. Cut the roof pitch at the top of the side, using the top rail as a guide. Attach the back retainers to each side, placing one above and one below the middle rail.

3. Make the back, attaching its two rails to the back boards. Leave a little space between each of the back boards to allow them to expand and contract with changes in the weather.

4. Attach the back to the sides.

5. Make the bottom by attaching two boards into the bottom side rails.

6. Make the front rail, which ties the top of the tool house together.

7. Add the roof, attaching it by driving screws into the pitched sides.

8. Make each door from three boards, attaching its two rails and the diagonal brace to the back surface.

9. Hang each door with three tee hinges, then make the door stop, which closes the gap at the top of the doors and gives you a place to mount the *strike* (or top component) of the barrel bolt. Attach the door stop to the back of the front rail.

10. Make the door batten and attach it to the outside edge of one door. The batten acts as a lip to hold the other door closed.

11. Mount the barrel bolt at the top of the door with the batten. Mount the strike on the door stop.

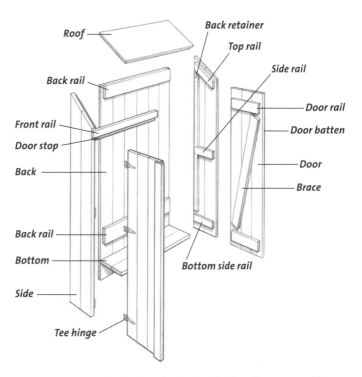

This shallow tool house is a handy place for hand tools. If you have reasonable carpentry skills, you should be able to build it in a day.

KNOTS FOR CLIMBERS

Give plants a lift with properly tied twine.

Next Year's Garden

Peonies with Good Posture

If your peonies have a tough time holding up those oversize blossoms, give them help next time around. Grow hoops specially made for peonies can give them help without being obvious. The hoops have a grid of wires through which the growing stems find their way. Eventually, the plant's generous foliage all but conceals the device. If you're not eager to add supporting peonies to your gardening chores, you can choose to plant single forms, rather than the heavy-headed doubles.

As a 1928 Kansas Agricultural Experiment Station guide to growing grapes put it, "Tie promptly and use only square knots." That bit of advice still is worth following, for all sorts of plants that need a lift. Make the knots as soon as they are needed, rather than trying to force a plant to conform to a trellis or other means of support and risk breaking a vine or stem. Use a square knot, as shown here. And keep plenty of sisal trellis twine on hand. Check with garden stores and look in catalogs for twine that hasn't been chemically treated, so that you won't have any qualms about tossing it in the compost bin when gathering plant waste at the end of the season.

Tie twine snugly around support

Create a loop to allow plant to grow freely

This hoop with its grid looks odd when the peony is just beginning its growth, but soon enough the hoop will be concealed by the plant, lending it support.

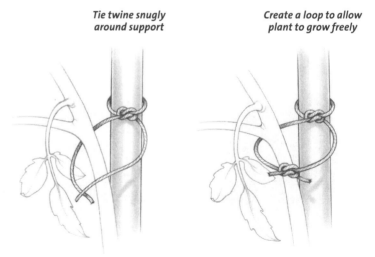

To tie up a plant, begin with a snug square knot on the support, as shown. Then make a loop to support the plant without binding it.

CHAPTER 10

Out in the Yard

How does your garden grow? Chances are it began with a particular focus, maybe as modest as belting the house with foundation plantings and the usual sort of cheery annuals. Other homeowners concentrate on growing vegetables, or perennials, or wildflowers, or fruit-bearing bushes. Whatever the case, one interest leads to another, and one gardening bed tends to become three or four, in various parts of the yard. In the process, gardeners learn the best qualities of their piece of land, in terms of soil and sun and gradient, and take advantage of these strong points by choosing certain kinds of plants. While most plants like lots of light and well-drained, humus-rich soil, that probably doesn't describe very many yards. And so, in addition to improving the soil, we learn to fit plant to place.

The result can be an interesting landscape, diverse and diverting, with features and varieties that are a bit out of the ordinary. Instead of tending a couple of isolated special-purpose beds, gardeners with some experience begin to think in terms of the entire yard, and how one part relates to all the rest. The reward is a great-looking piece of real estate. Beyond that, we enjoy a closer connection with the land. Rather than imposing our ideas upon it, we work with it. This final chapter suggests a few ways of enriching that relationship.

RADICAL PRUNING

Prune boldly and these shrubs will thank you for it.

When it comes to certain shrubs, it's easy to have too much of a good thing. Buddleia, caryopteris, forsythia, kolkwitzia (beauty bush), lilac, and mock orange have an exuberance that makes them easy to grow. But if you've skipped pruning them for several years, they may have become leggy and overgrown. When plants are dormant, lop them just above the ground. If stems are too thick for lopping, go at them with a saw.

This may seem like a drastic step, but it will hurt you more than it hurts the plants. Come next spring, they will sprout new growth and quickly revive.

WONDERING WHEN TO WATER?

A rain gauge takes some of the subjectivity out of judging the soil's moisture level.

It's easy to slip into a routine of watering plants according to some predetermined schedule. That's a good way to avoid forgetting to get out the hose, but it doesn't take rainfall into consideration. To make sure that vegetables and ornamentals get the moisture they require—no more and no less—it helps to have a simple rain gauge out in the yard. Attach one to a fence post, and check it each time it rains. Spend a bit more, and you can buy a gauge with a float that makes it easier to read the level. You might want a second gauge, to set out on the lawn or in a bed to determine how much water a sprinkler is delivering.

SHRUBS FREE FOR THE DIGGING!

Layering is one of nature's ways of propagating, and it can be one of yours, too.

To fill out sparsely planted beds and break up uninteresting expanses of lawn, shrubs can come to the rescue. Before going shopping, have a look at the shrubs you already have. They can be the mothers of a new generation of genetically identical shrubs, through *layering*—encouraging a branch to grow roots, then severing it to make an independent plant. In effect, the mother plant feeds and waters what will be the new shrub. Try layering with blueberry, daphne, hibiscus, hydrangea, kerria, lavender, mock orange, mountain laurel, spirea, viburnum, or any of the favorites growing in your yard.

1. In early spring when the mother shrub is growing vigorously, identify a low-growing branch.
2. Scoop out a shallow trough in which to lay the central portion of the branch.
3. Place the branch in the trough, with a few inches at the growing end left above ground level. To help ensure success, you can sprinkle the portion to be buried with rooting hormone.
4. Fill in the trough, and keep the branch in place either by weighing it with a brick or stone or anchoring it with a wire staple.
5. In fall, sever the branch close to the shrub. Lift the cutting with some soil intact, and plant it.

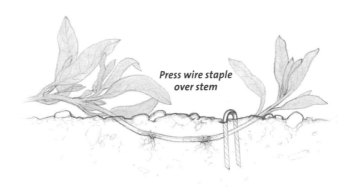

Press wire staple over stem

To get new plants off to a quick and sturdy start, try layering instead of growing from seeds.

WHEN PROPAGATION ISN'T A PLUS

If shrubs are too eager, think sterile.

Certain shrubs will give rise to a wealth of seedlings, more than you can use, so that controlling these freebies is added to your landscaping chores. Look for sterile hybrids of your favorite plants to keep these pets from becoming pests. For example, the Buddleia hybrids 'Lochinch' (with fragrant purple flowers) and 'Sungold' (yellow flowers) will stay politely within their bounds. Sterile Rose of Sharon cultivars, *Hybiscus mutabilis × syriacus,* include 'Tosca' (lavender flowers with a carmine eye) and 'Lohengrin' (white flowers). While winterberry euonymus (*Euonymus fortunei*) can be invasive, you can go with wintercreeper euonymus 'Purpurea' and sterile variegated forms.

FENCE POST FINIALS

Here's a quick way to dress up a humdrum vegetable patch. After all, we do like to have a nice-looking plot.

Sure, all you need to keep a fence from falling down is a row of 4 × 4s. But with little trouble and not much expense, you can dress up the garden with finials. Woodworker supply catalogs sell wooden balls equipped with screws set into the base. They're primarily intended as finials for banisters and such but will serve outside as well. Order balls with a diameter appropriate to the dimension of the posts—you wouldn't want them to look like golf balls balanced up there. Drill a pilot hole into the top of the post, then just give the ball a spin to install it. To keep these ornaments from cracking, it's best to apply a finish. For clear wood, use linseed oil or a commercial penetrating varnish. Or just paint both finials and posts.

A HEADBOARD GATE

For a stylish entrance to your beds, use part of a salvaged bed.

Old pipe-frame beds can be had cheaply at antique and used-furniture shops. Look at them with an eye to using an ornate, gracefully curving headboard as a garden gate. If it's from a larger bed, the headboard may be wide enough to admit a garden cart. Hang the headboard from a sturdily anchored metal post with two or three pairs of gate hinges. The two-part hinges shown here are clamped to the post and the headboard; to secure the swinging end of the gate, use a similar two-part latch.

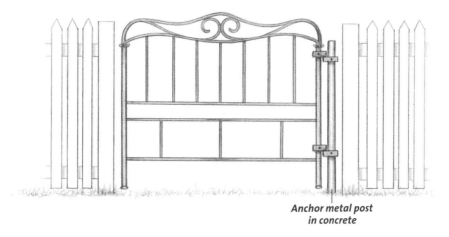

Anchor metal post in concrete

For a garden gate with a little flair, look for a headboard at a used-furniture store. You can add hardware cloth along the bottom to keep out nibbling wildlife.

GETTING A FORMAL YARD TO RELAX

Here are fixes for an all-too-proper property.

Want to break away from the lockstep routines of mowing, edging, and leaf blowing? First, *you* may have to relax. According to the Environmental Protection Agency (EPA), the key to having a more natural home landscape is to strive for a balance between your need for a controlled, attractive yard and the natural world's need for diversity. The weed ordinances of your municipality may also have to relax a bit, if you want to go with something other than a picture-perfect lawn.

A WILDFLOWER MEADOW

Convert part of the yard to a wildflower patch. It may be tempting to buy a "wildflower meadow in a can," scratch the ground, scatter the seed, and hope for the best. But if native perennials in a mix are to become established, you have to do some groundwork. To kill off competing weeds, you can *solarize* the meadow-to-be by laying a sheet of clear plastic over it and weighting the perimeter with rocks or a berm of soil. A month of sunny summer weather should do a good job of cooking whatever is underneath. Another strategy is to create a "stale bed" for the seeds. This involves tilling the soil and allowing a flush of weeds to sprout—as they probably will, having been brought close to the surface. Then till again to kill them, or cook them with a propane flamer, sold by mail-order garden supply firms. If you want to convert existing lawn to a meadow, roll off the sod to expose bare earth. You can rent a sod cutter to make the work go faster for a good-size area.

You're then ready for fall planting (the best choice for sites warmer than Zone 6) or planting the following spring (in cooler zones.) To make it easier to evenly distribute seed, you can mix it with light-colored sand. Broadcast the seed by hand over small plots, or use a crank-operated seed spreader for a larger meadow. Rake in the seed, then spread a light covering of straw. From there, it's a matter of watering if needed—and taking out weeds, which certainly *will* be needed. Mowing once a year will favor the plants

Good Grasses for a Mix

Big and little bluestem (*Andro-pogon geradii* and *A. sco-parios*)

Sideoats grama (*Bouteloua cur-tipendula*)

Lesser quaking grass (*Briza minor*)

Sheep fescue (*Festuca ovina*)

Indiangrass (*Sorghastrum nutans*)

you've planted, allowing them to self-seed more successfully. By doing this in late winter, you'll allow birds to nest and feed on seed undisturbed. You can use a lawn mower at a high setting, a weed whacker, or an old-fashioned scythe. For larger areas, you may want to hire a local farmer or landscape service to do the job.

Expect the ratio of species to change in the years to come. Mixes typically include annuals for an initial display of blossoms, and these may either disappear after the first season or reseed. Wild plants, desirable or not, can also be expected to show up. Manage the meadow with an eye to keeping a pleasing balance. You may want to selectively allow volunteer shrubs and trees to establish themselves, gradually changing the character of this piece of land.

A MEADOW OF GRASSES

Go with a grassy meadow. Again, you'll have to clear the area of weeds if you are starting from seed. Note that some named cultivars of ornamental grasses may not grow true from seed, and have to be grown from divisions. Also, divisions will compete with weeds and become established much sooner than plants grown from seed. *Clump-forming* grasses tend to become scraggly unless cut back in early spring, and they may need to be divided every 3 years or so. *Rhizome-forming* grasses, the other general category, spread via underground stems and may become invasive.

OUTDOOR ROOMS OF GREEN

You probably have a favorite room in your home. Why not set up an outdoor space that is especially welcoming?

Some folks like to set up folding chairs on the front lawn and watch the traffic go by. But most of us find ourselves hanging out in a more private part of the yard, one that offers some sense of enclosure. A traditional porch does that splendidly, of course, and with a little planning and planting you can do the same somewhere on your property. This spot is apt to catch the sun at the appropriate time of day, along with shade when necessary. It could offer a view to the front of the house so that you can keep an eye out for arriving visitors, or to the backyard so that you can monitor the kids' activities. And you might want to create the effect of walls with hedges, rock walls, or even just a row of potted plants. Add *comfortable* seating (a bench without a back might not qualify) and move right in.

A WOOD-AND-PLASTIC HYBRID FOR THE YARD

Plastic-based lumber is ideal for garden projects.

Take one part wood scraps, and one part plastic from shopping bags and pallet wrapping, and what do you get? Trex, a wood-polymer lumber now widely used for decking and railing intended for outdoor use. The stuff looks something like wood (unless you're giving it a close look), nails and saws like wood—and the similarities end there. The plastic component means that Trex won't splinter or rot, and there's no need for paint, stain, or preservatives. The wood, in turn, helps to protect the plastic from being damaged by UV rays. All of which is good news for gardeners, who have enough chores without maintaining wood decks, benches, and fences. Trex isn't a perfect building material, however. Unlike lumber from trees, it isn't suited for long spans, and it won't support considerable loads without intermediate support.

TURN A SLIPPERY SLOPE INTO A TERRIFIC TERRACE

You're only two or three steps from a more manageable yard—giant steps of stone, that is. Low stone walls can convert a steep pitch into an attractive landscaping feature.

A sloping yard makes a great place for sledding in winter. And that comes close to summarizing the benefits of having a small mountain behind your house. Slopes can be difficult (and downright dangerous) to mow; they tend to be prone to erosion; and it's a challenge to make them look like part of the natural landscape if they've been sculpted by a contractor's bulldozers.

With a shovel and a good back, you can *terrace* that pitch. It's a cut-and-fill procedure in which you move soil to make steps. To keep the soil in place, you need to make low walls of some sort, with stone either from the property or purchased, landscaping ties, or perhaps stuccoed concrete block. The trick is to conserve the topsoil taken from the uppermost layer of the slope, and then place it where plantings will go. Use inferior soil from the slope or elsewhere on the property for the basic form of the terracing. You can choose relatively neat, constrained plantings to show off attractive new terrace walls rather than conceal them. Note that the soil on a terrace is apt to drain quickly, favoring plants that like to have dry feet.

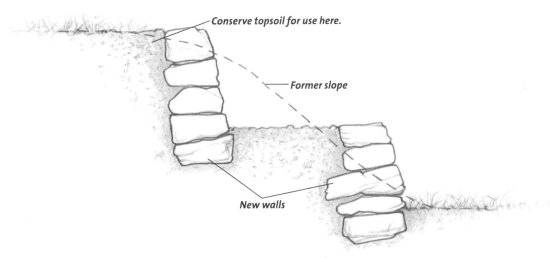

A difficult-to-mow slope can be eased away with two or three low stone walls. In the process, you create terraces ready for planting.

A ROCK WALL FOR THE AGES

One of the most lasting landscape features is one you can make yourself.

EASY DOES IT

Add a Faucet, Subtract a Lot of Steps

Having too few outdoor faucets can be as frustrating as having too few electrical outlets in a room, if you find yourself hassling with hoses and watering cans. Although it's not inexpensive to have a plumber add a tap or two to your foundation wall, consider the savings in time. Your plants are likely to benefit, too, because you'll be more likely to water them if a hose is handy.

Rock walls are one of the few improvements you can make to your property that will soon look as though they had been there for decades, if not centuries. They also sit well with the lay of the land. And you can't make either claim for a deck or even a patio. A wall of stone is also a handsome backdrop for flower beds. Roses will clamber along a low wall and up a tall one, in a highly picturesque way. You can tuck flowers and ferns into soil-filled interstices between stones. And if the wall faces the sun, the heat it absorbs might nudge the bed in front of it up a growing zone or so, allowing you to grow plants that won't make it elsewhere on the property, or to stretch the growing season.

FINDING GOOD STONES

Laying up stone for an attractive wall without mortar isn't all that difficult if you have good stones. In wall-building terms, that means they ideally will have some resemblance to building blocks, with a few parallel sides. Round, roly-poly stones tend not to stay put.

Chances are that you, as a gardener, already know if your yard can be counted on for some if not all of what you'll need. You may have to go to a garden center; or look in the yellow pages for a local stone dealer or quarry. The safest choice is to buy rocks that come from a nearby source, as a guarantee that they won't look exotic and out of place once you get them home. Also consider weight; the larger the stones, the sturdier the construction and the quicker the job will go, but you don't want to be saddled with massive boulders that you can't safely handle. To help move big rocks, you can use round posts as rollers, a ramp of ¾-inch plywood on which to slide them, and a long pry bar. See also "Heavy Lifting with a Wheeled Friend" on page 265. If the wall is to be any more than knee high, you'll want to run some longish stones back into the soil as "deadmen" that serve to anchor the structure.

BUILDING THE WALL

1. Lay out the base of the wall with string between stakes (for a straight wall) or a garden hose (for a curved wall).

2. In parts of the country where the ground freezes and heaves, anything but a low wall should start below ground level. Dig a trench about 12 inches deep where the wall is to go. Fill the trench nearly to ground level with gravel.

3. Lay the first course of stone, choosing the largest and most nearly rectangular beauties from whatever you have on hand; these stones will be supporting the weight of all that are to come. If the wall will be backed by soil rather than freestanding, tilt the stones *slightly* from front to back as shown to help throw their weight against the earth. A carpenter's level can help you maintain a consistent angle.

4. Continue adding courses. There should be a gradual tapering of the wall from top to bottom. Whenever possible, have each stone rest above the meeting of two stones below it. Shim with smaller rocks to help keep the courses level. Fill in behind the retaining wall with soil and smaller stones, tamping down with the end of a 2 × 4 or post as you go.

What You'll Need

Heavy work gloves

Work boots

Eye protection (if using hammer and chisel)

Shovel

Stake and string to lay out a straight wall; garden hose for a curved wall

Hammer and brick or stone chisel (for squaring rock, optional)

Rollers, plywood ramp, pry bar (for moving stone, optional)

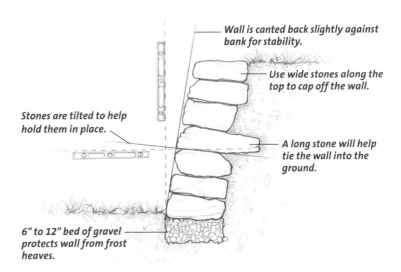

Wall is canted back slightly against bank for stability.

Use wide stones along the top to cap off the wall.

Stones are tilted to help hold them in place.

A long stone will help tie the wall into the ground.

6" to 12" bed of gravel protects wall from frost heaves.

Laying a stone wall is potentially one of the most satisfying yard improvements and (given care in the process) one of the most enduring.

(continued)

5. If your wall will have one or more corners, reserve large, flat rocks with a crisply defined 90-degree angle to use at these points. For the sake of stability, have some cornerstones run back into the soil as deadmen.

6. Use large, flat stones to cap off the top of the wall. These are the most visible stones, and they will help to keep the wall in place. If you will be having a planting bed at the top of the wall, use good soil for filling in the top foot or two.

SHAPING STONE

As you work with stone, you develop an eye for those that will serve well in a wall. But few rocks are without odd bumps that can make them teeter when stacked. You can use a hammer and brick or stone chisel to lop them off. Wearing safety eyewear and work gloves, rest the rock in a bed of sand or soil to keep it steady. Place the edge of the chisel against the protrusion, and begin tapping lightly with the hammer.

A GARDEN IN A WALL

Is the yard already crowded with plantings? Let's rock your world with a new idea.

An often-unexploited part of the yard is the face of a rock wall. The spaces between rocks are custom-made for certain plants, which aren't at all inconvenienced by having to reach into the wall to contact soil or crane their necks to catch the sun.

Left to its own devices, a wall is apt to become home to an interesting mix of self-seeding plants. If not, consider adding ferns, spirea, coralbells, oregano, thyme, pinks, and mints. You might include a prostrate variety of rosemary or creeping phlox for their interesting effect.

There's no special technique for giving these wallflowers a start. Just tuck some good soil into a crevice, insert the plant roots first, and follow up with more soil to both hold the plant in place and to surround its roots. You may have to add soil occasionally if rainwater courses through the wall and washes it out. If plants become straggly over time, prune them back for a tidier appearance.

CREATE A SOUNDSCAPE

Bugged by a noisy neighborhood? Water trickling into a backyard pool, rustling leaves, and sighing evergreens can ease the irritation.

One of the reasons that a walk in the woods—even a small patch of trees—feels so peaceful is that the natural sounds subtly soothe away the clatter of the outside world. You can get the same effect working for you. A small pool with a simple pump or fountain, either plugged in or solar powered, will contribute a pleasing background sound. Quaking aspen are noted for the white noise they generate as their leaves shiver. A breeze will set pines to sighing. Come fall, beech and oak trees hang on to some of their leaves and continue to add a dry rustling. You even can enlist the help of singing birds, which will serenade you if your yard has been planted to attract them.

A discretely placed solar panel can supply power for a small fountain, adding a lovely sound to the background call of birds and creating a sense of coolness on hot summer afternoons.

A DIFFERENT PERSPECTIVE ON LANDSCAPING

Use optical illusions to stretch the apparent size of your yard.

Here's a nifty trick for making a piece of property look more generous in size, employed by landscape painters for centuries. Called *forced perspective*, it exaggerates the way lines seem to converge when you look into the distance. Thomas Jefferson used the effect at Poplar Forest, his less-well-known home in Virginia; archeologists confirm that he had workers taper the opposite sides of what had been a rectangular lawn.

Even if your own yard is less than presidential in scale, try one of these techniques to fool the eye.

❖ Starting from a common vantage point on a lawn, add plantings along one or both sides so that they gradually come closer.

❖ Taper a path as it leads from the house. Or, line the path with shrubs and have these rows come closer together with distance.

❖ Plant the yard with trees and shrubs that are largest near the house, then gradually diminish in size.

Use plantings to bring in the sides of a lawn.

Plant shrubs and trees of decreasing size.

Lay out a tapering path.

You can use optical tricks to make a lawn look either deeper or wider, such as bringing in the sides of the yard with plantings, placing smaller shrubs in the distance, and even laying out a path that becomes narrower as it recedes from view.

THE LAYERED LOOK FOR VEST-POCKET YARDS

Back to basics—arrange plantings from short to tall to give an impression of depth.

If your property looks small and confined, try bordering it with a layered succession of plantings, incorporating low plants in the first rank, then medium-size, then tall. It's the same principle as overlapping hills and mountains to give depth to a landscape painting. Heighten the effect by choosing large-foliaged plants for the foreground, and shrubs and trees with an increasingly finer appearance as you go back. The eye is apt to read this progression as receding over a considerable distance.

EDGING BEDS FOR A TIDY LOOK

A little "trench warfare" can help to keep grass in the lawn and out of flower beds.

Although you can buy different sorts of edging to surround flower and garden beds, a little easy maintenance with a straight-bladed shovel will accomplish the same. Dig a 3-inch-deep V-shaped trench around beds, slicing at a 45-degree angle along either side. This will both define the beds crisply and also prevent grass and plants from invading each other's turf.

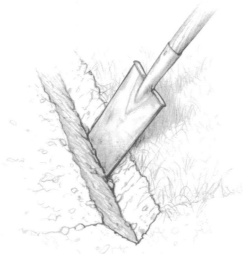

When garden beds begin looking a bit scruffy around their margins, spruce them up by edging with a trench. To keep the trench straight as an arrow, you can lay down a 2 × 4 as a guide.

A POOL FOR PLANTS, WILDLIFE, AND YOU

You'll appreciate a backyard water feature, and so will dozens of other species— both plant and animal.

Shallow backyard pools using durable PVC and butyl rubber liners have become popular for wildlife and aquatic plants. A good-quality liner should last at least 20 years. And there's no need to invest in all the water-feature gadgets now on the market. You can buy pumps and filters, test kits, submersible heaters, and even an electric fogging device that spreads a scented, glowing mist over the pond!

Keep it shallow and keep it simple. Water plants can help keep the pool water clean. Helpful species include water lettuce (*Pistia stratoites*), duckweed (*Lemna minor*), and water hyacinth (*Eichhornia crassipes*); note that plants recommended for small containers may be invasive elsewhere. When necessary, you can remove built-up sediment by first bailing the pool or using a sump pump. But for the most part, it's just a matter of topping off the pool with water as necessary, and sitting back to enjoy this pint-size water feature. Even the smallest of backyard pools can seem to have a cooling effect on a hot day. And you can expect all sorts of wildlife to come calling.

❖ Some 15 percent of our dragonfly species are thought to be endangered, as more of their watery habitat gives way to development. A small pool in the yard can encourage them to move in. The pool should be at least 18 inches deep and edged with vegetation. Fish will prey on dragonfly eggs and larvae, so it's best to try to raise either one or the other.

❖ Frogs may take up residence. Toads live on land in their adult stage, but they're apt to visit the pool to mate and lay eggs. If you want to make it possible for salamanders to overwinter in the pool, allow a layer of leaf litter to build up on the bottom.

❖ Expect to see birds stopping by for a splash and a sip. A platform of concrete block or stone will provide them with a shallow spot (1 or 2 inches deep is best) and good footing.

DIGGING A POOL

A small pond begins with a shovel. You can dig a hole sized to take a preformed liner. Or, for a more natural, informal shape, drape a durable rubber or plastic liner over the hole and keep it in place with either a single layer of flagstones or a built-up stone wall around the perimeter.

1. Find a good site. Besides being attractive, it must be level so that the water won't pour out a low side of the pool. Picking a spot directly under trees may mean trouble, starting with trying to dig in soil full of roots and then dealing with leaves falling into the pool each autumn.

2. Determine the shape, size, and depth of the pool. To come up with a graceful shape, use a garden hose or length of rope. Mark this outline with a can of spray paint. As for the depth, 18 inches will do for growing aquatic plants and encouraging wildlife to visit. The deeper you go, the more you'll have to stomp on that shovel. And local ordinances may require a fence around deeper ponds; it's best to investigate before you excavate.

3. Dig the pond. Ensure that it is level in all directions by spanning the hole with a 2 × 4 and placing a carpenter's level on the board. If the soil is rocky or has stubborn tree roots, you may want to dig deep enough to allow adding a 4-inch layer of sand for a smooth surface on which to place the liner. Shallow sides work best for wildlife and also help to keep a sand layer in place.

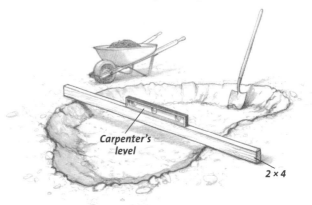

As you dig the pond, use a carpenter's level on a long board to make sure that the water won't drain out of a low spot.

(continued)

4. Lay down the liner, allowing for folds as need be. Add a few large rocks or concrete blocks for birds to perch on and as a platform for aquatic plants that don't need much depth.

5. Place flagstones around the perimeter of the pond, projecting just slightly over the pond's edge in order to conceal the liner. Or, build up a low fieldstone wall. Trim the excess liner as you go along.

6. Add water. The hose should have an anti-siphoning device to prevent pond water from running back into the home's supply. Put potted aquatic plants on the liner or on the platform of rocks or concrete blocks—water lilies, yellow flag iris, cardinal flowers, water poppies. You can also place plants outside of the pond's edge to help it fit naturally into the yard and also to provide cover for wildlife.

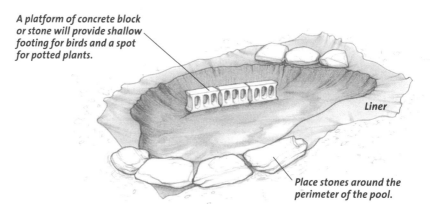

A platform of concrete block or stone will provide shallow footing for birds and a spot for potted plants.

Liner

Place stones around the perimeter of the pool.

To hold the liner in place and make the pond fit into the landscape, run stones around the edge.

POOL MATH

To make sure the liner matches the size of the excavation, you can use a simple formula: For either the width or length, find the sum of that dimension, plus double the maximum depth, plus 2 feet to serve as a border. So, to line a pool that's 6 feet wide and 18 inches deep, the calculation would be 6 plus 3 plus 2, meaning you'd need at least 11 feet to handle the width. Calculate the length in the same way.

A WATERFALL WITHOUT THE FUSS

Don't want to bother with electrical gadgetry? A solar-powered waterfall can be an ecofriendly addition to the yard.

The sound of a trickling home-scale waterfall can be as effective as deep shade in helping you to feel cool on a summer day. Trouble is, circulating the water means bringing in electrical wiring—at least it did until recently. You now can buy solar-powered pumps that use a collector placed inconspicuously below the surface of the pool at the bottom of the waterfall. Because you are dealing with a low-voltage system, installation is simple and safe.

LIGHT UP A GARDEN PATH IN 1 HOUR

Tap the sun's energy for landscaping lights.

That's right, you can install lights along a path in about an hour, with a kit that includes a solar panel and low-voltage wiring running to several lighting fixtures. These systems typically have an electric eye that turns the lights on at dusk and off at daybreak, conserving the electricity the panel generates by day. The beauty of solar outdoor lighting is that you don't have to fish a line to the home and hassle with the transformer needed to knock the power down for low-voltage lights. And there's no need to place the lights in a sunny spot; your only restriction is that the panel must bask in direct sunlight for most of the day. Because so little current runs through the system, you don't have to worry about getting an electrical jolt. Just snake the wire along a narrow cut made in the ground with a spade, or run it through a bed of pachysandra or vinca. The lights are mounted on stakes inserted in the ground, and you can move them freely about for best effect.

AUTUMN LEAVES TO THE RESCUE

By mounding leaves—nature's loose-fill insulation—you can protect heavy potted plants without moving them.

A sure way of protecting potted plants is to bring them indoors before freezing weather. But if you don't have the space (or the muscle) to drag larger plants into the house, make use of autumn's litter—fallen leaves. Either protect plants singly or gather three or four of them together. Rake up those leaves and pile them around the containers, heaping them up well over the pots. To keep the leaves in place through the cold months, cut a slit to the middle of an opaque plastic tarp and slide this cover over the heap. Overlap the cut edges, then place bricks or rocks around the perimeter as anchors.

Another cold-weather strategy is to make a cylinder of chicken wire and slip that over a large plant, pot and all. If the branches spread too wide, you can coax the plant into a narrower shape by wrapping it with twine. Save some of the leaves you've been raking up and pour them into the cylinder as insulation. You can help keep the cylinder upright in the same way that you would a tomato cage, by driving one or two stakes into the ground just inside the cylinder. Finally, wrap the cylinder with a plastic sheet or tarp, keeping it in place by belting it with loops of twine or rope.

You also can give plants some protection from a light frost by purchasing cleverly designed bags made of breathable polypropylene. The bags cinch shut with just a tug on a drawstring. They can be installed upside down to protect hanging plants, as well. Look for them at garden centers and on the Internet.

Pile up autumn leaves to help potted plants make it through the winter. You'll spare yourself the trouble of lugging heavy pots inside in fall, then back outdoors the following spring.

A FALL GROUND COVER PALETTE

Give the vinca and pachysandra a break and consider plantings that will enliven your vista in fall and winter.

Come fall, we tend to look *up* for our dose of autumnal color. As grand and noble as sugar maples and the rest may be, there's an opportunity to spread brilliant swaths over the yard as well—pools of outrageous scarlet and luminous school-bus oranges. Here are some plants worth investigating.

Kinnikinick (*Arctostaphylos uva-ursi*)

Bunchberry (*Cornus canadensis*)

Cranberry cotoneaster (*Cotoneaster apiculatus*)

Deutzia gracilis 'Nikko'

Virginia sweetspire (*Itea virginica*) 'Short and Sweet'

Virginia creeper (*Parthenocissus quinquefolia*)

Plumbago (*Plumbago auriculata*)

Spirea japonica 'Magic Carpet'

Stephanandra incisa 'Crispa'

Woolly thyme (*Thymus pseudolanuginosus*)

Lowbush blueberry (*Vaccinium angustifolium*)

CURRANT EVENTS

Try growing currants for attractive landscaping shrubs as well as berries that come in red (with a tart flavor), black (having a rich flavor all its own), and white (a mild-mannered variation).

For many years, currants and gooseberries were scarce in catalogs and nurseries because the plants were hosts of white pine rust, a disease afflicting that tree. The federal government banned the planting of currants and gooseberries back in the early 1900s, then lifted the restriction in 1966 so that states could tailor their own laws. Today, the plants can be purchased and planted in much of the United States; check with your state's agricultural department for guidelines. These bushes are easy to maintain and produce a reliable crop of fruits that are widely known in Europe but just now returning to the yards of this country.

REJUVENATE WITH A LAWN MOWER

Mowers can manage more than just bluegrass. Put them to use right on your garden plants.

ADVICE OVER THE FENCE
Mower Tune-Up Checklist

Tune up your walk-behind mower after every 25 hours of mowing to keep trouble to a minimum, especially if you're mowing over low-growing plants as well as turfgrass. Here's your to-do list:

- Change the spark plug
- Clean the cooling fans
- Change the engine oil
- Clean or replace the air filter
- Remove, sharpen, and balance the blade
- Clean the underside of the deck
- Lubricate the wheels and controls

A lawn mower can be used to stimulate growth as well as give grass a close haircut. Here's how.

- **Herb beds.** If a bed of herbs has lost its zest and you're tempted to yank all those lazy plants for a fresh start, wait. The mower may come to the rescue. Begin by doing a good job of plucking out weeds by the roots. Then set the mower higher than usual— from 3 to 5 inches—and go over the bed to trim it back. Rake away the tattered remains, uncovering the trimmed herbs. Mulch around these survivors for a bed that immediately looks presentable. In time, the plants may fully reestablish themselves.

- **Strawberry beds.** Strawberries can't be left to their own devices if they are to remain a productive part of your yard. Once the harvest is over for the year, set the mower at between 1½ and 2 inches to remove the leaves and stems; you may have to adjust the height to avoid damaging the crowns. The cut plant matter should be blown off the bed, deposited into the bagger attachment, or atomized if yours is a mulching mower. Next, reestablish the rows by removing plants that have strayed beyond their boundaries. Turn your attention to weeds, digging them out as well. While you're at it, take out enough strawberries for a spacing of a good 6 inches between plants. Finally, mulch the beds with straw until next growing season.

- **Raspberry beds.** 'Heritage', a highly popular raspberry, will turn into a thorny jungle unless cut back forcefully. You can simply mow the canes just above the ground late each fall. New growth, called *primocanes,* will appear the next year and bear a crop late in the season. Once the harvest is over, go over the plants again with the mower.

- **Poison ivy.** The idea here is to *harm* the plants, of course, not help them. By repeated close mowings, you reduce the leaf area and gradually starve the roots. The clippings from this procedure can cause serious reactions, and you should treat them accordingly if they are gathered in a bagger attachment. Be careful to avoid contact with the spray of these fragments if the mower does not collect them. Consistency is key here: Unless you keep mowing to prevent the foliage from appearing, the plants may thrive.

- **Lawns.** You mow a lawn to trim it, of course. But you also can use the mower to deal with fallen leaves. A standard mower will act as a somewhat inefficient leaf blower, gradually nudging the leaves to one side as you make repeated passes. A better approach is to use a mulching mower at a moderate speed, getting out there when there is just a scattered layer of leaves. The mulching action will turn the dead leaves into tiny particles that filter down through the grass blades, returning some nutrients to the soil. In a year, you may be recycling the equivalent of 1 pound of nitrogen fertilizer per 1,000 square feet of lawn. And the leaves won't contribute to thatch or significantly alter the pH of the soil.

MOWING WITH THE REEL DEAL

It's a good bet that you could walk around the block on a sunny afternoon and not spot a single reel mower. Rotary blades seem the only way to go these days. But reel mowers can do a better job, which is why you *will* see them at work on golf courses. If you like a close-shorn sward, a reel mower is particularly effective, according to trials at Ohio State University at heights of 1 and 2 inches. And Bermuda and zoysiagrass lawns are best cut with a reel mower. But a rotary is the better choice if you want to mow less often by cutting only when the grass reaches 3 inches or so. The exception is with an old-fashioned nonpowered reel mower; models are available that can be set at 3 inches. Another factor to keep in mind is that reel mowers tend to need professional attention for sharpening and adjusting the blades.

THE ORGANIC LAWN

Many homeowners are dependent on a host of chemicals in hopes of having a perfect lawn. Here's how to get unhooked.

You can eliminate or greatly reduce the synthetic fertilizers and pesticides used on your lawn. And that will mean one less source of worry about the health of your family, pets, and the home environment. While chemical-based lawn care treats the soil as a passive blotter, the organic approach focuses on improving the lawn from the ground up. Good soil gives rise to healthy lawns, with less trouble from pests, diseases, and adverse weather conditions. You also may find that the lawn has a reduced need for watering and fertilizer.

WORKING WITH AN EXISTING LAWN

Unless you're moving into a new home, or are expanding your lawn into what had been a field or garden beds, you probably are looking at a reasonably well-established lawn. You can bump up its appearance a couple of notches by core aeration, adjusting mowing height, and top-dressing with a fine, sifted compost.

Increasing the level of organic matter will improve the soil's structure, with a few benefits. The soil will be better able to hold on to moisture and nutrients, while promoting good drainage. Roots will grow more easily, so that the grass will hold up better against an assault from weeds. Finally, organic matter contributes to nitrogen fixation and helps resist soilborne plant diseases.

All of this won't take place overnight. While chemical approaches can have an almost immediate effect, organic improvements are gradual. And you'll be a happier homeowner if you don't expect a totally weed-free lawn. A yard that is a bright, flawless green throughout the year is probably a lawn heavily reliant on chemical help and a lot of irrigation. The organic way involves a more relaxed perspective.

MOW SMART

You may prefer the crisp look of a closely mowed lawn, but many common weeds also like it. By allowing the grass to grow a bit longer, depending on the varieties in the lawn's mix, you can shade out weed seeds so that they are less likely to sprout and cause trouble. Also, if grass is given periodic crew cuts, its roots don't grow as deeply and the lawn may be more susceptible to diseases.

Instead, mow to the height given below. Try to cut the lawn often enough that you're never lopping off more than one-third of the blade length. So, to mow at a height of 3 inches, you should get out the mower when the lawn measures 4½ inches high.

Here are the heights to shoot for.

GRASS VARIETY	HEIGHT (INCHES)
Kentucky bluegrass	2½–3½
Tall fescue	3–4
Fescue/bluegrass	3–4
Bluegrass/ryegrass	2–3½
Creeping red fescue	3–3½
Zoysiagrass	1½–2½

KEEP SHARP

The whirling blade of a mower is out of sight, and it tends to be out of mind as well. But if it has become dull, it may be beating the grass into submission rather than cutting it cleanly. Inspect the ends of a few clippings. If they are frayed, that's a sign that the blade needs attention. The entire lawn may take on a somewhat brownish tinge. A dull blade also puts a greater load on the mower, consuming more gas and contributing to wear and tear. Shredded grass may be more susceptible to lawn diseases. Finally, the blade has to be sharp in order to cut damp grass without serious tearing.

(continued)

Sharpening a blade isn't an easy task, no matter what the operating manual for your mower may suggest. You have to make sure the engine won't start up while you're removing the blade, and that means knowing where the spark plug is and how to remove the wire running to it. Getting at the blade is a challenge if you have a riding mower. And even a dull blade can cut you, meaning you need to be mindful when removing it. Finally, a blade may need routine balancing as well as sharpening, and that's a job beyond the skills and aptitude of most homeowners. The easiest solution is to have the mower dealer pick up the machine and do the sharpening, as well as balancing the blade if necessary. Second easiest is for you to deliver the mower. If you have no way of transporting a riding mower and the pickup charge is prohibitive, you can follow the operating manual's directions for removing the deck, then take it to the dealer.

REPLACING THE LAWN

If your lawn is chronically bare and riddled with weeds, you can take the somewhat drastic measure of reseeding after solarizing it. Solarizing involves tarping the area with sheets of clear plastic, so that a long stretch of sunny midsummer weather can cook the lawn below, including both grass and weeds. You then start from scratch, improving the quality of the soil with compost, manure, and natural amendments, followed by choosing grasses that are suited to your climate and your particular lawn. This is a radical approach, one that will deliver results much faster than if you top-dress the lawn in small amounts over a period of years.

FERN AFFAIRS

Try going with fronds, not just flowers, to add interesting textures to the yard.

Next Year's Garden

Install a Stumpery

Most yards have at least one unloved and all but unredeemable spot, where low light, so-so soil, and inaccessibility seem like unsolvable issues. These odd nooks are candidates for a *stumpery*, a modest-size landscape feature arranged around one or more stumps for a woodsy, picturesque effect.

Farmers and contractors routinely yank stumps of felled trees from the ground when clearing land, and you may be able to pick them up for no charge. If you can't find stumps, sections of log will do. Either way, you'll have a centerpiece around which to grow ferns and woodland plants, just as Victorian gardeners did during the stumpery fad (yes, there really was one) of more than a hundred years ago.

To make the stumps or logs look as though they've been moldering for decades, use a blender to process moss, yogurt, and water into a slurry, then spread it on these objects. If there's room enough, install a rustic bench on which to contemplate your romantic woodland niche.

If you're considering what to do with a shady area of the yard, give the hostas and pachysandra a rest and investigate the many shapes and textures and personalities to be found among ferns. That's not to say they make a visual splash. Ferns mostly come in shades of green, and these so-called primitive plants don't produce flowers. Still, once you begin noticing ferns, their individual personalities can be very charming. For a quick introduction to these plants, here are three very different forms.

- The **ostrich fern** (*Matteuccia struthiopteris*) is an eager grower, quickly reaching 4 to 6 feet, and it looks like what you'd expect of a fern. It will succeed in either sunny or shady spots if the soil is moist.

- The dainty **Japanese painted fern** (*Athyrium nipponicum*) is shaped like a fern, but its coloration is mildly outrageous. The stems are deep red, and the leaves are frosted with silver. To bring out the best color, place them in light shade with perhaps some morning sun. They also tend to be brighter in areas with cooler summer temperatures.

- The **maidenhair fern** (*Adiantum raddianuma*) is conventional ferny green (except for the contrasting black stems), but its form is strikingly different. The delicate fronds are low-growing fans, making this species a good choice for the front of beds and for easing the edges of a shady path. Maidenhairs do best under bright filtered light rather than in deep shade.

MULCH AS YOU MOW

Place grass clippings where they'll work for you best—back on the lawn.

ADVICE OVER THE FENCE

Mow Twice to Make It Nice

If you mow when the grass is damp or a bit too long, and the mower spits out clumps rather than clipping, there's still a chance to incorporate the cut grass with the soil. The next day (or as soon as the lawn dries somewhat), mow again at right angles to the first cutting.

Grass clippings can be a pain, if you rake them up after each mowing or collect them while you mow and then empty the bag. Sure, you can use the clippings as mulch around plants or as a compost ingredient. But it's easier—and smarter—to return them to the lawn. You're best off with a mulching lawn mower. It has a specially designed blade and mower deck that pulverize the cut grass so that it can be deposited in a form that decomposes quickly, returning organic matter and nutrients to the soil. Finely minced clippings can contribute up to 30 percent of a lawn's nitrogen requirement, and they aren't responsible for building up thatch.

FERTILIZING NATURALLY

First, the basics. The three major nutrients plants need are nitrogen (N), phosphorus (P), and potassium (K). Nitrogen is required for growth and an attractive green color. Phosphorus is key for root development and various growth processes. Potassium is essential for various physiological functions, as well as disease resistance and standing up to winter conditions. A fertilizer is called *complete* if it includes the three—nitrogen, phosphorus, and potassium. The relative amounts of each will be given on the packaging.

If you choose organic products over synthetic chemicals, the effects will be more gradual and also longer lasting. Just as important, organic fertilizers don't interfere with life in the soil; both microorganisms and earthworms will flourish. Organic fertilizers come from four main sources.

❖ Animal sources, including manure, bonemeal, and bloodmeal

❖ Plant sources, including seaweed, alfalfa meal, and cottonseed meal

❖ Composted sewer sludge products such as Milorganite

❖ Naturally occurring minerals, such as rock phosphate and greensand

STUDY THE FERTILIZER LABEL

A fertilizer labeled as organic or natural may not necessarily fit the description. Check the ingredients list for synthetic chemical fertilizers. You'll also find the overall percentages of nitrogen, phosphorus, and potassium yielded by whatever is in the mix.

FERTILIZER	% N	% P	% K	POUNDS TO SUPPLY 1 POUND ACTUAL N
Alfalfa pellets	5	1	2	20
Bloodmeal	10	1	0	10
Bonemeal	3	15	0	33
Cottonseed meal	3	1	1	33
Greensand	0	1	6	—
Kelp meal	2	1	3	50
Manure, composted chicken	0.5	0.3	0.5	200
Manure, composted cow	0.5	0.3	0.5	200
Rock phosphate	0	3	0	—
Seabird guano	12	8	2	8
Shellfish fertilizer	3	3	1	33
Soybean meal	7	1	3	14
Erth Rite	3	2	2	33
Milorganite/Com-Til	6	2	0	16
ReVita Compost Plus	3	4	3	33

A LAWN WITH LESS LABOR

To gain more time in the hammock, all you have to do is become more tolerant of a less-than-manicured appearance.

ADVICE OVER THE FENCE
Beware of Seedy Clippings

Although clippings contain nutrients that will enrich the soil, they also may contain weed seeds. If your mower doesn't mulch, but blows clippings out the side, don't shoot them out over garden beds if you see weeds bearing seeds—quackgrass seeds, in particular. Otherwise, you may be sowing your garden with a fine crop of trouble.

Americans spend some $30 billion a year on lawn maintenance—and a lot of lovely summer days, as well. If you feel like a slave to your sward, consider switching to other grass species for a low-maintenance lawn, also known as an ecolawn to play up its environmental benefits. You'll mow and water less often, and use fewer chemicals for fertilizing and weed control.

So, why doesn't everybody make the switch? A main reason is that a low-maintenance lawn just won't look quite as finely textured and lushly green as one that's primped. If you want to see firsthand what one of these yards looks like before committing yourself, ask a county extension agent (check the phone book under county or federal USDA listings) if there is a low-maintenance lawn in the area that you might drive past.

Here is a step-by-step guide for making the switch in gradual fashion. Specific procedures and grass varieties may differ depending on where in the country you live, so check with the extension agent for recommendations.

1. In late summer, mow the lawn as usual.
2. For a small area (1,000 square feet or less), use a metal rake to gather up loose grass and break up the surface of the soil. For larger lawns, you'll save time and energy by renting a verticutter, a powered machine that slices the surface lawn and may also do the job of sowing seed.
3. Sow about 1½ times the amount of seed recommended on the packaging. You can scatter the seed by hand or use a spreader. The varieties most often recommended include the fine-leaved fescues (including Chewings fescues, creeping red fescues, and the hard fescues), supplemented with Kentucky bluegrass and perennial ryegrass.

4. Rake the lawn just enough to help settle the seed into the soil. Water the lawn regularly, but allow it to naturally turn brown and dormant if midsummer weather is hot and dry. Mow at 2 or 2½ inches, and leave clippings on the lawn, ideally using a mulching mower.

5. Feed the lawn with a fertilizer containing a slow-release form of nitrogen, applying no more than 1 pound of actual nitrogen per 1,000 square feet.

CREATE A WILDFLOWER MEADOW

If you're determined to leave a lighter footprint and want to encourage Mother Nature, consider the advantages of turning lawn into meadow. However, it's one thing to look at the pretty label on the packaging of wildflower mix and another to study a blooming meadow close up. Try to find a meadow in your area, in a public garden or in someone's yard, and note which plants seem to be thriving. If possible, ask the person responsible for details on how the meadow was established and is kept flourishing. Then start making plans for next year's meadow.

A THORNY ISSUE SOLVED WITH NEWSPAPER

The thoughts of those raspberry and blackberry canes heavy with incredible ripe fruit can be painfully interrupted when you remember the thorns.

The scrapes and punctures associated with berry picking are hard-won signs of triumph but there's one relatively easy solution right on your doorstep. Pick up a few pages of today's newspaper, crumple it around the thorny canes where you're picking, then edge a shoulder into the newspaper area to reach the fruit hidden within. After you've harvested the berries in that area, (carefully!) move the crumbled newspaper to other canes, and continue picking.

A STRAIGHT AND SIMPLE STONE PATH

Serpentine walks take more time to lay out, and those curves tend to look contrived rather than relaxed.

What You'll Need

Rectangular flagstones of three or more different lengths

String and stakes

Square-bladed shovel

Work gloves

Work shoes

Much of the challenge of installing a flagstone path is getting those odd-shaped puzzle pieces to fit. They're heavy, sharp-edged, and seem to resist snuggling close to one another. You can make matters easier for yourself by visiting a home and garden center or stone dealer and buying rectangular stones. Be equipped with the overall length you need, so that you can order pieces of varying lengths that will do the job. If you have the choice of different *thicknesses* of stone, the thinner stuff is easier to move and less expensive, but it may be more prone to cracking over time.

Because rectangular stones are cut with some precision, the cracks between them are smaller and weeds have less of an opportunity to establish themselves along the walk. In fact, you can skip the usual step of laying down a bed of sand before putting the stones in place, although it may be easier to provide a level layer with sand than with stony or clumping soil.

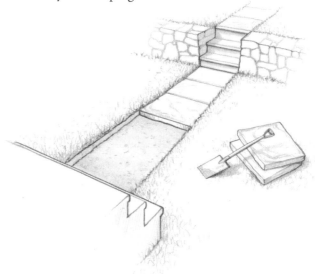

When it comes to putting down a walk of stone, straight is simpler than serpentine. Quarry-cut stones in squares and rectangles will go down quickly.

Walking a Stone

One nifty thing about using large rectangular stones is that you can "walk" them across the yard rather than risk wrecking your back by doing heavy lifting. Wearing sturdy work shoes to protect your toes, stand the stone upright. Hold it by the top corners, then alternately lift and advance each side forward. You won't win any footraces, but this method requires little strength.

Whenever possible, move heavy stones without hefting their entire weight. You can "walk" a large stone by lifting and advancing one side, then the other.

1. Lay out the walk with string stretched between two stakes tapped into the ground. If you place the string outside of where the walk will go, it'll be less likely to get in your way as you dig the trench. Alternately, you can lay out the string along both edges of the path's intended course and make lines with aerosol paint.

2. Dig a trench for the walk so that the top of the stones will be at ground level.

3. Wearing work gloves, put the stones in place. Vary their lengths randomly along the walk. If the last stone isn't the right size for the length of the walk, you can ask your supplier to saw it. Or do the job yourself with a circular saw and masonry blade, wearing safety glasses.

4. Put your weight on the walk to test it for stability. Tuck small stones and soil under the stones as necessary to level them. Finally, place soil along the outside edges and tamp it down. In time, grass will spread into this new strip of soil, making the walk look like it has been there for years.

STUMPED?

There's no speedy way to remove stubborn stumps, but you can help nature to do the job.

ADVICE OVER THE FENCE

Use Old Tires for Stump Bumpers

You can hide tree stumps from view by allowing a meadow to grow up around them, mowing occasionally. But low-cut stumps are a hazard to mowers and can bend blades or snap the belts that drive them. Repairs are costly and time consuming. To avoid running into these obstacles, ring them with old tires. The tires won't be an eyesore if the grasses grow fairly tall, and they'll keep you out of trouble. If you want to shovel soil over the stumps to speed their decay, the tires will help by keeping the dirt in place.

Ever since pioneers worked their way westward across the continent, stumps have been an inconvenient feature of the home landscape. They will rot over time, but not necessarily anytime soon—particularly cedar, cypress, locust, and mulberry. To speed things along a bit, the simplest step is to water the stump occasionally; this has the effect of promoting the growth of fungi that break up the wood. Or, take a battery-powered drill to the site and bore a number of 1-inch-diameter holes down into the top of the stump to further foster the fungi. You can even nourish organisms responsible for rot by occasionally dropping a pinch of nitrogen-rich plant fertilizer in each hole. Just don't fall for advertisements claiming that some miraculous chemical will make stumps vaporize overnight. If you really are desperate to be rid of the things, you can call a tree service to grind them to smithereens, an expensive process.

Or, if the stump is low enough, why not choose this spot for a nice raised bed? Plant it with flowers or shrubs to conceal the obstruction. You also will be speeding up the decomposition process by surrounding the stump with soil, rich in the organisms of decay.

HARVEST THE LEAVES, NOT JUST THE GRAPES

Grape leaves have a flavor and texture all their own.

Grape arbors once were fixtures in lawns of any size. They can still serve as an attractive way to set off a part of the yard. Or use a parallel pair of them to serve as an entryway to a fenced-in garden. In recent years, fruit developers have come up with flavorful seedless table grapes, as well as varieties for winemaking. The leaves can be harvested, too.

- Blanch the leaves and stuff them with seasoned rice and lemon to make dolmades.
- Wrap the leaves around Greek or Syrian cheese for baking in the oven.
- Wrap fish with the leaves before grilling.
- Add the leaves to soups for a subtle, intriguing flavor.
- When making a favorite casserole, line the dish with leaves and place them over the top as well.

Harvest the leaves when young, just as they are nearing their full size but before they become tough and bug battered. To have grape leaves on hand year-round, you can steam them and then freeze them in plastic bags. Just make sure that the leaves haven't been sprayed to control pests and diseases.

OFFER BIRDS "NEST LUMBER"

Attract birds by putting out scraps that they can turn into nests.

One way to encourage birds to take up residence in your yard is by providing nesting materials. Nail or tie a wire basket to a tree in the yard at about head height. Stock it with yarn, narrow strips of cotton fabric, cotton batting, feathers, or dried grasses. Just for fun, when the leaves fall from the trees in fall, tour the property to see if you can spot your materials woven into nests.

A BACKYARD BOG

Establish a wild bog garden and you greatly expand the number of plants you can grow, some of them highly unusual.

You don't need to have a stream coursing through your property or to live next to a swamp in order to have a fascinating bog garden, with its mysterious ecosystem. A bog does have to be somewhat wet, of course, with an acidic mix of sand and humus. Those conditions can be met by beginning with a hand-dug dish in the yard, equipped with a liner of the sort used to form the standard sort of pool (see "A Pool for Plants, Wildlife, and You" on page 298). Poke a few holes in the liner to allow some drainage. This will help to prevent the water from becoming stagnant—even natural bogs lose some water. Cover the bottom of the pool with a mix of one part soil, two parts sand, and three parts peat.

Maintain the bog garden by yanking weeds and dividing clumps of overgrown plants. By occasionally adding small amounts of compost, you add nutrients and also help to control the pH level. And of course you'll want to make sure the bog never dries out. If you are north of Zone 7, it's a good idea to mulch the bog with pine needles or oak leaves from late fall until above-freezing temperatures return in early spring.

PLANTING THE BOG

Arrange plants at the same depth they had been growing, whether it was in a pot or in the ground. Or you can keep them in their containers, placing them on bricks or stones to keep them at the proper depth.

You'll have a good time selecting plants for the bog—carnivorous and otherwise. Sweet flag (*Acorus calamus*) can be had in standard green and in ornamental variegated forms. Flag iris (*Iris ensata*) reaches 3 to 4 feet and is seen primarily in blue and yellow. A good choice for a small bog is the shorter Japanese iris (*Iris japonica*), with flowers of white to pink to purple. Native plants include yellow water canna (*Canna glauca*), with its vivid yellow flowers. Swamp hibiscus (*Hibiscus coccineus*) is a tall plant with pink blossoms 6

Don't Fight a Flood

If heavy rains tend to create a torrent that rips your lawn and flower beds, consider offering a path of less resistance—a waterway with gravel or larger rocks to prevent erosion. If this occasional stream has a curving course and a mix of large, attractive stones, it may look like a natural feature of the landscape even when not a drop is flowing.

inches across, and although it looks as though it would thrive only in the South, it can be grown in Zone 5. Cardinal flower (*Lobelia cardinalis*) was once a common wildflower along our waterways, but it has become relatively scarce; use it for a jot of brilliant red in the late-summer bog. Turtlehead (*Chelone glabra*) also blooms toward the end of summer, with white tubular flowers.

As for the remarkable bug-eating plants that make their home in bogs, many varieties are available through mail order. Pitcher plants (*Sarracenia* spp.) are tall and brooding in appearance, with a veined, oddly shaped hood and a large flower that may be a deep blood red or a more cheerful lemon yellow. Another favorite with gardeners are the sundews (*Drosera* spp.), low-growing plants that trap insect prey with sticky, scented leaves. The best-known carnivore may be the Venus fly trap (*Dionaea muscipula*), with leaves that close upon its victims.

PLANTS FOR THE BACKYARD BOG

It takes a special sort of plant to handle wet feet, as well as the acidic conditions found in bogs. Note that some species like to be around the edge of the body of water, while others are happy in it.

Swamp milkweed (*Asclepias incarnate*)
Milkweed (*Asclepias lanceolata*)
Black birch (*Betula nigra*)
Swamp buttonbush (*Cephalanthus occidentalis*)
Turtlehead (*Chelone glabra*)
Joe-Pye weed (*Eupatorium maculatum*)
Sneezeweed (*Helenium autumnale*)
Wild blue flag (*Iris versicolor*)
Cardinal flower (*Lobelia cardinalis*)
Great blue lobelia (*Lobelia siphilitica*)
Beebalm (*Monarda didyma*)
Yellow pond lily (*Nuphar luteum*)
Fragrant water lily (*Nymphaea odorata*)
False dragonhead (*Physostegia virginiana*)

WHEN STONES ARE A BLESSING

You can look at rocks as impediments to gardening, or as the bones for a rock garden.

Rock gardens are a one-eighty departure from standard gardening practice, making an advantage out of adversity. They play plants off of a rugged mini-landscape of stones placed artfully about (unless there is a handy outcropping on the property). Rock garden specimens typically are small and modest in habit, so that they appear to be challenged by their setting rather than luxuriating in it. Many favorite species are from alpine habitats, where the elements favor low, compact plants that look something like bonsai.

Unlike a garden bed, with its carefully leveled soil and neatly defined border, a rock garden suggests a natural setting in which the plants have to accommodate themselves to their less-than-ideal surroundings. In fact, this setting can be very hospitable to small species, in that they don't have to compete with big neighbors and aren't likely to be stepped upon. A rock garden also may prove to be a low-maintenance part of the yard, once you have it established. Weeds are less likely to go rampant, and pruning the little plants is a matter of taking a few minutes with a pair of scissors. Also, a rock garden can save you time and labor in the long run, if it takes the place of a slope that is difficult to mow, a sunny bank with indifferent soil, or a chronically eroding embankment.

WORK THE SITE

A bit of sloped land, studded with rocks and getting sun most of the day, will be the ideal. Add or subtract rocks to play up the site's appearance. You can remove some soil to make existing rocks look more dramatic.

So, what if you have the slope but not the stones? Either bring them in from elsewhere on your property or have them delivered by a stone yard. Visit the yard and ask to tour their stock so that you can pick out individual picturesque rocks, rather than settling for a

You can suggest a natural slope where none exists by backing up piled rocks against a fence, rock wall, or side of a building. The idea is to suggest that this really is a slope, and not just a bump in the yard.

random truckload. Although you're apt to see a mouthwatering assortment of colors and textures of rock, it's best to stick to one type that will look at home in your yard—perhaps rocks that have been quarried or gathered locally. If they have recently been unearthed and look a little too squeaky clean, don't worry; they gradually will take on a patina. Pick out a mix of sizes, not just impressively large ones, or your rock garden may look artificial.

Once you have the rocks, remove 1 foot or so of the soil where the garden is to go. This will allow you to fill in around the rocks and make it look as though they've rested there since the last Ice Age instead of having been plunked down last week. If you keep coming up with artificial-looking arrangements, it's time to take a drive out into the countryside to study natural formations.

GET READY FOR THE PLANTS

As you work, keep an eye out for attractive niches in which to put the plants. Partially fill these spots with garden soil, making sure that you first tamp ordinary soil into crevices so that the good soil doesn't wash away during your next heavy rainstorm. For rock gardening, a good mix is equal parts loamy soil, humus (screened leaf mold or compost), and fine, pea-size gravel.

PLANT THE PLANTS

Dwarf conifers will serve as visual anchors, while suggesting an Alpine landscape. Add a mix of low-growing cushionlike plants, prostrate varieties, and miniature flowering bulbs. Annuals can be called on to fill in the blanks, as long as they bear small blossoms and won't try to steal the show. If you have some species that aren't happy under the full brunt of the sun, the remedy is already in place—situate them on the shady side of big rocks.

GOOD ROCK GARDEN CHOICES

To get an idea of what you'd like to grow in a rock garden, see if you can sign up for a tour of a regional rock garden society. You also may be able to find a nursery within driving distance that

(continued)

specializes in these plants. And the Internet is a great backup for both plants and information.

Here are some of the plants that can be expected to fare successfully in the special environment of the rock garden.

Balsam (*Abies balsamea*)
Alpine yarrow (*Achillea jaboneggi*)
Wooly yarrow (*Achillea tomentosa*)
Alpine lady's mantle (*Alchemilla alpina*)
Mountain alyssum (*Alyssum montanum*)
Wild columbine (*Aquilegia canadensis*)
Rock cress (*Arabis caucasica*)
Carpathian bellflower (*Campanula carpatica*)
Weeping Alaskan cedar (*Chamaecyparis nookatensis*)
Clematis heraclifolia
Corydalis lutea
Rockspray cotoneaster (*Cotoneaster horizontalis* 'Variegatus')
Pinks (*Dianthus deltoides*)
Dalmatian cranesbill (*Geranium dalmaticum*)
Hosta 'Rock Princess'
Candytuft 'Weisser Zwerg' (*Iberis sempervirens*)
Japanese roof iris (*Iris techtorum*)
Alpine catchfly (*Lychnis alpina*)

Pink showy primrose (*Oenothera berlandieri* 'Siskyou')
Chilean oxalis (*Oxalis adenophylla*)
Alpine poppy (*Papaver alpinum*)
Fountain grass 'Little Bunny' (*Pennisetum alopecuroides*)
Moss phlox (*Phlox subulata*)
Norway spruce 'Little Gem' (*Picea abies*)
Rock soapwort (*Saponaria ocymoides*)
Saxifraga spp.
Sedum spp.
Sempervivum spp.
Blue-eyed grass (*Sisyrinchium bermudianum*)
Spiraea 'Little Princess' (*Spiraea japonica*)
Weeping threadleaf arborvitae (*Thuja occidentalis* 'Filiformis')
Wooly thyme (*Thymus lanuginoisis*)
Late tulip (*Tulipa tarda*)
Speedwell (*Veronica*)
Violets (*Viola* spp.)

THIS BERRY IS FOR THE BIRDS

One elderberry shrub is all you'll need for jams and pies, but recipes should include bird netting along with the lemon and sugar!

Read anything about growing elderberries, and you're apt to find a lot of grumbling about the way that birds manage to harvest the crop the day before the gardener gets around to it. You can try all sorts of stunts and devices to keep the birds away. Most practical is to toss netting over the shrubs until you're ready to pick. Or just stick a couple of plants in a relatively unused part of the yard and enjoy them and the wildlife they attract, without necessarily thinking of the elderberry pies and wine you might be making.

The plants are a bit straggly and free-growing, so they aren't the best choice for a tiny yard. Choose a site with moist, fertile, well-drained soil. Once plants are established, you can keep them vigorous by pruning 3-year-old canes. This encourages new growth and makes the overall form a little tidier.

An informal grouping of them won't attract much attention until the flowers appear—large, lacy umbrels of tiny cream-colored flowers. You can snip them for use in making fritters and pancakes, but you'll want to spare some in order to have berries. The inky berries find use in jam, pie, and wine. While the standard garden-variety elderberry remains popular, you have your choice of several that either offer generous harvests or add remarkable colors to the home landscape.

- ❦ 'Johns' is a selection of familiar native elderberry, *Sambucus canadensis,* chosen for its superior yield.
- ❦ 'Goldbeere' (*S. nigra*) produces stunning yellow berries.
- ❦ 'Black Beauty' (*S. nigra*) is just that, with purplish-black foliage setting off pink, lemon-scented blossoms.
- ❦ Variegated elderberry (*S. nigra*) has foliage patterned with cream and dark green.

THE HEALTHFUL BLUEBERRY

Recent medical studies have turned the blueberry into a nutritional star because of its high levels of antioxidants, credited with preventing cancer and even postponing the effects of aging.

EASY DOES IT

Easy with the Sulfur

Sulfur has long been a handy way to lower soil pH. But at higher levels, it can act as a fungicide and insecticide, making trouble for beneficial soil organisms and earthworms. So use sulfur moderately, and conduct frequent tests of the soil's pH to ensure that you don't overdo it. You also can follow the practice of the Ozark Organic Growers Association and lay on the peat moss rather than rely on sulfur. They recommend using up to 10 gallons of peat per plant, which will improve the soil while bringing down the pH. See "A Sour Test for Limey Soil" on page 89.

Blueberries aren't just for muffins and pancakes. Eaten frequently, they can have a range of beneficial health effects; in fact, in tests of some 40 fruits and vegetables, these little blue morsels ranked highest in antioxidants, including the anthocyanins responsible for their vivid color. And among blueberry varieties, 'Rubel' is a standout, with nearly double the antioxidant level. That doesn't mean they taste like vitamin pills. In fact, 'Rubel' has an excellent flavor. As a bonus, the small-size berries won't collapse in baked goods to leave the pockets created by super-size blueberries from the supermarket. 'Rubel' is a reliable producer, too, and although the small berries mean more picking, they are a relatively easy variety to harvest.

BLUEBERRIES IN A POT

Smaller blueberry varieties make handsome potted plants. And growing them in pots may be the way to go if you live in parts of the country with high-pH soils. To keep the soil cool and moist, it helps to dig a hole and sink the pot level with the ground. For the acid medium, mix $\frac{1}{3}$ pine bark, $\frac{1}{3}$ peat moss, and $\frac{1}{3}$ potting soil. Stir in $\frac{1}{2}$ ounce of sulfur for each cubic foot of soil. Fertilize with products labeled for use with azaleas. And top the pots with mulch to retain moisture and lower the temperature around the shallow roots. That's it—for the next 3 or 4 years. At that time, you'll want to replace the soil and prune back the roots, then repot.

USE A VINEGAR DRESSING FOR SOURER SOIL

While there are a number of things you can do to lower the pH of soil or growing medium, the easiest way to treat potted plants or a few in the ground is to include vinegar when watering. Stir 2 tablespoons of distilled household vinegar into 1 gallon of water, and monitor the effect this has over time by testing the pH.

WALLS OF GREEN

Instead of putting up a fence, consider planting a hedge.

It takes some time, but you can grow your own garden walls. A dense, formally pruned hedge will keep out many would-be animal intruders; it serves as an excellent windbreak; and it looks lovely. You don't even have to paint it! Think about leaving a gap for an attractive gate, suspending it from a sturdy post and having it close against another post. The short list below suggests a few shrubs that eventually will grow up into living walls. But feel free to use any shrub that has done well for you.

- Box
- Privet
- Shrub rose
- Spirea
- Weigela
- Yew

HAND-ME-DOWNS FOR THE YARD

Just as antiques grace the rooms of a home with their patina and lived-in appearance, recycled landscape elements can fit in with your yard better than any home center purchase.

If you like to haunt antique shops and vintage clothing stores, try shopping for lawn accoutrements at yard sales, household auctions, and renovation supply firms. You never know what you'll find, unlike visiting a home center chain store. And that's part of the fun. You might come away with Victorian cast-iron fencing, an ornate birdbath, a park bench, Belgian block paving stones, a vintage wooden wheelbarrow, or a stained glass window for the garden shed. With their built-in history, these objects instantly seem right at home.

IF YOUR GARDEN IS TOO BIG OR TOO SMALL

Whether your garden is too cramped or you have more space than you know what to do with, the answer may be the same: community.

Many of us find ourselves ordering far more seeds each year than we can cram into our tillable square feet. If your gardening ambitions are too big for your property, look into community gardens—at least for such large or sprawling plants as squash and corn. While you'd probably prefer to keep salad greens and herbs close at hand, try to come up with a list of crops that need space but don't need pampering. They might include potatoes, garlic, and cabbage for starters. When gardening alongside others, you might also harvest valuable hints either by chatting or just by observing over the fence. And there is apt to be a spirit of camaraderie, while tilling one's own backyard may be a solitary activity. In Broome County, New York, the Otsiningo Community Gardener's Association rents plots at a nominal annual fee to dozens of enthusiastic gardeners who live in apartments, condos, or houses with postage-stamp yards. To find a community garden, check with your parks department or with a local natural foods store.

And what if you're fortunate in having more good soil and plentiful sunshine than you can possibly use? Give some thought to offering a patch of ground to a friend who likes to dig in the soil but doesn't own much of it. You might try planning complementary crops, with each of you specializing in those vegetables he or she has succeeded with in the past. If you can't produce a decent melon to save your life, perhaps your friend will have the knack. You and the friend also may have complementary summer plans, so that you can garden-sit while the other is on vacation.

SOURCES FOR GARDENERS

The ideas in this book will help you turn a good garden into a great garden. These sources, listed by chapter, will help you find mail-order nurseries, garden supplies, and product manufacturers. When you contact small businesses, please enclose a self-addressed, stamped envelope with your inquiry.

Chapter 1: Seed Starting and Saving

SEED CATALOGS

The Cook's Garden
PO Box C5030, Warminster, PA 18974
www.cooksgarden.com
An interesting but not overwhelmingly huge listing of vegetable seeds, including a particularly good range of mesclun mixes.

Johnny's Selected Seeds
Foss Hill Road, Albion, ME 04910-9731
www.johnnyseeds.com
This catalog sets the standard, with wide and interesting selections of vegetables, herbs, flowers, and gardening supplies.

John Scheepers Kitchen Garden Seeds
23 Tulip Drive, PO Box 638, Bantam, CT 06750-0638
www.kitchengardenseeds.com
A good selection of vegetables and herbs, with occasional recipes and gardener's tips in its pages.

Native Seeds/SEARCH
526 North 4th Avenue, Tucson, AZ 85719
www.nativeseeds.org
A nonprofit organization dedicated to preserving Native American seeds suited to the Southwest. The catalog is strong on beans, especially hard-to-find tepary and limas.

Nichols Garden Nursery
1190 Old Salem Road NE, Albany, OR 97321-4580
www.nicholsgardennursery.com
An intriguing collection that runs from vegetable and herb seeds to such unusual items as olive, tea, and kaffir lime trees.

Pinetree Garden Seeds
Box 300, 616A Lewiston Road, New Gloucester, ME 04260
www.superseeds.com
A good source of reasonably priced seeds.

Renee's Garden
6116 Highway 9, Felton, CA 95018
Reneesgarden.com
A well-thought-out selection of vegetables, herbs, and cottage flowers, sold only through an online catalog.

Seed Savers Exchange
3094 North Winn Road, Decorah, IA 52101
www.seedsavers.org
A nonprofit organization dedicated to discovering precious old varieties and making them available through its catalogs as well as through a network of backyard growers.

Seeds of Change
PO Box 15700, Santa Fe, NM 87506-5700
www.seedsofchange.com
Organic seeds and seedlings, with a good selection of hand tools.

Southern Exposure Seed Exchange
PO Box 170, Earlysville, VA 22936
www.southernexposure.com
Concentrates on heirlooms and open-pollinated varieties, with a Mid-Atlantic focus.

Territorial Seed Co.
PO Box 158, Cottage Grove, OR 97424-0061
www.territorial-seed.com
Many of the selections are available through mail order as plants, shipped at any of several dates best suited to your conditions.

(continued)

Chapter 2: Planting and Transplanting

RED PLASTIC MULCH

Harris Seeds
355 Paul Road, PO Box 24966, Rochester, NY 14624-0966
www.harrisseeds.com

Chapter 3: Soil, Compost, and Fertilizing

DRIP IRRIGATION SYSTEMS

Johnny's Selected Seeds
Foss Hill Road, Albion, ME 04910-9731
www.johnnyseeds.com

Chapter 4: Weeds and What to Do about Them

HORTICULTURAL VINEGAR

Nature Hills Nursery, Inc.
3334 North 88th Plaza, Omaha, NE 68134
www.naturehills.com

PORTABLE FLAMER

Planet Natural
1612 Gold Avenue, Bozeman, MT 59715
www.planetnatural.com

SWAN'S-NECK HOE

Gardener's Supply Company
128 Intervale Road, Burlington, VT 05401
www.gardeners.com

Chapter 5: Getting a Leg Up on Pests and Diseases

PREDATORY MITES

Hydro-Gardens
PO Box 25845, Colorado Springs, CO 80936-5845
www.hydro-gardens.com

BENEFICIAL PREDATORY NEMATODES

Orcon
PO Box 781147W, Los Angeles, CA 90016
www.organiccontrol.com

LADYBUGS, PRAYING MANTISES, GREEN LACEWINGS

Home Harvest Garden Supply
East Lansing, Michigan, 4870 Dawn Avenue, East Lansing, MI 48823
www.homeharvest.com

SCAREY MAN INFLATABLE SCARECROW AND LASER GUN

Reed-Joseph International Co.
PO Box 894, Greenville, MS 38702
www.reedjoseph.com

Chapter 6: The Vegetable Plot

WILD GREENS

The Cook's Garden
PO Box C5030, Warminster, PA 18974
www.cooksgarden.com

Gourmet Seeds International
HC 12, Box 510, Tatum, NM 88267-9700
www.gourmetseed.com

Territorial Seed Co.
PO Box 158, Cottage Grove, OR 97424-0061
www.territorial-seed.com

Chapter 7: Flowers in Beds and Pots

HEIRLOOM FLOWER BULBS

Old House Gardens
536 Third Street, Ann Arbor, MI 48103
www.oldhousegardens.com

LIGHT MOVER

AHL Garden Supply
1051 San Mateo SE, Albuquerque, NM 87108
www.ahlgrows.com

Chapter 8: Growing and Enjoying Herbs

THYME VARIETIES

Well-Sweep Herb Farm
205 Mount Bethel Road, Port Murray, NJ 07865
www.wellsweep.com

WHITE SAGE SEEDS

Horizon Herbs, LLC
PO Box 69, Williams, OR 97544
www.horizonherbs.com

Chapter 9: Tools, Supports, and Storage

HORTICULTURAL KNIVES

Orchard's Edge
836 Arlington Heights Road #346, Elk Grove Village, IL
60007
www.orchardsedge.com

ROBOMOWER

System Trading Corp., USA
450 7th Avenue, Suite 2803, New York, NY 10123
www.friendlyrobotics.com

SCYTHES

Scythe Supply
496 Shore Road, Perry, ME 04667
www.scythesupply.com

Chapter 10: Out in the Yard

RUBEL BLUEBERRY

Hartmann's Plant Co.
PO Box 100, Lacota, MI 49063-0110
www.hartmannsplantcompany.com

Raintree Nursery
391 Butts Road, Morton, WA 98356
www.raintreenursery.com

SOLAR FOUNTAIN

Silicon Solar Inc.
2917 State Highway 7, Bainbridge, NY 13733
www.siliconsolar.com

INDEX

Underscored page references indicate tables or marginalia.
Boldface references indicate illustrations.

Perennials. *See also* Bulbs; Herbs
    advantages of crops, 64
    asparagus, 65–66
    geraniums as, 234–35
    horseradish, 67
    pruning after flowering, 195
    rhubarb, 64–65
    root division for, 192–93, **192**,
        193, 194
    unattractive to deer, 123
    untouchables, 194
    weeds, 116–17
    white flowers, 214
Pesticides
    eliminating for lawn, 306
    environmental impact of, 119
    organic, 143
Pests. *See also* Insects, beneficial;
        specific pests
    bean, avoiding, 53
    benign neglect of, 119
    birds, 146, 146
    on cabbage, 129, 135, 138, 141
    caterpillar appreciation, 136, **136**
    codling moths, 138
    colored mulches for discouraging,
        54
    cutworms, 128
    deer, 122–23, 142
    earwigs, trapping, 134
    fencing out, 121–22, 126, 127,
        127
    hot water for controlling, 139
    on houseplants, 142, **142**
    monocropping and, 56
    organic pesticides, 143
    from over-fertilizing, 135
    planting times for controlling, 129
    plants that protect against, 128
    protecting bulbs against, 52,
        124–26
    rock music for repelling, 145
    row covers for controlling, 120,
        120
    scarecrows for, 145, 146, 328
    sprays for, 144
    squirrels, 126
    vacuuming bugs, 129

as vectors for diseases, 11
    voles and moles, 52, 124–25
    yellow jackets, 140–41, **140**, **141**
Phlox, 206, 206
pH of soil
    composting and, 87
    impact of, 87
    for lavender, 241
    lowering, 87, 88, 89, 324
    for moss, 116
    raising, 87, 88, 89
    sulfur treatment for, 324
    weeds indicating, 71
Phosphorus. *See also* Fertilizing
    fish emulsion for, 76
    low, signs of, 71
    in N-P-K balance, 78
Phytolacca americana (pokeweed),
    115
Picking. *See* Harvesting
Pigweed (*Amaranthus hybridus*), 103
Pillowcase, for compost tea, 76
Pillow, herbal, 253
Pines, blue or blue-green, 202
Planting. *See* Seeds, starting;
        Transplanting
Planting mixes. *See* Mixes
Plant stands, modular shelves for, 48
Plastic-based lumber, 290
Plastic films and tarps
    colored mulches, vi, 54, 54, 328
    for greenhouses, **16**, 17
    for insulating plants, 151
    for poison ivy control, 109
    row covers, 120
    straw vs., 108
    for weed control, 104
Platform bed, 273, **273**
Poison hemlock (*Conium
        maculatum*), 115
Poison ivy (*Toxicodendron radicans*),
    109, 115, 304
Poisons. *See* Toxins
Pokeweed (*Phytolacca americana*),
    115
Pollination
    avoiding cross-pollination, 26
    making hybrid plants, 27

open-pollinated plants, 26
    rolling back row covers for, 120
    shaking tomatoes for, 181, 181
Polycarbonate glazing
    for cold frames, 9, **9**, 15, **15**
    for greenhouses, 17
Pools
    fitting liner to, 300
    with fountain, 295, **295**
    shallow, benefits of, 298
    shallow, digging, 299–300, **299**,
        300
Portulaca oleracea (purslane), 102
Potassium, 71, 78. *See also* Fertilizing
Potatoes
    cleaner harvest of, 49
    companion plants, 56
    crop rotation, 187
    date for planting, 21
    diseases resisted by, 11
    growing from market, 38
    harvesting, 49
    mulching, 49, **49**
    pest control for, 129
    presprouting, 49
    storing, 152, 187
    weeds suppressed by, 109
Potpourris, 236–38, 236, 238
Pots. *See also* Container gardening;
        Houseplants
    anchoring outdoors, 84
    cat-proofing, 134
    dollies for moving, 46
    drainage holes in, 47
    insulating against frost, 302, **302**
    keeping from tipping, 278, **278**
    plastic vs. terra cotta, 47
    within pots, for watering, 46
Potted plants. *See* Container
        gardening; Houseplants
Potting bench, making, 42–43, 43
Potting mixes. *See* Mixes
Potting plants
    bare-root plants, 59
    basil, 161
    blueberries, 324
    geraniums, 234–35
    herbs, 245

USDA Plant Hardiness Zone Map

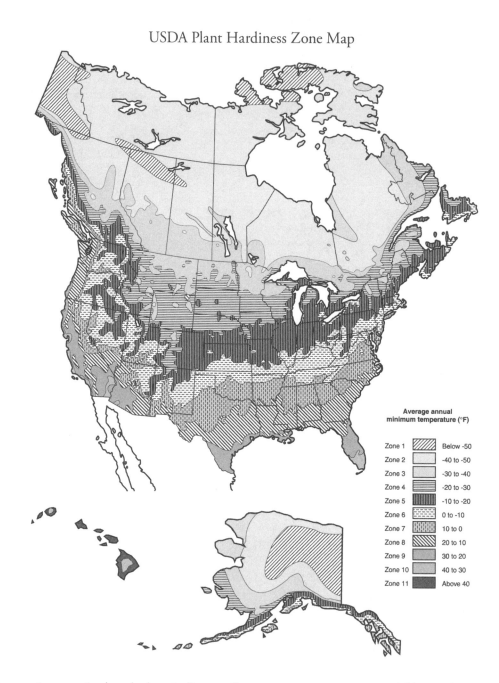

Average annual minimum temperature (°F)

Zone 1		Below -50
Zone 2		-40 to -50
Zone 3		-30 to -40
Zone 4		-20 to -30
Zone 5		-10 to -20
Zone 6		0 to -10
Zone 7		10 to 0
Zone 8		20 to 10
Zone 9		30 to 20
Zone 10		40 to 30
Zone 11		Above 40

This map is recognized as the best indicator of minimum temperatures available. Look at the map to find your area, then match its pattern to the key above. When you've found your pattern, the key will tell you what hardiness zone you live in. Remember that the map is a general guide; your particular conditions may vary.

346